Visions of Xanadu

MARSHALL SUTHER

Visions of Xanadu

Columbia University Press
New York and London, 1965

Marshall Suther is Associate Professor of Comparative Literature at Columbia University and is the author of THE DARK NIGHT OF SAMUEL TAYLOR COLERIDGE

N.C.
821.09
S

Copyright © 1965 Columbia University Press
Library of Congress Catalog Card Number: 65-10356
Manufactured in the United States of America

TO MY FATHER

Acknowledgments

Of the numerous debts I owe to the readers of Coleridge, most I believe are acknowledged in the notes. But to two very close readers I owe especial thanks, to my colleagues Professor Carl Woodring and Professor Alan Purves, each of whom is responsible for the absence of a good number of errors without having incurred any responsibility for the drift of what remains.

Chapter One has appeared in different form in the *Bucknell Review,* and is used here with their kind permission.

I should like to express my appreciation to copyright holders and publishers for permission to quote from the following works: to The Bollingen Foundation for *The Notebooks of Samuel Taylor Coleridge,* edited by Kathleen Coburn; to Chatto & Windus for *Coleridge the Visionary,* by J. B. Beer; to Harcourt, Brace, & World, Inc., for "The Waste Land," *Collected Poems, 1909–1962,* by T. S. Eliot; to Longmans, Green, & Co. for *The Consecrated Urn,* by Bernard Blackstone; to Oxford University Press for *Biographia Literaria,* edited by J. Shawcross, *The Collected Letters of Samuel Taylor Coleridge,* edited by E. L. Griggs, and *The Poetical Works of Samuel Taylor Coleridge,* edited by E. H. Coleridge, including the complete text of "Kubla Khan;" and to Rupert Hart-Davis for *Coleridge,* by Humphry House.

Contents

Visions of Xanadu

KUBLA KHAN

In Xanadu did Kubla Khan
A stately pleasure-dome decree:
Where Alph, the sacred river, ran
Through caverns measureless to man
  Down to a sunless sea.
So twice five miles of fertile ground
With walls and towers were girdled round:
And there were gardens bright with sinuous rills,
Where blossomed many an incense-bearing tree;
And here were forests ancient as the hills,
Enfolding sunny spots of greenery.

But oh! that deep romantic chasm which slanted
Down the green hill athwart a cedarn cover!
A savage place! as holy and enchanted
As e'er beneath a waning moon was haunted
By woman wailing for her demon-lover!
And from this chasm, with ceaseless turmoil seething,
As if this earth in fast thick pants were breathing,
A mighty fountain momently was forced:
Amid whose swift half-intermitted burst
Huge fragments vaulted like rebounding hail,
Or chaffy grain beneath the thresher's flail:
And 'mid these dancing rocks at once and ever
It flung up momently the sacred river.
Five miles meandering with a mazy motion
Through wood and dale the sacred river ran,
Then reached the caverns measureless to man,
And sank in tumult to a lifeless ocean:
And 'mid this tumult Kubla heard from far
Ancestral voices prophesying war!

The shadow of the dome of pleasure
Floated midway on the waves;
Where was heard the mingled measure
From the fountain and the caves.
It was a miracle of rare device,
A sunny pleasure-dome with caves of ice!

A damsel with a dulcimer
In a vision once I saw:
It was an Abyssinian maid,
And on her dulcimer she played,
Singing of Mount Abora.
Could I revive within me
Her symphony and song,
To such deep delight 'twould win me,
That with music loud and long,
I would build that dome in air,
That sunny dome! those caves of ice!
And all who heard should see them there,
And all should cry, Beware! Beware!
His flashing eyes, his floating hair!
Weave a circle round him thrice,
And close your eyes with holy dread,
For he on honey-dew hath fed,
And drunk the milk of Paradise.

The Perennial Problems

For a long time, encouraged by Coleridge's own statements concerning the poem, critics refrained from interpreting "Kubla Khan," content to appreciate it as a piece of glorious, wonderfully musical nonsense, a beautiful but inconsequent description of an opium paradise. But at the same time, some of the same critics persisted in referring to it as one of the great poems in the English language. In recent times a few, struck before any reflection perhaps by its beauty—

> In Xanadu did Kubla Khan
> A stately pleasure-dome decree:
> Where Alph, the sacred river, ran
> Through caverns measureless to man
> Down to a sunless sea.

—and rendered uncomfortable by the idea that such an effect of beauty could be produced in the absence of meaning, have sought for a symbolic content in the images and for some intelligible relation among the symbols, a content and a relation that would together account more adequately for the initial impact of the poem. (The presence of such intelligibility, though only glimpsed, only virtual in respect to the reader, is probably an indispensable condition of powerful impact.) Their efforts vary in interest and plausibility. But an eminent and careful student of the poem has subsequently cast them all into limbo, reopening the whole question of the relevance of attempts to interpret the poem, and has done so in such a way as to pose anew certain general and perennial questions in the field of criticism.

Miss Elisabeth Schneider, in her book *Coleridge, Opium and Kubla Khan*,[1] makes invaluable contributions to the understanding of the poem, and, because of its peculiar place in Coleridge's works, to the general understanding of its author. Having made a thorough reexamination of the known facts concerning Coleridge's opium addiction, she weighs their significance in relation to his work and character in the light of modern clinical knowledge and arrives at what seem to be eminently sane and probable conclusions, among others that the account given by Coleridge in the 1816 preface to "Kubla Khan" must be largely discounted as a literal description of the poem's composition and therefore as a key to its interpretation. Her study of the literary "echoes" in the poem, with the emphasis on those derived from works with which he was quite consciously concerned around the probable time of its composition, notably works of Landor, Southey, Wieland, and Milton, tends to weaken still further the assumption of Lowes and others that the poem issued full-born out of the unconscious, an assumption whose implications have laid the foundation for a good deal of the interpretation of the poem—or failure to find it interpretable. Finally, Miss Schneider would seem to have made a very good case for supposing that the poem was written not in 1797 as Coleridge stated, or in 1798, as later editors have been inclined to think, but either in the fall of 1799 or in May or June of 1800.

But Miss Schneider's treatment of the critical problems posed by the poem seems on the whole much less convincing than her treatment of the influence of opium on its composition and the problems of its date and literary influences. She takes up two interrelated critical questions: whether the poem is a fragment or a whole, and what kind of interpretation it is susceptible to. Briefly, she concludes that it *is* a fragment, and that it is *not* susceptible to a "symbolic" interpretation. Any new approach to this seductive but difficult poem must necessarily begin with a consideration of these views,

[1] (Chicago: University of Chicago Press, 1953), pp. ix, 378.

which reflect the opinion of many readers and find in Miss Schneider's work a persuasive and authoritative expression.

The biographical reasons for arguing that the poem is a fragment rather than a complete whole are strong ones. In the first place, Coleridge himself called it a fragment, and, "haunted as he was by the ghosts of his many unfinished works," Miss Schneider thinks, "it is unlikely that he would have added by a deliberate falsehood to the number of that congregation in limbo." [2] She also points out that he treated it as he did other fragments, not publishing it for many years after its composition, though his general custom was to publish very promptly.

The arguments from internal evidence are less persuasive, and they are of some importance in virtue of their relation to Miss Schneider's dismissal of "symbolic" interpretations of the poem. Such interpretations necessarily treat it in some sense as a complete whole. Some of the critics who so interpret it, notably Professor Knight,[3] make a great point of its being a whole. If in fact it is not, they look rather foolish, and some of that foolishness rubs off on their method of analysis, with which Miss Schneider is clearly rather impatient. One measure of this impatience is the fact that, having previously spent eighty-nine pages arguing that although Coleridge stated at least twice in writing that the poem was composed in an opium-dream, the overwhelming probability is that it was not, she takes only six and a half pages to dismiss the possibility that his statement that it is a fragment may also be in error.

She reads the poem as "a fragment with a postscript added at some later time when it has become obvious to the poet that he cannot finish the piece," [4] the postscript constituting an explanation of his not being able to finish it; and she finds no other unity between the two parts of the poem. The repetition of images from

[2] *Ibid.*, p. 246.
[3] *The Starlit Dome* (London: Oxford University Press, 1941), pp. 83–178, "Coleridge's Divine Comedy."
[4] Schneider, p. 247.

the first part in the second is a mere skillful link, contributing no additional dimension of meaning to the poem (the two poems, rather). "If a man begins a poem, gets stuck, and then adds the comment, 'I cannot finish this,' even though he versify his comment to match his fragment, he is not likely to produce a whole in the poetic or aesthetic sense, though he does bring his piece to an end beyond which it could not be continued." [5]

The substantive disagreement apparent here between Miss Schneider, whose book is the most nearly definitive study of the various problems surrounding the poem and as such carries great weight, and critics like Professor Knight, Professor Humphry House,[6] and Miss Maud Bodkin,[7] who offer more or less complex interpretations of the poem, can best be explored initially, I believe, by an examination of the ambiguities involved in the uses of the word "fragment." The question is whether the poem can be, as Coleridge called it, a "fragment," and at the same time be a complete whole in the sense that it lends itself to an integral interpretation, "symbolic," psychoanalytic, or other.

The following are some revelant ways in which the word "fragment" is used to refer to literary productions:

1. A group of verses is called a fragment when it appears separately from a larger group of which it is a part, that larger group being actually in existence (as when we publish a fragment of *Paradise Lost*) or having been in existence at one time (as when we speak of fragments from the Greek dramatists, which we have reason to suppose are parts of complete plays now lost).

2. A group of verses is also called a fragment when it is the actually written part of a larger composition that the author was in the process of composing but for some reason did not complete.

3. There are also groups of verses that are called fragments, usually by their authors, because in the judgment of their authors they

[5] *Ibid.,* p. 248.
[6] In *Coleridge* (London: Rupert Hart-Davis, 1953).
[7] In *Archetypal Patterns in Poetry* (London: Oxford University Press, 1934).

do not merit on internal grounds to be called wholes. (These are often the results of momentary insights or reactions that the author thinks he may use in the construction of some future whole poem growing out of other stimuli, or that he hopes sometime to "work up," but that as they stand he does not wish to present as finished wholes. They very frequently turn up in notebooks.)

It should be remarked in this connection that if for any reason whatever an author is dissatisfied with the development of a poem, one way of disclaiming it is to call it a fragment. Used in this way, the word "fragment" represents an aesthetic judgment, a qualitative judgment, although it may be true that improvement would involve expansion of the poem.

4. There are, finally, groups of verses that their authors may consider to be complete wholes, that in any case they publish as poems, but that one or another critic may consider "fragmentary," meaning perhaps that obviously possible and important implications of elements in the poem have not been sufficiently developed; that something indispensable to the interpretation or understanding of the poem is missing; or that as it stands it contains superfluous or irrelevant parts, that its parts do not cohere. (In this last case, its being made into a "whole" might involve shortening it. Cf. "Dejection: an Ode.")

There is a genuine ambiguity among these uses of the word "fragment," the relevant features of which may be summarized thus:

The statement that a group of verses is a fragment in Sense 1 or 2 represents a judgment of fact that can be conclusively verified only by external evidence. Thus, if we disagree with a person's statement that a group of verses is a fragment in Sense 1 or 2, we imply that he is lying, if he is its author, or, more probably, misinformed, if he is some third person.

The statement that a group of verses is a fragment in Sense 3 or 4 is an aesthetic judgment that can be supported only by internal evidence. Thus, if we disagree with a person's statement that a group of verses is a fragment in Sense 3 or 4, we are challenging his aesthetic judgment, whether he be its author or not.

It may be true that a given group of verses is a fragment in Sense 1 or 2, and not true that it is a fragment in Sense 3 or 4. Conversely, it may be true that a group of verses is a fragment in Sense 3 or 4, and not true that it is a fragment in Sense 1 or 2.

In his preface to the poem Coleridge obviously meant to convey that "Kubla Khan" was a fragment in Sense 1, an actually completed poem of some two to three hundred lines, all but fifty-four of which were "lost" by the accident of his being interrupted by the person on business from Porlock while he was writing the poem out from memory. This would not entail its being a fragment in any of the aesthetic senses of the term, but it would create the strongest kind of presumptive evidence. Miss Schneider's arguments for rejecting the veracity of the preface as an account of the actual composition of the poem, too long and complex to summarize here, seem to me convincing; and we are left with the conclusion that Coleridge's statement that the poem is a fragment in Sense 1 is deliberately misleading.

On the other hand, there seem to be no similarly persuasive reasons for rejecting the external evidence that the poem is a fragment in Sense 2, i.e., Coleridge's calling it a fragment, his statement in the preface that he "frequently purposed to finish" it, and his failure to publish it until some sixteen years after its composition. Miss Schneider suggests internal evidence as well in support of the contention that it is a fragment in Sense 2. She thinks the first thirty-six lines may have been composed as the opening lines of a "romantic narrative poem of some magnitude," like *"Oberon, Gebir, Thalaba,* the unwritten 'Mahomet,' *Christabel,* even Cottle's *Alfred,* to name only such poems as were present to Coleridge's mind in 1799." [8] This would indeed make it very likely that the tion of it as an integral whole be quite unjustified and irrelevant. poem be a fragment in an aesthetic sense, and that any interpreta-

[8] Schneider, p. 250.

But in suggesting reasons why, if this is the fact of the matter, Coleridge was unable to finish the poem, she points out that "the texture of the poem is exceedingly rich and concentrated for the opening of a long poem. The author could hardly sustain it, one feels, and if he could the reader could not. A narrative poet, almost of necessity, lets the reader into his tale more thinly, with his matter spaced more widely; or if the opening texture is extremely rich the pace will be slower, more leisurely or more dignified, as in *Paradise Lost* and *Lycidas*." [9] All of this seems quite true, but offers itself more readily as evidence that the poem was *not* begun as a long narrative poem, since Coleridge had at the time of composition of this poem some experience in the technique of long narrative poems. Having said that the lines "sound more than anything else like a fine opening for a romantic narrative poem of some magnitude," Miss Schneider is in effect explaining that it could not be finished because it does *not* sound like the opening of a narrative poem of some magnitude. One is inclined to agree that it does not sound like the opening of a long narrative poem, and to adopt the less paradoxical conclusion, that it probably was not begun as such, especially since the only external evidence, however doubtful, as to its projected length is Coleridge's statement that in its finished form as it existed in his dream, it consisted of "not less than" two to three hundred lines.

Miss Schneider's other hypothesis as to the poem's genesis is that Coleridge is just as likely "to have begun with only the vaguest plan in mind or even none at all. He may have begun the piece, as painters and other poets sometimes do, as a kind of glorified doodling—an accurate enough name for 'daydreaming' with pen or brush—which might or might not develop an intention as it proceeded." [10] This would place the poem squarely within the definition of a fragment in Sense·3, and the critic is at liberty to disagree even with the author's judgment as to whether in its actual state it constitutes an integrally interpretable whole. Sup-

[9] *Ibid.,* p. 252.   [10] *Ibid.,* p. 90.

posing "Kubla Khan" to fall roughly within this category, several things distinguish it from similar pieces by Coleridge. In the first place, as Miss Schneider points out, "there is no reason to think that it was printed without revision and polishing." [11] Her own analysis of its metrical perfections alone would lend positive weight to the opinion that it was extensively "worked on." There is also the fact that, although he waited sixteen years to publish "Kubla Khan," he did publish it. It is true that Coleridge produced many "fragments" (in Senses 3 and 2), although not more poetic fragments than a great many other poets. Evidently Coleridge himself used the term "fragment" in at least two distinct senses. In one case there is the fragment that is publishable, either because it constitutes enough of a whole to be of interest, to be understandable as a unit or, as in the case of "Christabel" and "The Three Graves," because it is a large enough fragment to suggest the main lines of the projected whole. In the other case, that of fragments published for the first time by E. H. Coleridge, the fragment is unpublishable. The determination of what Coleridge may have meant by the term is additionally complicated by his linking "The Pains of Sleep" with "Kubla Khan" in the preface as a fragment "describing with equal fidelity the dream of pain and disease." "The Pains of Sleep," however, is a very literal account of nightmarish dreams, an itemization of their contents, with their emotional effects upon the dreamer, and some moral speculation about their causes, ending very neatly with two couplets:

> Such griefs with such men well agree,
> But wherefore, wherefore fall on me?
> To be beloved is all I need,
> And whom I love, I love indeed.

Without the statement in the preface to "Kubla Khan," I think it would never have occurred to anyone that "The Pains of Sleep"

[11] *Ibid.,* p. 90.

was a "fragment." One is tempted to think Coleridge was simply tossing off the word carelessly, using it as a synonym for a small or inconsiderable thing, perhaps a thing without "poetic merit"—and in the case of "The Pains of Sleep" one would be less inclined to disagree than in the case of "Kubla Khan."

There would seem to be no way of deciding finally whether when Coleridge called "Kubla Khan" a fragment he was using the term in Sense 2 or Sense 3 (if we do not take seriously his intent to convey Sense 1). The examination of fourteen other poems that he referred to as fragments and published during his lifetime would make it seem more likely that he was using it in Sense 2, that a fragment was not just the momentary jotting down of an idea for a poem, but constituted some kind of deliberate project, that, in short, he thought it susceptible of further development, some at least vague idea of which he actually had in mind, and that he really did "purpose to finish" it. If this is true of "Kubla Khan," if the poem is something he purposed to finish and did not, for whatever reason, the aesthetic question, the question of interpretation, is still left open; and one possible answer to the question of why he failed to "finish" it is that it turned out to be, in the aesthetic sense, finished. Perhaps he found he had brought "his piece to an end beyond which it could not be continued" in the sense that it was, aesthetically, finished. And, as we have said, this can only be decided on internal evidence, and may, in a given case, even be properly decided against the artist himself. The consideration involves some important aesthetic conceptions, and misconceptions.

The idea of a work of art being a "whole" is very important in almost all aesthetic theories, from Aristotle's "beginning, middle and end" on; but in the course of time the idea has been associated with a kind of mystical biographical fallacy, which considers the poem not just as a distant analogy to the mass, but as being of the same nature, so that in order to say *missa est,* this is a complete poem, certain things must have been said and no others—and the poet knows this infallibly in each case. If the mass lacks a Consecration, it is not just a shorter and somewhat different mass, but no mass at all: the miracle has not taken place. But as like masses, sacraments, miracles, as poems may be, they are not like them in this way.

The interesting question is, how *does* the artist *know* when the work is complete? There is a great deal to be said on this subject, from a variety of aesthetic points of view, but the least acceptable answer to the question involves the idea that there is something mystical and absolute in his knowledge, the idea that it "could not have been otherwise," and that the artist knows this in some peculiar and absolutely certain way. All this derives in part from the wish to attribute perfection to the work of art, even a kind of mysterious, miraculous perfection. And we apply it not only to the matter of completeness of the work of art but to the choice of its elements. It is a kind of doctrine of poetic infallibility.

Coleridge is doing something like this when he says that "The collocation of words is so artificial in Shakespeare and Milton, that you may as well think of pushing a brick out of a wall with your forefinger, as attempt to remove a word out of any of their finished passages." [12] Now we feel a truth in this in relation to many works, we feel that they are, almost miraculously, consummate wholes and that the removal of even one brick would bring the edifice tumbling down; and I think we are right, the miracle does occur. But this perfection is in the thing *as it exists,* and cannot be read over into the process of its production. The revision and re-revision practices of nearly all poets serve as a warning. In terms of the author's plans or intentions, it is permissible to suppose that a great many works of art are "finished" at the point where, quite simply, the author cannot think of anything else to do to them. It probably seldom occurs that he has a sudden, apodictic conviction, *finis est.* If in a given case he tells us he had thought of doing something

[12] *Table Talk,* ed. H. N. Coleridge (London: John Murray, 1851), 3d edition, p. 263 (3 July 1833).

further, particularly in the way of adding to his poem, it is proper to call the work a "fragment," if this seems to be an important thing to communicate about it. In this sense there is perhaps little doubt that "Kubla Khan" is a fragment; but this does not at all prevent its being a "complete whole" in another sense, susceptible to a relevant integral interpretation, and Coleridge may have done his poem a gratuitous disservice in leading us to believe its being a fragment in this sense was one of the most important things to communicate about it. In this sense, most poems could be called fragments.

The same thing must be said about the infallibility of the elements within a work of art. It is quite conceivable that Milton might have changed many more things than he did in "Lycidas" without destroying it, even improving it (for instance it may be asked, would "Lycidas" be a "fragment" if Milton had omitted the flower passage, which he seems to have had trouble with?).

The decision as to whether a work is a fragment in the aesthetic sense must in many cases be a tentative one, and in every case it must be based on *what is there,* regardless of whether the author intended to add to it or not. It is quite conceivable that Coleridge might have added to "Kubla Khan," and if he had it would be a *different* poem, perhaps even a "more complete" one, which is just another way of saying a better one; but it does not at all follow that it is not a "complete whole" as it stands. If the foregoing analysis is valid, the critic is still warranted in his effort to interpret "Kubla Khan" as a poem, without running a serious risk of embarrassment through discovering that he has mistaken a part for a whole.

But Miss Schneider has still another reason for calling into question the validity of any "symbolic" interpretation of the poem— that Coleridge simply did not write that kind of poetry:

I think it will have to be agreed that this mode of thought was never in accord with Coleridge's conscious practice, and probably not with his theory either. His mind seems to have worked differently. Perhaps it was the preacher in him, which Lamb more than once remarked upon;

at any rate, his habit was to expound his interior meanings outright. Often enough he conferred upon images of nature some deep significance, but he regularly made that explicit.[13]

She gives as illustrations "A Wish" (1792), the jasmin and myrtle in "The Eolian Harp" (1795), and the verses to Charles Lloyd (1796), noting, however, that he does this sort of thing less blatantly as he goes along. Nevertheless, Miss Schneider knows of no poems that "one naturally feels to be symbolic, in which no specific meaning is avowed," and she attributes a kind of *ad hominem* fallacy to those critics who insist on symbolic interpretations of Coleridge's poetry:

The critic nourished on Donne, Yeats, and Mr. Eliot may be repelled— but, whether one likes it or not, this is the way Coleridge actually wrote. He often wrote much better but always in the same kind. Undoubtedly he was very modern in some ways; but he was neither modern nor medieval enough, he was still too close to the earlier eighteenth-century habits of thought, to transform symbol or allegory altogether into pure metaphor in such a way that the relation between different levels of meaning is wholly implied and not explicit. This open symbolism, with its obvious reference to the moral world, is the only kind that we are sure Coleridge practiced. We should have an exceptionally good reason before we suppose that in *The Ancient Mariner, Christabel*, and *Kubla Khan* he departed from it, yet at the same time departed so invisibly that posterity has required a hundred and some years to uncover the true meaning.[14]

There would seem to be a kind of impasse between the two points of view in question here, Miss Schneider's and that of the critics who interpret Coleridge's poems symbolically. Miss Schneider may be prejudicially indisposed to find symbolic meanings, and consequently not find them, and, in using this fact to argue against their presence, beg the question; Miss Schneider may say, on the other hand, that the "interpreters" are prejudicially disposed to find such

---

[13] Schneider, p. 254.   [14] *Ibid.*, pp. 255–56.

meanings, and, as a result, illicitly read them into poems in which they do not in fact or in intention exist. On the face of it, the dispute would seem to be unjudicable, since each side rejects the evidence of the other as invalid (somewhat in the way of those who see ghosts and those who do not). But the reader who fancies himself quite unprejudiced in the matter must in fact make some determination concerning the probable validity of these opposing positions if he is to read "Kubla Khan" at all, and a determination other than simply finding out whether when he reads it he does or does not find implicit symbolic meanings—since in either case he would be subject to the same strictures as the original disputants.

Fortunately, there are some avenues of appeal, more or less independent of direct observation, that may lead out of the impasse. One is a critical examination of Miss Schneider's charge of prejudice on the part of the "interpreters," an attempt to determine as accurately as possible what this charge really involves. If taken at its face value, it effectively invalidates a major bulk of recent critical interpretation of many poets besides Coleridge. Obviously, the danger to which Miss Schneider is pointing is a very real one. The danger of "reading into" poems meanings that are not "there" is a perennial danger for the critic, involving many vexing problems in the philosophy of criticism (or better, perhaps, many different ways of stating the same vexing problem), such as the limit of relevance of the artist's conscious *intent* at the moment of composition, the probable legitimacy of the reinterpretation each successive age is able to make of a given work of art, the problem of what the poetic act consists of generically, by proper definition, distinguishing it from other discourse different in kind, as opposed to subsidiary distinctions among the widely differing ways in which this identical generic act may be realized by different poets at different times (in other words, the distinction between poetry and philosophy as kinds of discourse as opposed to the distinction among different styles of poetry). A given critic may or may not address himself explicitly to the solution of these problems—that is perhaps more the work of the philosopher than of the critic *per se*— but some working determination concerning them necessarily underlies his interpretation of any poem. It is the critic's job to see how apparently widely differing poetic techniques participate in a common essence, which is *Poetry*. And it is equally his job not to identify one more or less specialized technique with *Poetry* and consequently either exclude other techniques from his working definition or try to squeeze other techniques into conformity with his favored technique and so do violence to these other techniques and diminish *Poetry* itself.

Now it is certainly true that critics do not always succeed in these respects. Some recent critics seem to have cut their teeth on a group of poets who may in the vaguest possible way be said to constitute a family, in the sense that in their way of handling symbols they are more like one another than they are like certain other poets (though the poets Miss Schneider singles out as furnishing their pattern of what poetry should be, to be poetry, are in fact separated by centuries and differ among themselves in important respects). Having cut their teeth on these poets, doubtless because for complex reasons the way these poets employ symbols is especially congenial to their methods of absorbing and analyzing poetry, these critics may sometimes tend to force other poets into the accustomed mold. When this happens, it does result in critical monstrosities.

But the question here, independent of the particular virtues and vices of their interpretation of individual poems, is whether these critics are guilty of the critical fallacy to which we have alluded, whether, that is, they are mistaking a particular symbolic technique peculiar to Donne, among others, for a generic and indispensable poetic operation, and insisting upon finding it in Coleridge's poetry in order to justify his being called a poet, and so doing violence to Coleridge and making themselves ridiculous; or whether the symbolic technique they may first have isolated for themselves in reading Donne is really a generic poetic technique, common, with variations, to all poets insofar as they are poets, and the differences between Donne and Coleridge therefore to be sought at other levels.

Is the distinction between a kind of discourse that characteristically delivers its meaning by implication (by precipitation, as it were, from the relations among its parts, by its very *way* of saying what it says—in more philosophical terms, by the relative identity between its form and content) and a kind of discourse that characteristically delivers its meanings "outright," by making them "explicit," by "obvious reference to the moral world" (in short, by discursive exposition), is this a distinction between two styles of poetry or a distinction between poetry and various other generically different kinds of discourse? Miss Schneider comes very near providing us unintentionally with the answer when she goes on to suggest, as an explanation of Coleridge's alleged exclusive practice of what she calls "open symbolism," that "perhaps it was the preacher in him." The distinction between poetry and preaching, if it is at all precise, is a distinction between two different kinds of discourse, as different as kinds of human discourse may be, not a distinction between two varieties of poetic technique. It is true that there was a great deal of the preacher in Coleridge—and that it not infrequently led him out of poetry while he was still versifying; but Coleridge was himself quite aware that everything in "poems" is not "poetry," as evidenced by his apologies in presenting such poems as "Sonnet on Receiving a Letter," "The Three Graves," "Dejection," "The Pains of Sleep," and even, annoyingly enough for the present purpose, "Kubla Khan."

The suggestion is that what Miss Schneider is accusing these critics of reading into Coleridge is not some specialized and alien symbolic technique, peculiar to a few metaphysical and a few modern poets, but the most characteristic operation of poetry, a "technique" in the absence of which a piece of discourse cannot intelligibly be said to be "poetry." To say that he does not write at all in this way would amount to saying that he does not write poetry. To say that he does not always write in this way, that he perhaps never writes purely in this way, is to say that, in common with all other known poets, he does not always succeed, perhaps never succeeds, in being poetic in the fullest sense of the word. Further, it is no doubt true to say that he is less often successful in being highly and purely poetic than some other poets; because it is certainly true, as Miss Schneider points out, that he very often "conferred upon images of nature some deep significance," but that he "regularly [not always] made that explicit," and that in doing so, he frequently ceased being the poet and became the critic, the interpreter, within his own poem, a strategy that reflects his own adverse judgment of the ability of his symbols, his "poetry," to stand alone. (We may legitimately agree or disagree with him in any given case.) It would seem to be self-evident that it is the peculiar excellence of the *poet* to confer significance upon images in such a way that it inheres in them without the necessity of "explanation," simply as a result of the choice and arrangement of the images within the poem. And this has nothing to do with being "metaphysical"—there are all kinds of choices and arrangements of images that stand an equal chance of success and that cannot in any useful sense be identified as "metaphysical" techniques.

Whether "pure poetry" in this sense is possible is a great question, one that I should be inclined to answer in the negative.[15] Perhaps all actual poetry is a compromise between what Miss Schneider calls "pure metaphor" (which is probably a contradiction in terms) and "explanation," a compromise necessitated by the fact that poetry is a *human* activity, starting out with ready-made and therefore somewhat recalcitrant materials, operated upon by a discursive and less than omnipotent intelligence [16]—Man's "creation" is only

---

[15] As Coleridge seems to do when he remarks "that a poem of any length neither can be, or ought to be, all poetry." *Biographia Literaria,* ed. J. Shawcross (London, Oxford University Press, 1939), II, 11.

[16] Coleridge was aware of the "obstacles [to be] . . . overcome" in "the subjection of matter to spirit so as to be transformed into a symbol, in and through which the spirit reveals itself; . . ." *Ibid.,* II, 239.

a partial, secondhand creation, not a creation *ex nihilo,* in which the "meaning," the intention, can be perfectly inherent in the object (God's creations never bear glosses with them).

Although "pure poetry" is surely not to be found in Donne, Yeats, or Eliot, I should think, it has been attempted, with indifferent success, by a few poets, most of them French; but short of such an attempt there is a wide range of relative purity in this respect within which what most people would agree to call "great" poems fall—on the condition that, whatever else they have in them in the way of "explanation," they have "enough" of this element of "poetry," this incarnation of meaning into an object. In these terms, the proportion of "poetry" in a great many of Coleridge's poems is relatively low (as he himself in some cases recognized), but even in those where it is heavily overlaid with explanatory material, it is none the less there, sometimes having its effect in spite of, even in contradiction to, the explanatory material, the built-in interpretation. In a few poems, the weight of poetry, of symbols effectively incarnate with meaning, is very great, and, surely not by accident, these are the poems in which there is the smallest proportion of interpretive material within the poem. Of these, "Kubla Khan" is the most extreme case. And it is an extreme case not only relative to Coleridge's poetry but relative to English poetry in general: it is not without reason that it has been considered one of the greatest poems in the language. Its weight of "meaning," taken absolutely, is less than that to be found in other poems of Coleridge and in a vast number of poems of other poets; but it is not inconsiderable, and it is about as nearly perfectly incarnate as possible. When we set ourselves to establish a kind of absolute scale of poetic worth, as most of us do at some time or other in spite of all disclaimers, one of the primary difficulties we face is that of determining priority between these two standards of excellence, weight of meaning, and the degree of perfection with which what meaning there is in the poem is embodied, or, significance and artistic perfection. There is surely no way, and happily no necessity, of coming to a final determination—another consequence of the human condition. But ordinarily we are fairly clear about the extremes.

Miss Schneider makes the point that it is curious, in view of Coleridge's habitual use of "open symbolism," that he should have departed from it in three and only three cases, "The Ancient Mariner," "Christabel," and "Kubla Khan," "yet at the same time departed so invisibly that posterity has required a hundred and some years to uncover the true meaning." (In the case of "Kubla Khan," the implication is clearly that, since there is no "open symbolism, there is no symbolism at all, and that the poem is meaningless.) [17] I have tried above to show (1) that the dichotomy between "open symbolism" and "pure metaphor" is misconceived as a distinction between two styles of poetry, that, taken as extremes, its two terms would correspond not to two styles of poetry but to poetry and not-poetry; (2) that in fact neither extreme exists in any actual poetry, that Coleridge, like all other poets, falls somewhere between the two in each poem; and (3) that his relation to poets like Donne, Yeats, and Eliot in this respect has nothing to do with a legitimate distinction among their poetic styles—if it is true, for instance, that Donne is more often a "purer" poet than Coleridge, that is not to say that Coleridge would become purer in proportion as he approached what we might legitimately determine to be Donne's "style."

But even if it were agreed that "Kubla Khan" has a meaning in very much the same sense that other poems have meanings and that, with due allowance for Coleridge's peculiar style, that meaning can be approached in very much the same way, what is to be said about its "true meaning" being invisible for over a hundred

---

[17] The suggestion that it represents a kind of "doodling," of course, far from eliminating the possibility of its being "interpreted," leaves it wide open to the most searching interpretation of the psychoanalysts.

years? The first thing to be said is that the phrase, its "true meaning," is Miss Schneider's, not that of any of the interpreters of "Kubla Khan" or of Coleridge's other poems. I should imagine all of them would disclaim it vigorously, not out of personal modesty, but for a reason having to do with the nature of poetry and of criticism. If poetic symbols are meanings incarnate, the nature of such incarnation is that the meanings can never be perfectly and exhaustively *dis*incarnated. One can determine exhaustively and beyond any doubt the "true meaning" of an allegory, but not of a symbol—as we shall see, Coleridge was himself quite clear on this point. A symbol, by its nature, is a kind of inexhaustible mine of meaning. It may be true that some recent critics have delved more successfully in this particular mine than anyone had previously done, or it may simply be that their particular critical apparatus was better adapted than previous ones for extracting and exhibiting their finds. Neither case is really beyond the realm of plausibility. In view of Coleridge's habit of expounding the meaning of his own symbols, even within the poem itself, it is a question whether we are to take his refusal to expound the meaning of the symbols in "Kubla Khan" as evidence that he did not himself "understand" them in a discursive way. (One thinks of his remark concerning some lines in "The Destiny of Nations": "These are very fine Lines, tho' I say it, that should not: but, hang me, if I know or ever did know the meaning of them, tho' my own composition."[18] I do not think that, even jokingly, Coleridge would have applied the term "fine lines" to lines he supposed to be meaningless.)

We may turn now to a second avenue of escape from the impasse between the symbolic interpreters and the antisymbolic interpreters, that is, to some of Coleridge's own statements concerning the nature of poetic symbolism. Miss Schneider, although admitting

---

[18] *The Complete Poetical Works,* ed. E. H. Coleridge (Oxford, 1912), I, 140, note. All future references to this volume will identify it simply as *Poems.*

that Coleridge's "remarks on symbolism are somewhat mixed," makes a good try at finding support for her position in Coleridge's own critical theory. She notes that he twice drew a distinction between allegory and symbol, but points out that these occasions were relatively late (1816 and 1818), and that in one case he was writing of religious faith rather than literature. The lateness of the statements may be discounted in the light of similar ones made earlier, and the fact that one of these later statements concerns religious faith may be discounted in view of the fact that the other statement concerns literature specifically and makes a similar distinction. Here is the principal text:

Eheu! paupertina philosophia in paupertinam religionem ducit:—A hunger-bitten and idea-less philosophy produces a starveling and comfortless religion. It is among the miseries of the present age that it recognizes no *medium* between literal and metaphorical. Faith is either to be buried in the dead letter, or its name and honors usurped by a counterfeit product of the mechanical understanding, which in the blindness of self-complacency confounds symbols with allegories. Now an allegory is but a translation of abstract notions into a picture-language, which is itself nothing but an abstraction from objects of sense; the principal being more worthless even than its phantom proxy, both alike unsubstantial, and the former shapeless to boot. On the other hand a symbol (ὁ ἔστιν ἀεὶ ταυτηγόρικον) is characterized by a translucence of the special in the individual, or of the general in the special, or of the universal in the general; above all by the translucence of the eternal through and in the temporal. It always partakes of the reality which it renders intelligible; and while it enunciates the whole, abides itself as a living part in that unity of which it is the representative. The other are but empty echoes which the fancy arbitrarily associates with apparitions of matter, less beautiful but not less shadowy than the sloping orchard or hill-side pasture-field seen in the transparent lake below.[19]

Here the symbol is conceived as a "medium" between literal state-

[19] *The Statesman's Manual, Complete Works,* ed. W. G. T. Shedd (New York: Harper & Bros., 1871–76), I, 437–38.

ment and metaphor, or allegory, and its prime characteristic is that it "always partakes of the reality which it renders intelligible." It delivers its meaning by a process of *translucence*. The word seems eminently appropriate to describe the manner of operation of the poetic symbol. Miss Schneider's description of what she finds to be Coleridge's habitual poetic technique seems rather clearly to correspond, on the one hand, to what Coleridge is here calling literal statement, when she says that "his habit was to expound his meanings outright," or, on the other hand, when she points out that "often enough he conferred upon images of nature some deep significance, but he regularly made that explicit," to what Coleridge calls allegory, a counterfeit product. Leaving aside the question of whether this was in fact Coleridge's universal or regular practice, it seems clear that a significance "conferred" upon an image (the very term has a mechanical ring in the context—*conferred upon* rather than *found* or *felt in*) in such a way that the connection must be explained is the antithesis of a "translucent" symbol. As a matter of fact, Coleridge makes it quite plain that what he conceives of as a symbol does not require explication:

The Symbolical cannot, perhaps, be better defined in distinction from the Allegorical, than that it is always itself a part of that, of the whole of which it is the representative.—'Here comes a sail,' (that is, a ship) is a symbolical expression. 'Behold our lion!' when we speak of some gallant soldier, is allegorical.[20]

A much earlier statement bears upon the same point, and constitutes a similar condemnation of allegory, of the more or less mechanical *conferring* of significances upon images of nature as opposed to *finding* them *in* the images of nature:

never to see or describe any interesting appearance in nature, without connecting it by dim analogies, with the moral world, proves faintness of Impression.

[20] *Miscellaneous Criticism,* ed. T. M. Raysor (Cambridge: Harvard University Press, 1936), p. 99 (reprinted from *Literary Remains*).

He would seem up to this point to be condemning symbolism as well as allegory, in preference for straight description, but he goes on:

Nature has her proper interest; & he will know what it is, who believes & feels, that every thing has a Life of its own, & that we are all one Life. A Poet's *Heart and Intellect* should be *combined,* intimately combined *& unified* with the great appearances in Nature—& not merely held in solution & loose mixture with them, in the shape of formal Similies.[21]

Coleridge goes on to discuss a point of capital importance, the degree of consciousness involved in the creation of symbols:

Of most importance to our present subject is this point, that the latter [the allegory] cannot be other than spoken consciously;—whereas in the former [the symbol] it is very possible that the general truth represented may be working unconsciously in the writer's mind during the construction of the symbol;—as the Don Quixote out of the perfectly sane mind of Cervantes, and not by outward observation, or historically. The advantage of symbolical writing over allegory is, that it presumes no disjunction of faculties, but simple predominance.

Again this would lead one to expect rather highly implicit symbols, even symbolic significances not necessarily fully or explicitly recognized by the poet; and Miss Schneider is aware that this poses a difficulty relative to her contention that even in theory Coleridge probably did not lean toward implicit symbolism (if we take Coleridge at his word, it also makes delays in the interpretation of given poems seem less remarkable). She points out that "he did not, however, imply that the poet remains ignorant of the symbol he has been constructing." True, but neither does he rule out the possibility, and he is far from suggesting that the poet should expound the meaning of the symbol if he is explicitly conscious of it. Professor Muirhead, in his *Coleridge as Philosopher,* quotes a passage from the *Semina Rerum* manuscript that bears upon this point:
Beauty too is spiritual, the shorthand hieroglyphic of Truth—the medi-

[21] *Collected Letters of Samuel Taylor Coleridge,* ed. E. H. Griggs (Oxford: Clarendon Press, 1956–   ), II, 864.

ator between Truth and Feeling, the Head and the Heart. The sense of
Beauty is implicit knowledge—a silent communion of the Spirit with
the Spirit in Nature, not without consciousness, though with the consciousness not successively unfolded.[22]

It is undeniable that Coleridge did often expound, successively
unfold his meanings, either because he himself felt the symbol he
had created to be less than adequate, or even quite unnecessarily,
when he might better have left it to stand for itself; but he cannot
be said to have approved of the practice in theory, much less to have
erected it into a principle. Still another passage cited by Professor
Muirhead tends, though less explicitly, in the same direction:

To make the external internal, the internal external, to make Nature
thought, and thought Nature—this is the mystery of genius in the Fine
Arts.[23]

As a matter of fact, this whole question of the nature of symbolism, of the poetic act, is central in Coleridge's aesthetic, involving
such master conceptions as that of the union of all the faculties in
the creative act, the "Will," and the "Imagination," which he
defines in one place as

that reconciling and mediatory power, which incorporating the reason
in images of the sense, and organizing (as it were) the flux of the senses
by the permanence and self-circling energies of the reason, gives birth
to a system of symbols, harmonious in themselves, and consubstantial
with the truths of which they are the conductors.[24]

At least in his theory of the creative act, far from being opposed to
the principles on which symbolic interpretation is based, he may
be said to have enunciated many of them far in advance of anyone
else.

Coleridge also has several things to say concerning the matter

[22] J. H. Muirhead, *Coleridge as Philosopher* (London: Macmillan, 1930),
p. 195.
[23] *Ibid.*, p. 204.   [24] *Statesman's Manual*, p. 436.

of obscurity in poetry that are relevant to the charge that close symbolic analysis of the kind that may be appropriate to the poems of the Metaphysicals is not appropriate to his poems. In *Early Years and Late Reflections,* Clement Carlyon reports,

> He frequently recited his own poetry, and not unfrequently led us further into the labyrinth of his metaphysical elucidations, either of particular passages or of the original conception of any of his productions, than we were able to follow him . . . [he] very seldom went right to the end of any piece of poetry; to pause and analyse was his delight.[25]

In the notebooks we find these two entries:

> Canzone XIV, fra le Rime di Dante is a poem of wild & interesting Images, intended as an Enigma, and to me an Enigma it remains, in spite of all my efforts. Yet it deserves transcription, and translation— P.195—A.D. 1806.[26]

Years later he notes, in the same notebook:

> 2 Sept. 1819. Ramsgate. I *begin* to understand the above poem: after an interval from 1805, during which no year passed in which I did not reperuse, I might say construe, *parse,* and spell it, 12 times at least, such a fascination had it, spite of its obscurity! A good instance, by the bye, of that soul of *universal* significance in a true poet's compositions in addition to the specific meaning. S.T.C.[27]

Writing of Milton in 1796 he says:

> A Reader of Milton must be always on his Duty: he is surrounded with sense; it rises in every line; every word is to the purpose. There are no lazy intervals: all has been considered and demands & merits observation.
>
> If this be called obscurity, let it be remembered tis such a one as is

---

[25] *Early Years and Late Reflections* (London: Whittaker & Co., 1836–58), I, 138.

[26] *The Notebooks of Samuel Taylor Coleridge,* ed. Kathleen Coburn (New York: Pantheon Books, 1957–　　), Vol. II, 3014　24.7.

[27] *Ibid.,* Vol. II, 3014　24.7 n. Miss Coburn agrees with E. H. Coleridge in dating the first of these notes 1807 instead of 1806.

complaisant to the Reader: not that vicious obscurity, which proceeds from a muddled head & c.[28]

And finally, a notebook entry of one line, dating from one of the very periods when Miss Schneider thinks "Kubla Khan" may have been written: "A great Vice is *metaphysical Solution* in Poetry." [29] Whatever his practice, it seems safe to say that in theory Coleridge does not hold for "open symbolism," for expounding interior meanings outright, for making the significance of symbols explicit. One may, then, paraphrase Miss Schneider in reverse by saying that we should have an exceptionally good reason before we suppose that the poems in which he seems most nearly to have practiced what he preached, "The Ancient Mariner," "Christabel," and "Kubla Khan," have no symbolical depth susceptible to relevant and fruitful interpretation.

In the case of "Kubla Khan" in particular, a third related avenue of escape from our impasse lies open, an avenue that ought to contribute substantially to the understanding of the poem itself. The major images to be found in "Kubla Khan," far from being unique to it, are to be found in different versions in a wide variety of Coleridge's poems, written both before and after "Kubla Khan" itself: the women wailing for their demon-lovers; the demon-lovers wailing for their women; the castles-mountains-temples overlooking turbulent streams of violent and mysterious origin; the sun-ice juxtapositions; the isolated paradises; the caves and chasms; the witching melodies; and so on and on. Many of them use the very words of "Kubla Khan." Since the symbolism of many of these poems is, in Miss Schneider's terms, relatively "open," and remarkably consistent, a study of these symbols with "Kubla Khan" in mind makes a symbolic interpretation of that poem seem not only to be plausible in principle but to promise an appreciable degree of success.

[28] *Ibid.*, Vol. I, 276   G.273.
[29] *Ibid.*, Vol. I, 673   10.34 (February–March, 1800).

CHAPTER TWO

The Early Poems

Since John Livingston Lowes opened up the road to Xanadu in 1927, its lanes and byways have tempted a wide variety of scholars, and a great deal of careful and interesting work has been done in the effort to identify the materials that went into the composition of "Kubla Khan," so much, in fact, that it may never be possible to apply all of the information so gathered toward the elucidation of the poem. Thus Professor Raysor is doubtless right in saying of Lowes's work that it "has been a dominating influence on Coleridge studies ever since its publication"[1]; but it is perhaps also necessary to say that the influence has not been entirely salutary. When we are faced with a very beautiful poem, one that compels our imagination and yet refuses to give up its "meaning" (if it has one) in such a way as to allow of provisionally acceptable paraphrase, when we know that its author was a man of vast and highly various learning, and when the poem itself appears to be highly allusive, then the temptation is great to exceed the limits of useful elucidation in the search for "sources," to make of that search an end in itself, finally quite independent of any probable application of the results to the closer apprehension of the poem. Although some partial efforts have been made,[2] the vast and scattered accumulation of suggested sources of the imagery in "Kubla Khan" still awaits the student who will bring all the suggestions together, try to adjudicate the rival claims, and enable us to see how far the determination of the sources can aid us in reading the poem well.

[1] *The English Romantic Poets, A Review of Research,* ed. T. M. Raysor (New York: Modern Language Association, 1956), p. 93.
[2] See, for instance, J. B. Beer, *Coleridge the Visionary* (London: Chatto & Windus, 1959).

Meanwhile, the search undoubtedly continues, despite the volume of unused stock on hand, and somewhere in the distant background one hears the warnings voiced by Coleridge himself. It can hardly be unwholesome to repeat them. When Thomas Warton finds a source for the first line of *Lycidas* in Sydney's line "Yet once againe, my Muse," and says that poets often imperceptibly adapt phrases from contemporaries or immediate predecessors, Coleridge somewhat impatiently notes in the margin:

This, no doubt, is true; but the application to particular instances is exceedingly suspicious. Why, in Heaven's name! might not 'once more' have as well occurred to Milton as to Sydney? On similar subjects or occasions some similar Thoughts *must* occur to different Persons, especially if men of resembling genius, quite independent of each other. The proof of this, if proof were needed, may be found in the works of contemporaries of different countries in books published at the very *same time,* where neither *could* have seen the work of the other— perhaps ignorant of the language. I gave my lectures on Shakespeare two years before Schlegel *began* his at Vienna, and I was myself startled at the close even verbal Parallelisms.[3]

And when Warton cites another's opinion that lines 23-24 of *L'Allegro* are based on lines from *Pericles, Prince of Tyre,* it is obviously too much for Coleridge:

Perhaps, no more convincing proof can be given that the power of poetry is from a Genius, i.e. not included in the faculties of the human mind common to all men, than these so frequent "opinions," that this or that passage was formed from, or borrowed, or stolen, etc. from this or that other passage, found in some other poet or poem, three or three hundred years older. In the name of common sense, if Gower could write the lines without having seen Milton, why not Milton have done so tho' Gower never existed? That Mr. Bowls or Bishop Newton, or

---

[3] John Drinkwater, "The Notes of S. T. Coleridge in 'Milton's Poems'—by Thomas Warton," *London Mercury,* XIV (1926), 495. The fact that Coleridge may have had special reason for being sensitive in this matter of imputed borrowings does not really diminish the common sense of his remarks.

Mr. Cary, etc. should be unable to imagine the origination of a fine thought, is no way strange; but that *Warton* should fall into the same dull cant—!!![4]

These attributions by Warton are perhaps not very similar in character to most of those made for "Kubla Khan," and Coleridge's protests may only remotely apply to statements concerning, for instance, the possibility that Alph is a shortened form of Alpheus, related in some way to the letter Alph in the Amharic dialect of Ethiopic—though the warnings still have a certain force. But the name of Bartram calls up sharp echoes in the following note appended by Coleridge to line 74 of "This Lime-Tree Bower My Prison":

> Some months after I had written this line, it gave me pleasure to find that Bartram had observed the same circumstance of the Savanna Crane.[5]

And he goes on to quote Bartram.

Though the warning is clear, and dampening if heeded, one might regret less its being so little heeded were it not for the likelihood that the fascination of the search for outside sources has too much distracted the energies of many able searchers from another line of possibly fruitful investigation: the search for "sources" within Coleridge's own poetry, the effort to find out whether the images in "Kubla Khan," even clusters of those images, occur in other poems of Coleridge, and whether their use in those poems may not illuminate the use made of them in "Kubla Khan."[6] We

---

[4] *Ibid.*, p. 499.   [5] *Poems*, p. 181 n.

[6] Among those who have made some effort in this direction, and whose lead will be followed in this chapter, are J. B. Beer, *Coleridge the Visionary;* Bernard R. Breyer, "Towards the Interpretation of *Kubla Khan*," *English Studies in Honor of James Southall Wilson, University of Virginia Studies,* V (1951), 277–90, who points out interesting relations between "Kubla Khan" and the *Biographia Literaria;* H. J. W. Milley, "Some Notes on Coleridge's 'Eolian Harp,'" *Modern Philology,* XXXVI (1938–39) and G. Wilson Knight, *The Starlit Dome,* 83–178. Professor Knight's findings are by far the most extensive.

should of course be greatly aided on our way if we knew certainly the ultimate sources of the images in the poem that derive from Coleridge's readings; but wherever Coleridge originally found them, whatever weight of meaning and emotion they may have borne in their original contexts, his own use of them in other poems, especially in poems less resistant to interpretation than "Kubla Khan," is likely to bring us closer to an understanding of the significance they had for him. Even psychoanalytical researchers might do well to bear this in mind.

In this connection we ought to remind ourselves of the splendid irresponsibility that is characteristic of poets in this matter of sources, their way of gathering lilies out of dung heaps, of detaching fragments, even from highly integrated wholes, and turning them to their own purposes, having seen in them some virtualities that never entered the minds of their original authors. The problem is a delicate one, therefore. It is not enough to have ascertained beyond all reasonable doubt the source of an apparent "allusion": it remains to determine from the context in which it is used whether the author intends it as an "allusion," whether he is in effect depending on us as readers to import into our apprehension of his poem a certain weight of meaning from the original context, or whether he has simply appropriated it for his own purposes, even hoping we shall not know where it came from.[7] When T. S. Eliot writes,

> A crowd flowed over London Bridge, so many
> I had not thought death had undone so many.

we are in no uncertainty as to the properly "allusive" function of

[7] The so-called intentional fallacy need not come into question here. Certainly there are situations in which the author's "intentions," even if we knew them, are quite irrelevant to the task of interpretation; but clearly it is not an irrelevant matter if, for instance, we suppose an "allusion" to require importation of elements into the poem under examination, when in fact the author of the poem "intended" no such thing—possibly because he got the image in question from somewhere else.

the second of the lines, and lest any reader feel uncertainty, Mr. Eliot has furnished us with notes. Even without the notes, once allusions in *The Waste Land* were identified, it would be virtually impossible not to grasp at least their ironical function as allusions. But *The Waste Land* is an extreme case. More often, surely, the poet merely hopes, insofar as he has his eye on the audience, that we shall be able to import some of the allusive context into his poem, without depending for his indispensable effect on our being able to do so. When, in an early poem, Coleridge referred in a simile to "The white-robed multitude of slaughtered saints," [8] he surely thought, and we may think, of Milton's "slaughtered saints," but if we lose our way in "The Destiny of Nations" it will not be because we fail to spot such allusions.

The situation with images or clusters of images used repeatedly within an author's own works is somewhat different, and does not involve the same problem of attribution and intention. As for the problem of attribution, there are really only two possibilities: either the image in a later poem may be remembered from an earlier one, or it may come to the poet's mind again from the same source in the poet's reading or experience from which it came originally. For our purposes of interpretation, it will in most cases make little or no difference which of these things has happened, or whether—a third and more remote possibility—the image comes this time from a quite different source, but attracts him for the old reasons. We have only to move from one use to another, becoming familiar with the associations and emotions that seem habitually to cling to the image, and, in the case of an especially difficult poem, to use that familiarity, as tactfully as possible under the control of the immediate context, in our effort to grasp its significance in this particular poem.

Likewise the problem of the author's intention is of minimal

[8] "The Destiny of Nations," *Poems,* p. 142, line 334.

importance. There may be cases in which he achieves his effect by deliberately quoting himself with a difference, and wants us to know he is quoting himself and to observe the difference, but such cases are likely to occur infrequently, and to be obvious when they do occur—if the author has any modesty at all. It is much more likely that each use of an image be, from the poet's point of view, a *new* use, that it represent a new effort to realize virtualities he obscurely feels to inhere in that image. Such "obsessions" are not unfamiliar to psychologists, and their roots may well lie in the unconscious. What we have to deal with are the poetic results. The fact that the poet, on using the image this time, may momentarily have forgotten his previous use of it is not very important. *We* know how he used it before, and that knowledge provides, at the very least, a highly promising suggestion of its present significance.

If further justification were needed for what may ungracefully be called inter-poem analysis, it could be pointed out that there is surely an intelligible sense in which it may be said that most poets, even very great ones, write only one poem, or at most two or three. And this is not very strange; there are, finally, very few things to be said, and it can be a life's work to get any one of them said to one's own satisfaction (those of us who are not engaged in the effort to say things poetically ought perhaps to engage less glibly than we sometimes do in judgments about the "versatility" of poets). There is also the difficulty of discovering what it is one has or wants to say: a poetic career may be seen as a groping after *the* thing to be said, and most poems, all in the case of some poets, as relics left by the wayside, sketches, approximations, to be discarded and forgotten by the poet, but often containing miraculous scraps of incarnated meaning that the rest of us may treasure. Surely the poet *must* look at his past works in this way, if he is to continue to be a true poet, although if necessary we must protect his poems from his impatience—he must be strong enough to forget them rather than destroy them, for our sake. One thing we mean by a "great poet" is a poet who at least in one or two instances, with whatever inevitable deficiencies, really comes through, really finds a body that will *hold* a considerable piece of meaning, that will stand by itself as a body with the fewest members irrelevant to that meaning. Such a poem is likely to illuminate all of his other works, which will seem to have their meaning in function of it. And at the same time, all the other works, the approximations, the fragments, the outright failures, may be necessary *to us* for the understanding of the one success.

There should be little risk of dispute in classifying among Coleridge's outright failures his "Sonnet to the Autumnal Moon," (1788), a moon whose "weak eye glimmers through a fleecy veil." But it is of interest to the student of "Kubla Khan" because it includes his first poetic reference to "visions":

> Mild Splendour of the various-vested Night!
> Mother of wildly-working visions! Hail!   (1–2)

We should in the most general way expect visions to be desirable, and in a young man who was to become a Romantic poet we should not be surprised at the desirability of even "wildly-working" visions. But when we come to "Kubla Khan" we discover that there is a good deal of disagreement among its readers as to whether some of its images are to be taken as positive or negative, as good or bad things, whether, for instance, the scene described in the first part of the poem is a true or a false paradise, whether it *could* be a true paradise if it has anything to do with demonic love. In general, it is true, the vision of the Abyssinian maid in the second part of the poem has been taken in a favorable light, but those who take it so do not always account satisfactorily for its producing an effect upon the visionary that calls for the exorcism described in the last lines of the poem. And so it seems significant that already, at the age of sixteen, Coleridge is experimenting with the reconciliation of opposites, that visions work "wildly," and that the inspirers of visions (in this case the autumnal moon) are somehow morally ambiguous:

> I watch thy gliding, while with watery light
>   Thy weak eye glimmers through a fleecy veil;
> And when thou lovest thy pale orb to shroud
>   Behind the gather'd blackness lost on high;
> And when thou dartest from the wind-rent cloud
>   Thy placid lightning o'er the awaken'd sky.   (3–8)

If only we liked the word "placid" better, we might find in this last line a rather fine paradoxical climax, but the preceding context is too flaccid, and what follows ("Ah such is Hope!") too thoroughly trite. And yet we know from this poem that Coleridge, like many another seer of visions, was aware from the very first that what was "mild" might also and at the same time be "wild."

The first juxtaposition of fire and ice to be found in Coleridge's poetry occurs in the fourth, and last, stanza of a mock ode, "The Nose" (1789), written in honor of the then Lord Mayor's fiery proboscis. The "subject" is treated with heavy-handed parody, utilizing epic allusions, appeals to the Muse, and variegated mythological machinery. Happily, since Freud, we know that there are no jokes, and are presumably at liberty to find serious implications in even the most arrant nonsense. Coleridge describes the Mayor's nose as a Promethean fire, and as a source of poetic inspiration:

> Thus with unhallow'd hands, O Muse, aspire,
>   And from my subject snatch a burning brand!
> So like the Nose I sing—my verse shall glow—
> Like Phlegethon my verse in waves of fire shall flow!   (7–10)

After two intervening stanzas that magnify the flame by comparisons with Sirius and Satan, whose nose St. Dunstan pinched with red-hot tongs, the inspiration turns out to be overwhelming and destructive:

The Furies to madness my brain devote—
In robes of ice my body wrap!
On billowy flames of fire I float,
Hear ye my entrails how they snap?
Some power unseen forbids my lungs to breathe!
What fire-clad meteors round me whizzing fly!
I vitrify thy torrid zone beneath,
Proboscis fierce! I am calcined! I die!
Thus, like great Pliny, in Vesuvius' fire,
I perish in the blaze while I the blaze admire. (31–40)

There seems to be no record of the Furies' employing "robes of ice" as a means of punishment—this seems to be Coleridge's own importation into an otherwise totally fiery context, perhaps just out of a general taste for paradox. But the paradox in question came, as we shall see, to be freighted with meaning for him, and even here it does occur in connection with a somehow ruinous inspiration, involving madness.

In the sonnet "Life" (1789) we have an early use of the river as a symbol of life, and associated with it is a "verdant hill," a dreary "steep," a "quick succession of delight," a "Wood" and a "Meadow" (cf. the "wood and dale" of "Kubla Khan"). Most of the basic landscape of "Kubla Khan" is there, and the result is "ravishment."

As late I journey'd o'er the extensive plain
Where native Otter sports his scanty stream,
Musing in torpid woe a Sister's pain,
The glorious prospect woke me from the dream. (1–4)

Here a dream of a maid associated with pain instead of delight is broken by the existing landscape, instead of giving rise to the recreation of that landscape.

At every step it widen'd to my sight—
Wood, Meadow, verdant Hill, and dreary Steep,
Following in quick succession of delight,—
Till all—at once—did my eye ravish'd sweep!

May this (I cried) my course through Life portray!
New scenes of Wisdom may each step display,
    And Knowledge open as my days advance!
Till what time Death shall pour the undarken'd ray,
    My eye shall dart thro' infinite expanse,
And thought suspended lie in Rapture's blissful trance.   (5–14)

Although there are none of the complications of "Kubla Khan"—
he knows little yet of the *dangers* of Knowledge—and certainly
none of the beauty of the later poem, still the "succession of delight," "Rapture's blissful trance" may bear some relation to the
delight induced by the song of the Abyssinian maid. At any rate,
we ought to note that here this peculiar landscape is associated with
Knowledge, a knowledge that issues in Rapture, thought suspended in a blissful trance. If the right people were near, they
might weave a circle round him thrice.

In "Anna and Harland" (1790?) we have another case of vision
of the past induced by surroundings both forbidding and beautiful.
Here a ghost maiden is moaning—"t'was the passing blast"—for
her ghost lover, whose death at the hands of her brother in mutually
fatal combat was quickly followed by her own.

I love to sit upon her tomb's dark grass,
    Then Memory backward rolls Time's shadowy tide;
    The tales of other days before me glide:
With eager thought I seize them as they pass;
For fair, tho' faint, the forms of Memory gleam,
Like Heaven's bright beauteous bow reflected in the stream.   (9–14)

The grass, though dark, not sunny, and the shadowy tide may
remind us vaguely of the environs of Kubla's dome ("Death's
dark house" at any rate is nearby), but the most striking detail is
the comparison of the fair, faint forms of Memory to "Heaven's
bright beauteous bow reflected in the stream," like the shadow of
the dome in "Kubla Khan." [9] Involving one of the half-lights that,

[9] See "To Robert Southey" (1795), *Poems,* p. 87, for a repetition of this
image.

like the wind, found earlier in the sonnet, Coleridge habitually associates with the poetic experience, it is also the first of many instances, culminating in "Kubla Khan," of edifices real or imaginary reflected in streams. And the vision of the past is called up under the influence of a maid.

"Pain" (1790?), another sonnet probably belonging to the same period, describes a condition in which not only the ordinary stimuli, "the Morn's first beams, the healthful breeze, / All Nature," but what are singled out as the most powerful stimuli, "Music's self," the "fragrant bower," are impotent to awaken the senses. Even could he revive within him the symphony and song of the Abyssinian maid, find himself in a garden "Where blossomed many an incense-bearing tree," it would be in vain, no "music loud and long" would issue forth, and it is just this that he regrets in this early sonnet; he thinks and sighs—

> I too could laugh and play
> And gaily sport it on the Muse's lyre,
> Ere Tyrant Pain had chas'd away delight,
> Ere the wild pulse throbb'd anguish thro' the night! (11–14)

In "Kubla Khan" it is "delight" to which the symphony and song would win him, "delight" and "joy" being Coleridge's perennial characterizations of the poetic experience.[10]

After the examination of even so few poems as we have considered here, it should not seem strange that Coleridge chose to translate into a poem called "A Wish Written in Jesus Wood" (1792) a Latin ode of John Jortin (1698–1770),[11] and send it to Mary Evans. As he renders it, the landscape is already a familiar one:

[10] For an interesting discussion of the anatomy of "Joy," see Hisaaki Yamanouchi, "The Shaping Spirit of Imagination," Master's thesis, University of Tokyo, 1959.

[11] John Sparrow, *Times Literary Supplement,* April 3, 1943, p. 163. The original may be found in *Poems in Latin,* comp. John Sparrow (London: Oxford University Press, 1941), p. 16.

> Lo! through the dusky silence of the groves,
> Thro' vales irriguous, and thro' green retreats,
> With languid murmur creeps the placid stream
>   And works its secret way.
>
> Awhile meand'ring round its native fields
> It rolls the playful wave and winds its flight:
> Then downward flowing with awaken'd speed
>   Embosoms in the Deep!   (1–8)

At twenty he can still conceive of *life* in these terms, and need not confine them to privileged moments whose magic boundaries are achieved through art. Yet although a natural phenomenon, not a work of art, is being described, the circuitous progress of the placid stream is presented as if the stream had a will of its own, as if, while it is "meand'ring" within the confines of its "native fields" (not everyone, perhaps, would translate *flexas* "meand'ring"), it can play, can deliberately make of itself and its environs a kind of garden—and a garden strikingly similar in certain details to that of "Kubla Khan," without the aid of a decreeing artist. The "groves" in their "dusky silence," the "vales irriguous," the "green retreats," and the stream that "works its secret way," all suggest a landscape more exotic than Jesus Wood, although the translation is rather close. Like the more familiar landscape, it is also distantly threatened by sordid realities:

> Thus thro' its silent tenor may my Life
> Smooth its meek stream by sordid wealth unclogg'd,
> Alike unconscious of forensic storms,
>   And Glory's blood-stain'd palm!   (9–12)

As in "Kubla Khan," the merely temporal threat is quickly dismissed, yet once beyond its in this case indefinitely prescribed limits, out of its "native fields," the meek stream is "awaken'd" from something like a trance, a vision, and falls precipitously into the Deep. The meter—"Embosoms in the Deep!"—gives the effect, as does that of "Down to a sunless sea." No more meandering, no more playing. Again, it may not be stretching a point to notice that "Embosoms in the Deep" is not a quite inevitable translation of "miscetur gremio maris." In the final stanza of the poem the Deep is replaced by "slumbrous Death."

> And when dark Age shall close Life's little day,
>   Satiate of sport, and weary of its toils,
>   E'en thus may slumbrous Death my decent limbs
>   Compose with icy hand!   (13-16)

The general tone of the poem, its apparent level of complexity, hardly seems to justify the suggestion of a significant paradox in the fact that the stream, or Life, is "awaken'd" to fall into the bosom of the deep, into "slumbrous Death," but it may not be irrelevant to notice that even in this poem what is valuable in life is associated with dream images.

Although E. H. Coleridge points out, in reprinting "Ode" (1792) for the first time since its appearance in the *Watchman,* that it was never claimed by Coleridge or assigned to him,[12] certain of its images might argue for Coleridge's authorship. Its theme, reduced to abstract essentials, recalls that of "A Wish": it deals wistfully with the possibility of productive isolation from the woes of life, particularly those occasioned by war, aspiring to "The cloudless Azure of the Mind / And Fortune's brightening Hue"—a stroke of Aristotelian realism. It is almost as if Coleridge in these early years had a premonition of the difficulties he was to face in achieving the circumstantial autonomy indispensable to artistic creation. Here a haven for the poor Pilgrim from the midnight whirlwind is thus envisaged:

> Where'er in waving Foliage hid
> The Bird's gay Charm ascends,

[12] *Poems,* p. 35 n.

Or by the fretful current chid
Some giant rock impends—
There let the lonely Cares respire
As small airs thrill the mourning Lyre
And teach the Soul her native Calm;
While Passion with a languid Eye
Hangs o'er the fall of Harmony
And drinks the sacred Balm.   (11–20)

The landscape is familiar enough—the sheltering wood, the stream overhung by a kind of natural dome—but it is not so easy to determine precisely what happens there. The "gay charm" of the bird is doubtless its song, but how is a song to be thought of as "hid" *in* the wood, and if hid, then how ascending? It would seem that the bird must be hidden and its song ascending. (This kind of syntactical confusion is not common in Coleridge's verse, and may heighten doubt as to his authorship of the poem.) In the lines that follow, the weary Pilgrim is evidently seen as working his own cure: the act of sighing out his cares teaches the soul her native calm, but the sighs themselves are compared to "small airs" that cause a lyre to sound, and so it is in making music of his cares that he is cured, inspired perhaps by the music of the bird. Whether the "fall of Harmony" over which Passion hangs with a languid Eye is that produced by the bird or the mourning lyre is not easy to determine, the less so when the "fall" apparently turns into a waterfall, from which Passion drinks the "sacred Balm." A remarkable number of the elements of "Kubla Khan" are here, in a state of baffling confusion, but if we have already read the later poem it is not so difficult to guess the implied relations among them. In the usual privileged surroundings a troubled, distracted soul is restored to harmony through the inspiration of and consequent participation in the poetic experience in its purest form, that of music, whose "sacred Balm" has not yet the ambivalent characteristics of honeydew.

It is, however, already threatened by the voice of war, at considerable length and still in lines of somewhat puzzling logic:

> Slow as the fragrant whisper creeps
>   Along the lilied vale,
> The alter'd Eye of Conquest weeps,
>   And ruthless War grows pale
> Relenting that his Heart forsook
> Soft Concord of auspicious Look
>
> *   *   *
>
> Then cease, thy frantic Tumults cease,
>   Ambition, Sire of War!
> Nor o'er the mangled Corse of Peace
>   Urge on thy scythéd Car.   (21–26, 31–34)

The "fragrant whisper" adds another note from Xanadu, and the "lilied Vale" adds to the sense of enclosure, but is the Eye of Conquest weeping "slow"? In the latter lines the advance echo of "Kubla Khan" extends to the very words: we have tumults, "war" as a rhyme word (no closer than the war-far rhyme of "Kubla Khan"), and a Sire if not ancestors. But the prospect is at least tentatively favorable here, the tumult hopefully relegated to the past. And the poem ends with a "holy Spell" that is completely innocent in character:

> And oh! that Reason's voice might swell
> With whisper'd Airs and holy Spell
>   To rouse thy gentler Sense,
> As bending o'er the chilly bloom
> The morning wakes its soft Perfume
>   With breezy influence.

Under Reason's spell, the Tumult distracting the poet, not the poet himself, is exorcised. The poet is left to enjoy the breezy and benign influence of nature. Clearly the total psychological complex of "Kubla Khan" does not yet obtain.

The setting for "Songs of the Pixies" (1793), as indicated in Coleridge's preface to the poem, is topographically similar to the setting of "Kubla Khan":

At a small distance from a village in Devonshire, *half-way up a wood-covered hill,* is an *excavation called the Pixies' Parlour.* The roots of *old trees* form its ceiling; and on its sides are innumerable cyphers, among which the author discovered his own cypher and those of his brother, cut by the hand of their childhood. *At the foot of the hill flows the river Otter.*[13]

Here the pleasure dome *is* a cave, though not of ice, actually formed by the roots of the ancient trees, which, however, cannot be expected to be incense-bearing in Devonshire. And the event commemorated bears a vague resemblance to events in "Kubla Khan":

To this place the Author, . . . conducted a party of young ladies; one of whom, of stature elegantly small, and of complexion colourless yet clear, was proclaimed the Faery Queen. On which occasion the following Irregular Ode was written.

In the first two stanzas of the poem the Pixies' abode is characterized as a retreat from the workaday world, congenial to these children of Fancy, whose proper atmosphere is that provided by the fading moon and fragrant flowers, as contrasted to the morning world of "lusty Labour." [14] The Pixies are creatures of the half-lights—moonlight, rainbow hues, shooting gleams, and of the gale, perennial symbolic accompaniments, for Coleridge, of the poetic experience. In Stanza III something very near the sun-ice opposition is introduced:

> But not our filmy pinion
> We scorch amid the blaze of day,

[13] All italics in quotations from the poems are mine, unless indicated as Coleridge's.

[14] Although it is a natural structure, not a decreed one, the "rudely sculptured names" (line 41) carved on its walls make of it a kind of temple, touched by art.

> When Noontide's fiery-tresséd minion
>   Flashes the fervid ray.
>   Aye from the sultry heat
>   We to the cave retreat
> O'ercanopied by huge roots intertwin'd
> With the wildest texture, blacken'd o'er with age:
> Round them their mantle green the ivies bind,
>   Beneath whose foliage pale
>   Fann'd by the unfrequent gale
> We shield us from the Tyrant's mid-day rage.   (21–32)

Most often in Coleridge's poetry the half-lights associated with poetic inspiration are contrasted with the sun as dimness opposed to brightness. Here the contrast is between the heat of the sun and the coolness of the cave, the former associated with "the Tyrant's mid-day rage." When, however, in Stanza IV, the Bard is placed in this setting to woo "the Queen of Solemn Thought," the Pixies inspire him thus:

> Weaving gay dreams of sunny-tinctur'd hue
>   We glance before his view:
> O'er his hush'd soul our soothing witcheries shed
> And twine the future garland round his head.   (43–46)

The dreams in the cave are tinctured with the sun! Indeed a miracle of rare device, this abode of the Pixies.

In Stanza VI we are outside the curious edifice and beside the river, which is described in both its tumultuous and its meandering phases, with a shadow sleeping upon its breast:

> Then with quaint music hymn the parting gleam
> By lonely Otter's sleep-persuading stream;
> Or where his wave with loud unquiet song
> Dash'd o'er the rocky channel froths along;
> Or where, his silver waters smooth'd to rest,
> The tall tree's shadow sleeps upon his breast.   (67–72)

The tall tree, no doubt, whose huge roots intertwine to form the Pixies' cave. So the shadow of the dome of pleasure, reared over the caves of ice, floats midway on the wave. As so often, the music is "loud." In Stanza VII we come to the high point of the Pixies' celebrations, with the approach of Night, whose features are elaborately but with surprising accuracy described as those of a goddess, who, like the moon of the early sonnet, is "Mother of wildly-working dreams," a "Sorceress." Mid the quivering light of a pale moon the Pixies play, "Aye dancing to the cadence of the stream." (88) So, if there were Pixies in Xanadu, they might dance to the mingled measure from the fountain and the caves.

The maid in the last stanza is not precisely the woman wailing for her demon lover:

> Unboastful Maid! though now the Lily pale
>   Transparent grace thy beauties meek;
> Yet ere again along the impurpling vale,
> The purpling vale and elfin-haunted grove,
> Young Zephyr his fresh flowers profusely throws,
>   We'll tinge with livelier hues thy cheeks
> And, haply, from the nectar-breathing Rose
>   Extract a Blush for Love!   (102–109)

Obviously, we have caught her before the fact, but in such an elfin-haunted grove the peril is imminent.

It cannot be a great pleasure to explore a poem like "An Effusion at Evening" (1792), a first draft, or its revised version, "Lines on an Autumnal Evening" (1793), some lines of which Coleridge himself characterizes as "intolerable stuff," [15] but it contains a liberal sprinkling of "Kubla Khan" motifs, with emphasis upon the inspirational maid. The draft begins with an address to "Imagination, Mistress of my Love," who possesses an "elfin Haunt," and is

---

[15] *Poems*, p. 52 n. Although Coleridge entreated pardon for printing the stuff, E. H. Coleridge records the fact that he republished it five times before his death.

capable of flinging the flowers of *Spring* over *"Winter's* icy plains" (Coleridge's italics). With a "faery wand" this "lovely Sorc'ress," to aid the poet's dream, is to bid his Love arise with "soul-entrancing mien." One way of reminding oneself of the virtue of "Kubla Khan" is to note the absence in it of all this cumbersome machinery. His prayer is answered, the absent Maiden flashes on his eye, and together they walk "along the streamlet's brink" and listen to "the warblings of the Grove." A passage added in the published version reveals that the Maiden's name is a "powerful spell," and her voice when she speaks a "passion-warbled song":

> Still, Fancy! still that voice, those notes prolong.
> As sweet as when that voice with rapturous falls
> Shall wake the soften'd echoes of Heaven's Halls!   (54–56)

This song, and its celestial symphonic accompaniment, it is to be remembered, he has revived within him under the impulse of Imagination. And, as a result, he imagines building, or rather, in this case, becoming, something very remotely comparable to that dome in air:

> O (*have I sigh'd*) *were mine the wizard's rod,*
> Or mine the power of Proteus, changeful God!
> A flower-entangled *Arbour* I would seem
> *To shield* my Love *from Noontide's sultry beam:*
> Or bloom a Myrtle, from whose *od'rous boughs*
> My love might weave gay garlands for her brows.   (57–62)

Since these are among the very lines that Coleridge found intolerable, we need read no further. He is doubtless right in saying that every thought in them is to be found in the Greek Epigrams, but in pillaging these he has lit upon one or two of his favorite images. The tone of line 57 recalls one way of reading "could I revive within me," the arbor he imagines becoming is both sunny and cool, and there are od'rous boughs in the poetic neighborhood.

The spring described in "Lines to a Beautiful Spring in a Village" (1794) is one that, although "zephyr-haunted," seems to be explicitly *un*like the fountain in "Kubla Khan":

> For not through pathless grove with murmur rude
> Thou soothest the sad wood-nymph, Solitude;
> Nor thine in unseen cavern depths to well,
> The Hermit-fountain of some dripping cell!   (7–10)

It is a highly domestic spring, on whose stream the schoolboys launch paper navies, but still it is remarkably like the stream of "Kubla Khan" *in parvo:*

> Unboastful Stream! thy fount with pebbled falls
> The faded form of past delight recalls,
> What time the morning sun of Hope arose,
> And all was joy; save when another's woes
> [like ancestral voices prophesying war?]
> A transient gloom upon my soul imprest,
> Like passing clouds impictur'd on thy breast.
> Life's current then ran sparkling to the noon,
> [like gardens bright with sinuous rills?]
> Or silvery stole beneath the pensive Moon:
> Ah! now it works rude brakes and thorns among
> Or o'er the rough rock bursts and foams along!   (23–32)

This, of course, is one of the many uses of the stream as a symbol of "life," its hopefully turbulent beginning, its placidly productive middle course threatened only by more or less remote perils, and the tumult of its final disappearance. The tumult here is, to be exact, an intermediate one—the lifeless ocean is still far away. But then there is no pleasure-dome, no walled garden to furnish a privileged refuge.

Coleridge once envisaged, on the banks of another stream, the Susquehanna, a real encinctured paradise, where with like-minded friends he might escape not only the political and social evils of contemporary England but the temptation of his "visionary soul" to dwell "On joys that were."[16] We have a poetic reverberation in the sonnet "Pantisocracy" (1794). It was to be a thoroughly domestic paradise, a "cottag'd dell / Where Virtue calm with careless step may stray," as safe as one might suppose oneself to be within the wall and towers of Kubla's garden. But Virtue calm would be ill-advised to step carelessly in a place where "dancing to the moonlight roundelay, / The wizard Passions weave an holy spell"—the exact geographical relation of the dell or dale to the chasm is as difficult to fix here as in "Kubla Khan." In "Pantisocracy" this contradictory juxtaposition, unsupported by all that surrounds it in "Kubla Khan," seems quite inadvertent. Certainly Coleridge was hardly ready in 1794 deliberately to attempt a reconciliation, nor was he at the time of "Kubla Khan" in terms of life (as distinguished from art).

It is tempting to seek in Coleridge's own remarks about the projected settlement on the banks of the Susquehanna, or in the sources of his information about the region, other affinities with the paradise of "Kubla Khan," but the evidence seems to be scanty. He reports, for instance, a conversation with a land agent from America who "recommends Susquehanna for its excessive beauty and its security from hostile Indians,"[17]—forgetting that the "wizard Passions" are going to be inside the walls. And two of his main sources of information, Jean-Pierre Brissot and Thomas

[16] I have emphasized elsewhere (*The Dark Night of Samuel Taylor Coleridge* [New York, Columbia University Press, 1960], pp. 35–36, 78, 86) the importance of the personal as distinguished from the political element in Coleridge's impulses toward "Pantisocracy," suggesting that one of these supposed "Joys that were" may well have been his dream of happiness with Mary Evans.

[17] *Biographia Epistolaris*, I, 42–43, quoted by J. R. MacGillivray, "The Pantisocracy Scheme and Its Immediate Background," *Studies in English by Members of University College Toronto* (Toronto: University of Toronto Press, 1931), p. 161.

Cooper, emphasize the "fertility" of the land there.[18] Coleridge's dreams of isolated retreats were not always sweetly communistic. Sister Eugenia quotes a letter to Southey [19] in July, 1801, in which Coleridge is proposing an island retreat most unpantisocratic on St. Nevis in the West Indies, where they might through influence get sinecures as slave drivers and "make the island more illustrious than Cos or Lisbos! A heavenly climate, a heavenly country, and a good house! The seashore so near us, hills, and rocks, and streams." Perhaps, in the absence of any clear pejorative hints in the poem, we need not suppose Coleridge to have been automatically shocked by the idea of Kubla's "decreeing" a pleasure-dome.

The theme of Coleridge's "Elegy Imitated from One of Akenside's Blank-Verse Inscriptions No. III." (1794?), the death of a poet from unrequited love for an undeserving maiden, is not one that we should be surprised at his attraction for,[20] and at least some traits of the adaptation suggest his hand, so that it is not immediately apparent why Derwent and Sara Coleridge omitted it from their edition of 1852 "as of doubtful origin," [21] in spite of Coleridge's having reprinted it as his own in four editions of his poems. Akenside's poem [22] begins with an extended description of the site of the lover's tomb, including a "rural palace old" imbosomed in a grove of branching oaks, the seat of a local potentate named Albert, "generous lord / Of all the harvest round." Coleridge, somewhat

[18] Brissot, *New Voyage,* p. 474, quoted by MacGillivray, p. 142; Thomas Cooper, *Some Information Concerning America,* p. 13, quoted by MacGillivray, p. 151.

[19] *Letters of Samuel Taylor Coleridge,* ed. E. H. Coleridge (Boston & New York: Houghton, Mifflin, 1895), I, 360, quoted by Sister Eugenia, "Coleridge's Scheme of Pantisocracy and American Travel Accounts," *PMLA,* XLV (1930), 1083.

[20] See, for instance, "A Lover's Complaint to his Mistress, Who Deserted Him in Quest of a More Wealthy Husband in the East Indies" (1792), *Poems,* pp. 36–37.

[21] *Ibid.,* pp. 69–70 n.

[22] *A Collection of Poems in Six Volumes by Several Hands* (London: J. Dodsley, 1775), VI, 31–32.

disconcertingly for the present context, leaves all of this out, and begins in the graveyard itself, near what in Akenside was "A low plain chapel":

> Near the lone pile with ivy overspread,
> Fast by the rivulet's sleep-persuading sound,

[In Akenside the rivulet is "silent," but that would hardly do for Coleridge.]

> Where 'sleeps the moonlight' on yon verdant bed—
> O humbly press that consecrated ground!   (1-4)

This consecrated ground is the grave of a *poet,* "famed for each harmonious strain, / And the sore wounds of ill-requited love," closely following Akenside. But Coleridge adds:

> Like some tall tree that spreads its branches wide,
> And loads the West-wind with its soft perfume,
> His manhood blossom'd;   (9-11)

All but the first of the following four lines describing Matilda's punishment are Coleridge's additions to the picture:

> But soon did righteous Heaven her Guilt pursue!
> Where'er with wilder'd step she wander'd pale,
> Still Edmund's image rose to blast her view,
> Still Edmund's voice accus'd her in each gale.   (13-16)

The poem ends with a very conventional moral ("That Riches cannot pay for Love or Truth"), but Matilda, who pines away amid an Affluence impotent to "lull the wakeful horror from her mind," (19) reminds one sharply of the woman wailing for her demon-lover—she is a woman haunted by her murdered lover.

"To the Nightingale" (1795) involves a triple comparison, issuing in what it is hard not to think of as an anticlimax. The bird is first praised as natural and rural, in comparison with the watch-

men of the city "(Those hoarse unfeather'd Nightingales of
Time!)," and is said to have produced a poetic trance:

> O! I have listen'd, till my working soul,
> Waked by those strains to thousand phantasies,
> Absorbed hath ceas'd to listen!   (12–14)

The praise of nature above art extends to a comparison with a
figure who has characteristics of both of the females in "Kubla
Khan":

> Oft will I tell thee, Minstrel of the Moon!
> 'Most musical, most melancholy' Bird!
> That all thy soft diversities of tone,
> Tho' sweeter far than the delicious airs
> That vibrate from a white-arm'd Lady's harp,
> What time the languishment of Lonely love
> Melts in her eye, and heaves her breast of snow,   (16–22)

And then the anticlimax:

> Are not so sweet as is the voice of her,
> My Sara—best beloved of human kind!
> When breathing the pure soul of tenderness,
> She thrills me with the Husband's promis'd, name!   (23–26

The white-armed Lady is surely the same kind of lady as the one
or ones appearing in "Kubla Khan." It is even likely that Coleridge
in speaking of her "delicious airs" is not being, shall we say,
Keatsian, but is thinking of the common root behind "delicious"
and "delight," which involves the idea of enticement—"to such
delight 'twould win me" and "the long sequacious notes / Over
delicious surges sink and rise." But here the Lady is a mere intru-
der. One is tempted into biography, at this point, but then so has
Coleridge been. It is plausible to think that at the time this poem
was written Coleridge was trying desperately to acclimate himself
to the domestic world offered by Sara Fricker, not to the exclusion

of the more benign types of nature influence, which he still hoped
would prove themselves amenable to both a healthy poetic activity
and a manageable, placid exploration. If we follow Coleridge's
winding path up to the point of "Kubla Khan," through the circuitous obstacle course of inhibitions, one of the great pleasures of
that poem is the sense of liberation it breathes, its total freedom
from any of the *arrières pensées* that consistently dogged him.

The very title given to "Lines Composed While Climbing the
Left Ascent of Brockley Coomb, Somersetshire" (1795) suggests
an attempt at accurate, sensitive nature description, based upon
close observation, the eye on the object, and that is what we find.
But there is an indefinite number of things to be described in such a
scene, and when Coleridge climbs a mountain we may expect a
certain characteristic choice of detail:

> With many a pause and oft reverted eye
> I climb the Coomb's ascent: sweet songsters near
> Warble in shade their *wild-wood melody:*
> For off the unvarying Cuckoo soothes my ear.
> Up scour the startling stragglers of the flock
> That *on green plots o'er precipices* browze:
> From the *deep fissures of the naked rock*
> The Yew-tree bursts! Beneath its *dark green boughs*
> (*Mid which the May-thorn blends its blossoms white*)
> Where broad smooth stones jut out in mossy seats,
> I rest:—and now have gain'd the topmost side.
> Ah! what a *luxury of landscape* meets
> My gaze! *Proud towers* and Cots more dear to me,
> Elm-shadow'd Fields, and *prospect-bounding Sea!*
> Deep sighs my lonely heart: I drop the tear:
> *Enchanting spot!* O were my Sara here!

There is, as always, music, a "wild-wood melody" furnished in
this case by the birds. The sheep are seen on "green plots o'er
precipices," and there are "deep fissures of the native rock." The
yew's "dark green boughs" are mingled with the Maythorn's

"blossoms white," an ancient tree with a fragrantly blossoming one. One of the charms of Kubla's garden is the combination of the blossoming incense-bearing trees and the forests ancient as the hills —one has the best of all worlds in that miraculous garden. There are, also, "proud towers" (as well as "cots more dear to me") overlooking the "prospect-bounding sea." The whole landscape is characterized as an "Enchanting spot!" One understands well enough, but one is not poetically prepared for "O were my Sara here!" if one has been following the description with "Kubla Khan" in mind, and has overlooked the "cots more dear to me." I. A. Richards has suggested [23] that the use of poems to illuminate biography is more likely to be fruitful than the use of biographical fact to elucidate the meaning of poems; and it may be that we can best trace the progress of Coleridge's wistful-desperate hope for solution of the enigma in terms of domestic tranquility, and his ultimate disillusion, most closely in the poems leading up to "Kubla Khan," in which the domestic element is, perhaps for the first time since his marriage, completely absent.

Affinities between "Kubla Khan" and "The Eolian Harp" (1795) have been noticed by a number of critics,[24] concentrating mainly upon the second section, in which the echoes are verbal and unmistakable. The opening scene of the poem is both very like, and very unlike "Kubla Khan":

> My pensive Sara! thy soft cheek reclined
> Thus on mine arm, most soothing sweet it is
> To sit beside our Cot, our Cot o'ergrown
> With white-flower'd Jasmin, and the broad-leav'd Myrtle,
> (Meet emblems they of Innocence and Love!)
> And watch the clouds, that late were rich with light,
> Slow saddening round, and mark the star of eve
> Serenely brilliant (such should Wisdom be)

[23] *Coleridge's Minor Poems* (Montana State University, 1960), p. 11.
[24] E. G. Brandl, Lowes, Graves. See H. J. W. Milley, "Some Notes on Coleridge's 'Eolian Harp,'" *Modern Philology*, XXXVI (1938-39), 359-75.

Shine opposite! How exquisite the scents
Snatch'd from yon bean-field! and the world *so* hush'd!
The stilly murmur of the distant Sea
Tells us of silence.   (1–12)

As in "Kubla Khan," we are in a garden spot, but the atmosphere is altogether different. This garden is unprotected by walls and towers because it would seem to need no protection. The two plants first mentioned, the Jasmin and Myrtle, expressly stated in all but one version of the poem [25] to be emblems of Innocence and Love, do not seem quite the right plants for Kubla's garden. None of the plants in the latter are named, but surely neither "forests ancient as the hills" nor even "incense-bearing trees" are meet emblems of innocence and love. Instead of the incense-bearing trees, we have the exquisite scents "Snatch'd from yon bean-field," a very different perfume. Milley sees a correspondence between the "distant sea" that "Tells us of silence" in this poem and the "sunless sea" in "Kubla Khan," [26] but, like many of the parallels he points out between the two poems, this one seems merely verbal—the silence this sea tells us of is surely *this* side of the "caverns measureless to man," of which there is no suggestion here. What we have here are the lovely elements of Kubla's garden perfectly isolated from any suggestion of its exotic features, or its ominous surroundings. It would be very hard to imagine a woman wailing for her demon-lover in this environment.

But in the second section of the poem, which may in some respects be compared to the second section of "Kubla Khan," the atmosphere changes sharply:

And that simplest Lute,
Placed length-ways in the clasping casement, hark!

[25] For some unknown reason, Coleridge decided in 1803 that the somewhat intrusively interpretive parentheses of lines 5 and 8 were unnecessary. *Poems*, 100 n.
[26] "Some Notes," p. 373.

How by the desultory breeze caress'd,
Like some coy maid half yielding to her lover,
It pours such sweet upbraiding, as must needs
Tempt to repeat the wrong! And now, its strings
Boldlier swept, the long sequacious notes
Over delicious surges sink and rise,
Such a soft floating witchery of sound
As twilight Elfins make, when they at eve
Voyage on gentle gales from Fairy-Land,
Where Melodies round honey-dropping flowers,
Footless and wild, like birds of Paradise,
Nor pause, nor perch, hovering on untam'd wing!   (12–25)

Unlike the second section of "Kubla Khan," which begins *"But oh!* that deep romantic chasm," this section begins *"And* that simplest Lute,"[27] as if what is to follow were just a continuation of the same, but that is not at all the case. In "Kubla Khan," the "and" would really *do* (though "but" is better), since Kubla's garden does not leave us wholly unprepared for romantic chasms and women wailing. It would doubtless be a slightly ludicrous refinement of interpretive reading to see an indication of Coleridge's increasing profundity of insight in the difference between his use of "and" in 1795 and his use of "but" in 1798–1800, yet the difference between these two conjunctions can certainly be crucial. In 1795 he failed to see an opposition where it patently existed. In 1798–1800 he insisted on noting it even where it came closest to being resolved.

The music of the Lute ("Placed *length-ways* in the *clasping* casement")[28] turns out to have an effect closely similar to that of the remembered music of the damsel with the dulcimer, and the

---

[27] In the edition of 1803 this line read "And th'Eolian Lute," an emendation consistent with the omission of the parentheses in lines 5 and 8. Along with the omission of lines 21–25 in that version, these changes might be seen as efforts to reduce the contrast, not to say inconsistency, between sections one and two. When lines 26–33 were added in 1817, all of these lines were restored.

[28] This line also was omitted in 1803.

lute itself is compared to a "coy maid," caressed by a present lover (the desultory breeze), and half-yielding. We know from a multitude of other contexts in Coleridge's poetry how the breeze is associated with the poetic experience, with poetic inspiration.[29] We have, in effect, arrived at the Abyssinian maid without having passed through the romantic chasm. In one early version of the poem, the song of the lute is actually compared to music issuing from a magic *mountain,* anticipating her song of Abora:

> And now its strings
> Boldlier swept, the long sequacious notes
> Over delicious Surges sink and rise
> In aery voyage, Music such as erst
> Round rosy bowers (so Legendaries tell)
> To sleeping Maids came floating witchingly
> By wand'ring West winds stolen from Faery Land;
> Where on some magic Hybla MELODIES
> Round many a newborn honey-dropping Flower
> Footless and wild, like Birds of Paradise,
> Nor pause nor perch, warbling on untir'd wing.[30]

The implications of this passage (in whatever version) are complex and highly suggestive. Here the lute clearly represents the poet, and the breeze what Coleridge was later to refer to as the "influxes" of nature.[31] But it must be noticed that the poet *is* the lute, a passive instrument simply played upon by the wind, and therefore, by implication, he *is* the maid—how far we are from "My pensive Sara!" The relation between the two—between lute and wind, maid and lover, poet and influx of nature—is graphically described in terms of sexual union (a case of *becoming* the *other*). Is it not

---

[29] See Warren, pp. 90–100; Suther, Chapter III *passim.*

[30] Version of 1797, *Poems,* p. 520. Milley (p. 374) points out that the expressions *"on* Hybla" "shows that Coleridge is thinking of a mountain. Of the three towns in Sicily named Hybla, that famous for its honey is near Syracuse. Coleridge has probably confused this with the one on Mt. Aetna, and then confused the mountain with the town on it."

[31] "The Nightingale" (1798), *Poems,* p. 265, line 27.

possible that this maid *is* the damsel with the dulcimer whom in a
vision once he saw? And this maid is *himself*, operating smoothly,
perfectly as a poet, a role conceived at this point as almost, though
not quite, completely passive (a maid is, after all, more voluntarily
responsive to a lover than a lute is to the breeze).[32] The result here
is the creation (beginning with the 1817 version) of a kind of
"dome" issuing out of the very experience itself—lines that express
the very grounds of the possibility of poetry:

> O! the one Life within us and abroad,
> Which meets all motion and becomes its soul,
> A light in sound, a sound-like power in light,
> Rhythm in all thought, and joyance everywhere—
> Methinks, it should have been impossible
> Not to love all things in a world so fill'd;
> Where the breeze warbles, and the mute still air
> Is Music slumbering on her instrument.   (26-33)

In the earlier versions, before these lines were added, the "dome"
was not built until later, after he had recalled being "on the midway
slope / Of yonder hill." In this section the comparison of poet to
lute is made explicit:

> And thus, my Love! as on the midway slope
> Of yonder hill I stretch my limbs at noon,

[It is perhaps not quite irrelevant to remember the lute placed
length-ways in the clasping casement.]

> Whilst through my half-clos'd eye-lids I behold
> The sunbeams dance, like diamonds, on the main,
> And tranquil muse upon tranquility;
> Full many a thought uncall'd and undetain'd,
> And many idle flitting phantasies,
> Traverse my indolent and passive brain,

---

[32] In "Kubla Khan" the pleasure-dome is "decreed" by Kubla, "built" in
the imagination of the poet—all is active.

> As wild and various as the random gales
> That swell and flutter on this subject Lute!   (34–43)

It is of little moment whether Coleridge was conscious of the sexual imagery, here repeated without the explicit comparison of the lute to the maid. It serves, if recognized, to place the poet in the position of the woman, and so to indicate that we must move *through* the specifically animal to the superhuman, where there is no distinction between the sexes, where all is "one Life within us and abroad." In fact, an even more theologically daring proposition is advanced here:

> And what if all of animated nature
> Be but organic Harps diversely fram'd,
> That tremble into thought, as o'er them sweeps
> Plastic and vast, one intellectual breeze,
> At once the soul of each, and God of all?   (44–48)

And it is this speculation that calls forth Sara's "mild reproof," summoning him back from these "dim and unhallow'd" thoughts to the "cot o'ergrown with / White'flowered Jasmin" of section one. In a later context we can easily imagine Sara as one of those who "Weave a circle round him thrice." Thus, although many earlier poems contain clusters of images that remind one more or less forcibly of "Kubla Khan," "The Eolian Harp" is the first to contain an extended passage whose language resembles that of "Kubla Khan," and the first to contain an all but complete paradigm of the later and greater poem.

In "To the Author of Poems" (1795), which distinguishes, by means of a continuing metaphor, among the ascending realms of poetry, we find that

> Circling the base of the *Poetic mount*
> A *stream* there is, which rolls in lazy flow
> Its coal-black waters from Oblivion's *fount:*   (10–12)

The stream is lethal to poets, and the only escape is to ascend the mountain, which in its higher reaches is "frowning" and "perilous." But about "midway," presumably, there is "A mead of mildest charm," which is easy of access. It is contrasted with the "cloud-climb'd rock, sublime and vast, / That like some giant king, o'er-glooms the hill," and with the "Pine-grove that to the midnight blast / Makes solemn music." Here in the mead,

> th 'unceasing *rill*
> To the soft Wren or Lark's descending trill
> Murmurs sweet undersong 'mid *jasmin* bowers.   (22–24)

And there are flowers and "herbs of med'cinable powers." This mead reminds one rather of the wood and dale through which the sacred river meanders with a mazy motion. There is a suggestion of pedantry in the effort to compare the two landscapes point by point, but it may be worth risking, especially since the precise disposition of the various features in "Kubla Khan" is a matter of considerable doubt and possibly of some importance.

Kubla decreed the pleasure-dome "where," indefinitely enough, "Alph, the sacred river, ran / Through caverns measureless to man." By "twice five miles," Coleridge must mean that the enclosure was five miles by five miles, a square, within which were to be found the gardens bright with sinuous rills, etc., since, in the second section, the sacred river is spoken of as "Five miles meandering with a mazy motion / Through wood and dale," presumably from one wall of the garden to the opposite wall. On one boundary of the enclosure is to be found the "deep romantic chasm," from which the "mighty fountain" momently is forced. From here it flows through the enclosure, diverted with a mazy motion into the sinuous rills, until, at the other boundary, it reaches "the caverns measureless to man." It is somehow natural to suppose that Kubla would build his pleasure-dome in the center of the enclosure, and it turns out that its shadow does float "midway on the waves" (in both dimensions?). At this mid-point, the noise of the fountain on the one side and the caverns on the other would necessarily be "mingled."

There is no sufficient reason to presuppose that the landscape of "To the Author" should correspond exactly to that of "Kubla Khan"—we analyzers are woefully tempted to make things *fit*. But we do have a fountain, *Oblivion's* fount, a fact that somehow makes up by an effect of foreshortening for the absence of any reference to the "sunless sea." Above it, as in "Kubla Khan," are the gardens, a "mead of mildest charms," in which there are "rills," flowers, med'cinable herbs, balmy sweets. But this is in the middle realm of poetry (the native realm of most if not all of author Cottle's verse)—the rill "Murmurs sweet undersong 'mid jasmin bowers." It is as if we were beside "our Cot o'ergrown / With white-flower'd Jasmin, and the broad-leav'd Myrtle, / (Meet emblems they of Innocence and Love!)" But, as in "The Eolian Harp," the strings are boldlier swept, and, as there, this suggests a physical ascent, a "perilous ascent": in "The Eolian Harp" it was perilous enough to result in heresy and a rebuke therefor. The ascent here is toward "the Mountain's lofty-frowning brow," "the cloud-climb'd rock, sublime and vast, / That like *some giant king* o'erglooms the hill," toward the "Pine-grove that to the midnight blast / Makes solemn music!" The shadow of the rock is like the shadow of the pleasure-dome of Kubla Khan, which floats midway on the waves, and which includes and transcends the dangers *and* the beauties of its surroundings. It recalls Mount Abora as well, the song about which would frighten all who heard. He tells Cottle that "Virtue and Truth shall love your gentler song; / But Poesy demands th'impassion'd theme," associated with the storm, the shrill gust, the "tempest-honor'd ground." So in "The Eolian Harp" the emblems meet of innocence and love were left behind, and something beyond truth and virtue passionately invoked, something that inspired unhallowed thoughts, "shapings of the unregenerate mind." And in "Kubla Khan," the music loud and long to be inspired by the song of the damsel would both build a dome (no mention of the gardens) and result in the singer's requiring exorcism.

Coleridge was not the man to exult for long in overleaping truth and virtue.

> Low was our pretty Cot: our tallest Rose
> Peep'd at the chamber-window. We could hear
> At silent noon, and eve, and early morn,
> *The sea's faint murmur.* In the open air
> Our *Myrtles blossom'd;* and across the porch
> *Thick Jasmins twined;* the *little landscape round*
> Was *green and woody,* and refreshed the eye.
> It was a *spot* which you might aptly call
> The Valley of Seclusion!   (1–9)

It is not hard to tell, in these lines, that we are in the same year with "The Eolian Harp" and "To the Author." "Reflections on Having Left a Place of Retirement" (1795) continues, "Once I saw . . . ," but instead of a damsel with a dulcimer the reference is to "A wealthy son of Commerce . . . Bristowa's citizen." And he turns out to be quite capable of appreciating the virtues of this scene. "A Blesséd Place," he sighs. There is a fine pathos in Coleridge's congratulating himself on being envied by a commercial citizen of Bristol (his intrusion, by the way, is not superfluous in the economy of the poem, which ends with a resolve on the part of the poet to enter into the life of action, albeit not by the way of commerce). But into this placid scene a supernal note is introduced:

> Oft with patient ear
> Long-listening to the viewless sky-lark's note
> (Viewless, or haply for a moment seen
> *Gleaming on sunny wings*) in whisper'd tones
> I've said to my Beloved, 'Such, sweet Girl!
> The *inobtrusive song of Happiness,*

> *Unearthly minstrelsy!* then only heard
> When the soul seeks to hear; when all is hush'd
> And the Heart listens.'   (18–26)

In so many of these early poems Coleridge seems to slip insensibly from the domestic into the exotic. Here, as in "The Eolian Harp," it is music that strikes the new note, there the music of the lute, here the music of the lark, but here no comparable flight of fancy is produced. Yet, just as in "The Eolian Harp," he recalls being on the mountain. "But," he begins this time as in "Kubla Khan":

> But the time, when first
> From that low Dell, *steep up the stony Mount*
> I climb'd with *perilous* toil and reach'd the top,
> Oh! what a goodly scene! *Here* the bleak mount,
> Grey clouds, that shadowing *spot the sunny fields;*
> And *river* now *with bushy rocks o'er-brow'd,*
> Now *winding bright and full,* with naked banks;
> And *seats and lawns,* the *Abbey* and the *wood,*
> And cots, and hamlets, and faint city-spire;
> The Channel *there,* the Islands and white sails,
> *Dim* coasts, the cloud-like hills, and *shoreless Ocean*— [33]   (26–37)

This is a kind of compressed version of the first three descriptions in "Kubla Khan"—the opening description of the pleasure-dome, the romantic chasm, and, what was originally a third section, the redescription of the dome. And the speaker, without any intervention of a damsel, builds the dome, or conceives that God has built it for him:

> It seem'd like Omnipresence! God, methought,
> Had built him there a Temple: the whole world
> Seem'd *imag'd* in its vast circumference: (38–40, italics Coleridge's)

This is essentially the same "dome" that was built in "The Eolian Harp," but neither the dome itself nor the surroundings out of which it arises are so magical as in the former poem, perhaps be-

---

[33] Only "here" and "there" are italicized by Coleridge.

cause here there is no damsel. The lark, which provides the music in this poem, somehow does not call forth the same response from Coleridge. In an early published version the poem was subtitled: "A Poem which affects not to be Poetry." [34]

Having had the dome built for him in this case, the dome itself wins the poet to a remarkable delight:

> No *wish* profan'd my overwhelméd heart.
> Blest hour! It was a luxury,—to be!   (41–42, italics Coleridge's)

Here there follows no rebuke from Sara, and indeed, theologically speaking, there is not the same occasion for it as in "The Eolian Harp." In any case, here the speaker is no more than an innocent, unwishing bystander, not at all the making, decreeing Poet—a luxury indeed. But there is nevertheless a rejection of the experience, for a very different kind of reason—it is opposed to the life of action and responsibility (as in "To the Nightingale" is was opposed to domesticity, in "The Eolian Harp" to religious orthodoxy). There is a genuine, if not entirely convincing, attempt at excoriation of the sentimental humanitarian. He scans

> The sluggard Pity's vision-weaving tribe!
> Who sigh for Wretchedness, yet shun the Wretched,
> Nursing in some delicious solitude
> Their slothful loves and dainty sympathies!   (56–59)

(We may think how much it cost Coleridge to use "delicious" in this way.) And a kind of exorcism is performed. At least its results are registered:

> I therefore go, and join head, heart, and hand,
> Active and firm, to fight the bloodless fight
> Of Science, Freedom, and the Truth in Christ.   (60–62)

The last section of the poem sounds something like the note that Maud Bodkin finds one of the most haunting in "Kubla Khan," [35]

[24] *Poems,* p. 106 n.   [35] Bodkin, p. 95.

the expression of longing in "Could I revive within me. . . ." Only *something* like it, for the renunciation still seems voluntary and temporary, and nothing is said about the mount—only the emblems meet of Innocence and Love are recalled (it is as if Coleridge were not yet fully aware of the true relation for him of the symbols he is manipulating):

> Yet oft when after honourable toil
> Rests the tired mind, and waking loves to dream,
> My spirit shall revisit thee, dear Cot!
> Thy Jasmin and thy window-peeping Rose,
> And Myrtles, fearless of the mild sea-air.
> And I shall sigh fond wishes—sweet Abode!
> *Ah!*—had none greater! And that all had such!
> It might be so—but the time is not yet.
> Speed it, O Father! Let thy Kingdom come!   (63–71)

Yet this is real pathos, of which there is no suggestion in "Kubla Khan."

Critics old or new have ample warning from Coleridge himself that any effort to find in "Religious Musings" (1794–96) an organic structure is doomed to failure. As if it were not enough to characterize the composition as "musings," Coleridge appends a subtitle, "A Desultory Poem, Written on Christmas Eve of 1794," and in several editions furnishes an "Argument." What we have in fact is a pseudo-Miltonic mixture of contemporary politics and apocalyptic vision. The Miltonic tone and imagery, though hardly successful in the total absence of any unifying myth, are yet not inappropriate to the subject, which reflects a halting effort to justify the ways of God to man, to embrace divine order and perfection and terrestrial confusion and evil within a single view. It cannot, after all, have been easy to write a Christmas Eve poem in 1794, with the Red Terror still fresh in mind, expecially for one who still had an emotional investment in the Revolution. But for all its cumbersome machinery, the theme of this poem bears a recog-

nizable relation to that of "Kubla Khan." Here, in conventional
religious terms used for the most part in a secondhand way, we
have both order and violence, both beauty and terror, and we even
find a few of the images as well.

It is a "voice" that rouses him, "most divine to hear," and as a
result he sees a heavenly vision. Characteristically, the vision issues
in a landcape image, including vernal mead, high grove, sea, sun,
and stars, a natural garden reflecting the divine order, "The supreme beauty uncreate," but reflecting it less majestically than
Christ upon the cross. A long section (28–158) elaborates upon this
vision of order overcoming all the forces of division. But the vision
is interrupted by voices prophesying war, one of them identified
in a note as that of Lord Abingdon, who is quoted as having declared in Parliament that, "The best road to Peace, my Lords, is
WAR! and WAR carried on in the same manner in which we are
taught to worship our Creator, namely, with all our souls, and with
all our minds, and with all our hearts, and with all our strength." [36]
It would surely seem that the good lord fancied himself as an
"ancestral voice." He is seconded in the poem by "that foul Woman
of the North" and "each petty German princeling, nursed in
gore! / Death's prime slave-merchants!" The principle offered in
the poem to reconcile this opposition in the state of things between
order and violence is an old one—that evil is temporary, and a
means to good:

> Lord of unsleeping Love,
> From everlasting Thou! We shall not die.
> These, even these, in mercy didst thou form,
> Teachers of Good through Evil, by brief wrong
> Making Truth lovely, and her future might
> Magnetic o'er the fixed untrembling heart.   (192–97)

Not satisfied merely to enunciate the principle, Coleridge goes on
to offer a kind of historical analysis of the ambiguous development

[36] *Poems,* p. 115 n.

of society, an account vaguely reminiscent of that given by Socrates in the Republic (not to mention Hartley), and one that has a close bearing upon "Kubla Khan":

> In the primeval age a dateless while
> The vacant Shepherd wander'd with his flock,
> Pitching his tent where'er the green grass waved.
> But soon Imagination conjured up
> An host of new desires:

In the work of some other author we might suppose that we are here embarked upon an account of the golden age or the state of nature and its degeneration, but with Coleridge we know that, even as early as 1794, "Imagination" can hardly be an entirely evil word; and what follows is in effect a reconciliation of opposites by discursive philosophical rather than poetic means:

> with busy aim,
> Each for himself, Earth's eager children toiled.
> So Property began, twy-streaming fount,
> Whence Vice and Virtue flow, honey and gall.
> Hence the soft couch, and many-coloured robe,
> The timbrel, and arched dome and costly feast,
> With all the inventive arts, that nursed the soul
> To forms of beauty, and by sensual wants
> Unsensualized the mind, which in the means
> Learnt to forget the grossness of the end,
> Best pleasured with its own activity.   (198–212)

Here it may be useful to recall J. B. Beer's insistence that Xanadu is found in the context of a *fallen* world;[37] that Kubla is "the Tartar king of tradition: fierce and cruel,"[38] his genius "the manifestation of demonic powers," to be compared to that of Napoleon;[39] and the dome, in contrast to natural domes in other poems, which are seen as temples (and in contrast as well to the

[37] Beer, p. 216.   [38] *Ibid.*, p. 222.   [39] *Ibid.*, pp. 226–27.

dome built in the last section of the poem), a "man-made dome," a "mistaken ideal, an attempt to escape from the true temple and create a private world."[40] Beer sees all of the images in the second section as "anti-types of the true paradise,"[41] and finds the point of the poem in the contrast between the "pleasure-dome" decreed by Kubla in the first part, an artificial tour de force, and the "dome of pleasure," the harmonious symbol of paradise regained, described in the section beginning with line 30.

This interpretation presents a number of difficulties that we shall have to consider later on, but the passage quoted above from "Religious Musings" suggests that we cannot assume Coleridge to have thought of invention, building, material splendor as necessarily evil, or as pertaining in some special way to the fallen nature. He is concerned with man after the fall, presumably, though he makes no point of it here, but his conception of man's development is an evolutionary one, in which his powers for evil are inextricably bound up with his powers for good:

> From Avarice thus, from Luxury and War
> Sprang heavenly Science; and from Science Freedom. (224–25)

He is not here at least thinking in terms of contrast between the man-made as evil and the natural as good: Imagination itself is the source of the "arched dome" and costly feast, which may be a source of good or of evil, though at this time of life he envisaged a necessary progress toward the good. Amid "beauteous terrors" (236) he sees the phalanx of unnumbered tribes led by Philosopher and Bard

> o'er the wild and wavy chaos rush
> And tame the outrageous mass, with plastic might
> Moulding confusion to such perfect forms,
> As erst were wont,—bright visions of the day!—
> To float before them, when, the summer noon,

[40] *Ibid.,* p. 224. [41] *Ibid.,* p. 242.

Beneath some arched romantic rock reclined
They felt the sea-breeze lift their youthful locks;   (245-51)

To mould confusion "to such perfect forms" may well be to build
an "arched dome," even a pleasure-dome, which is both the place
and the product of visions. In 1794 he is still able to see the building
of the dome as a social enterprise, to imagine a "vast family of
Love" enjoying

> *Such delights*
> As float to earth, permitted *visitants!*
> When in some hour of solemn jubilee
> The massy gates of *Paradise* are thrown
> Wide open, and forth come in *fragments wild*
> Sweet echoes of *unearthly melodies,*
> And *odours* snatched from beds of Amaranth,
> And they, that from the *crystal river of life*
> Spring up on freshened wing, *ambrosial* gales!
> The favoured good man in his lonely walk
> Perceives them, and his silent spirit *drinks*
> *Strange bliss which he shall recognise in heaven.*
> And *such delights,* such *strange beatitudes*
> Seize on my young anticipating heart
> When that blest future rushes on my view!   (343-57)

Even in this solemn and pious atmosphere (the next lines read:
"For in his own and in his Father's might / The Saviour comes!"),
the beatitudes seem "strange," though they do not yet, as in "Kubla
Khan," call for exorcism.

The poem ends instead with an address to the "Contemplant
Spirits":

> ye that hover o'er
> With untired gaze the *immeasurable fount*
> *Ebullient* with creative Deity!
> And ye of *plastic power,* that interfused
> Roll through the grosser and material mass
> In *organizing surge!* Holies of God!

(And what if Monads of the infinite mind?)
I haply journeying my immortal course
Shall sometime join your mystic choir!   (402–10)

Fortunately or unfortunately, Sara was not by to reprove him as
she did in "The Eolian Harp," and he can look forward to partici-
pating in the divine creation as a Monad of the infinite mind, a
creation involving almost all the features of "Kubla Khan."

> Till then
> I discipline my young and novice thought
> In ministeries of heart-stirring song,
> And aye on Meditation's heaven-ward wing
> Soaring aloft I breathe the empyreal air
> Of Love, omnific, omnipresent Love,
> Whose day-spring rises glorious in my soul
> As *the great Sun,* when he his influence
> Sheds on the *frost-bound waters—The glad stream*
> Flows to the ray and *warbles as it flows.*   (410–19)

In the end he forgets the "unnumbered tribes" and looks forward
to the day when he will himself be able to build that dome in the
air, that sunny dome, those caves of ice.

In the "Monody on the Death of Chatterton" (1790–1834) Coleridge reviews the case of a poet whose discipline in the ministeries
of heart-stirring song was cut short in mid-progress toward mem-
bership in the mystic choir, allegedly by "freezings of neglect" on
the part of those very unnumbered tribes who, roused by eloquent
men in "Religious Musings," were to mould Confusion to such
perfect forms.

> Lo! by the grave I stand of one, for whom
> A prodigal Nature and a niggard Doom
> (*That* all bestowing, *this* withholding all)
> Made each chance knell from distant spire or dome
> Sound like a seeking Mother's anxious call,
> Return, poor Child! Home, weary Truant, home!
>   (10–15, italics Coleridge's)

Professor Knight connects the dome here with that in "Kubla Khan," and taken as a symbol of safety something might be made of it, but the connection seems tenuous. Closer would seem to be the association of the winding river with inspiration, the composition of verse described in terms of whirling eddies and thronging surges, the poetic *élan* itself, the poet's lifeblood, described as a flowing tide of power:

> Sublime of thought, and confident of fame,
> From vales where Avon winds the Minstrel came.
>   Light-hearted youth! aye, as he hastes along,
>   He meditates the future song,
> How dauntless Ælla fray'd the Dacyan foe;
>   And while the numbers flowing strong
>   In eddies whirl, in surges throng,
> Exulting in the spirits' genial throe
> In tides of power his life-blood seems to flow.   (43–51)

Even here the similarity is not very close, but up to 1829, for lines 47–56 appeared the following:

> How dauntless Ælla fray'd the Dacyan foes;
>   And, floating high in air,
>   Glitter the sunny visions fair,
> His eyes dance rapture, and his bosom glows! [42]

He is seeing a vision of the sunny dome in air, and the portrait of the poet that follows in the later version reminds one of the flashing eyes and floating hair of "Kubla Khan":

> And now his cheeks with deeper ardors flame,
> His eyes have glorious meanings, that declare
> More than the light of day shines there,
> A holier triumph and a sterner aim!
> Wings grow within him; and he soars above
> Or Bard's or Minstrel's lay of war or love.   (52–57)

[42] *Poems*, p. 127.

It is appropriate, then, that as one of his accomplishments "On many a waste he bids trim gardens rise," (62) and discloses his early bloom "Filling the wide air with a rich perfume!" (68)

We have even a version of the woman wailing for her demon-lover. When the poet is contemplating suicide, oppressed by the "hard world" without and "canker" within, Affection appears to him—"(Her bosom bare, and wildly pale her cheek)"—(83) and tries to deter him by inducing visions of his native cot and his sister's and mother's woe at his fate, but in vain. Just so had the image of Sara invoked domestic responsibility to combat the dangers of the poetic trance, and for a time successfully, as in "Shurton Bars" and "The Eolian Harp."

Returning from meditation on Chatterton's fate to the consideration of his hours of inspiration, Coleridge depicts as the scene of his roving a landscape that recalls "Kubla Khan" in many of its features:

Ye *woods!* that wave o'er Avon's *rocky steep,*
To Fancy's ear sweet is your *murmuring deep!*
For here she loves the cypress wreath to weave;
Watching with wistful eye, the saddening tints of eve.
Here, far from men, *amid this pathless grove,*
In solemn thought the Minstrel wont to rove,
Like star-beam on the slow sequester'd tide
Long glittering, through *the high tree* branching wide.
And here, in Inspiration's eager hour,
When most the big soul feels the mastering power,
These wilds, these *caverns* roaming o'er,
Round which the screaming sea-gulls soar,
With wild unequal steps he pass'd along,
Oft pouring on the winds a broken song:
Anon, upon *some rough rock's fearful brow*
Would pause abrupt—and gaze upon the waves below.   (114–29)

The poet sees himself escaping Chatterton's fate by fleeing o'er the ocean swell to seek the cottag'd dell

> Where Virtue calm with careless step may stray;
> And, dancing to the moon-light roundelay,
> The wizard Passions weave an holy spell!   (145–47)

I have pointed out elsewhere the inconsistency between the cottag'd dell and the wizard Passions. In this poem he is still hoping to combine them. In "Kubla Khan" the cottag'd dell has completely disappeared. In fact, the scene he imagines o'er the ocean swell is closer to Xanadu than to Clevedon:

> Yet will I love to follow the sweet dream,
> Where Susquehanna pours his *untamed stream;*
> And on some hill, whose *forest-frowning side*
> *Waves o'er the murmurs of his calmer tide,*
> *Will raise a cenotaph to thee,*
> Sweet Harper of *time-shrouded Minstrelsy!*
> And there, sooth'd sadly by *the dirgeful wind,*
> Muse on the sore ills I had left behind.   (158–65)

"The Destiny of Nations" (1796) is a kind of apocalyptic fantasy in somewhat the same vein as "Religious Musings," and, if possible, even more "desultory," consisting as it does of a series of fragments the majority of which were fitted into Southey's epic poem *Joan of Arc*.[43] It is subtitled "A Vision," and opens with an invocation to the Eternal Father, in "symphony" and "song" that casts a "soliciting spell." Its "strong music" played upon a harp induces a Platonic apperception of reality, with political overtones:

> For what is Freedom, but the unfettered use
> Of all the powers which God for use had given?
> But chiefly this, him First, him Last to view
> Through meaner powers and secondary things
> Effulgent, as through clouds that veil his blaze.
> For all that meets the bodily sense I deem
> Symbolical, one mighty alphabet

[43] *Poems,* p. 131 n. See Knight, pp. 136–42 on the echoes of "Kubla Khan" in this poem.

For infant minds; and we in this low world
Placed with our backs to bright Reality,
That we may learn with young unwounded ken
The substance from its shadow.   (13–23)

As in many other contexts, the melody-inspired vision is one
involving knowledge, metaphysical knowledge, wisdom perhaps.

There follows a critique of contemporary cosmologies, including
one that posits "Infinite myriads of self-conscious minds" (43) in
explanation of the forces of the universe. In this view, even the evil
spirits contribute positively to the whole:

And what if some rebellious, o'er dark realms
Arrogate power? yet these train up to God,
And on the rude eye, unconfirmed for day,
Flash meteor-lights better than total gloom.   (60–63)

And their action is compared, interestingly enough, to an action
involving sun and snow. Again we may have a hint as to the force
of the juxtaposition in "Kubla Khan":

As ere from Lieule-Olaive's vapoury head
The Laplander beholds the far-off Sun
Dart his slant beam on unobeying snows,
While yet the stern and solitary Night
Brooks no alternate sway . . .
                         he the while
Wins gentle solace as with upward eye
He marks the streamy banners of the North,
Thinking himself those happy spirits shall join
Who there in floating robes of rosy light
Dance sportively.   (64–68; 75–80)

The idea, somehow a plausible one, seems to be that contradictories
reconciled, at least existing together in act, provide a hint, a
glimpse, of the absolute. For, he continues, echoing a passage
quoted from "Religious Musings,"

> Fancy is the power
> That first unsensualizes the dark mind,
> Giving it new delights; and bids it swell
> With wild activity; and peopling air,
> By obscure fears of Beings invisible,
> Emancipates it from the grosser thrall
> Of present impulse, teaching self-control,
> Till Superstition with unconscious hand
> Seat Reason on her throne.   (80–88)

So we may see, perhaps, how the creation of Kubla, even though obscurely involved with evil forces, may serve as the type of the ultimate in human accomplishment:

> Wherefore not vain,
> Nor yet without permitted power impressed,
> I deem those legends terrible, with which
> The polar ancient thrills his uncouth throng:
> Whether of pitying Spirits that make their moan
> O'er slaughtered infants, or that Giant Bird
> Vuokho, of whose rushing wings the noise
> Is Tempest, when the unutterable Shape
> Speeds from the mother of Death, and utters once
> That shriek, which never murderer heard, and lived.   (88–97)

We may see also on the basis of what conviction Coleridge accepted his share of the dual project envisaged in the poems of *Lyrical Ballads,* that of dealing with "incidents and agents . . . in part at least, supernatural; and . . . the interesting of the affections by the dramatic truth of such emotions, as would naturally accompany such situations, supposing them real." "It was agreed," he goes on, "that my endeavors should be directed to persons and characters supernatural, or at least romantic; yet so as to transfer from our inward nature a human interest and a semblance of truth sufficient to procure for these shadows of imagination that willing suspension of disbelief for the moment, which constitutes poetic faith." [44] As the project is described here in the *Biographia Literaria,* it can easily be taken to entail simply a technical exercise, and certainly that is intended; but underlying the technical exercise is a deeper and quite genuine poetic faith, or more properly, faith in poetry, faith in its ability by combining the supernatural and the natural to open a window upon ultimate reality. Coleridge says that "with this view I wrote 'The Ancient Mariner,' and was preparing among other poems, 'The Dark Ladié' and the 'Christabel,' in which I should have more nearly realized my ideal, than I had done in my first attempt." The failure to mention "Kubla Khan," unless it be included "among other poems," suggests that, as Miss Schneider argues, it was of somewhat later date than the three poems mentioned, but surely it falls within the same category.

In a second illustration of salutary legend culled from northern mythology, symbols reminiscent of "Kubla Khan" float indefinitely:

> Or if the Greenland *Wizard in strange trance*
> Pierces the untraveled realms of Ocean's bed
> Over the abysm, even to *that uttermost cave*
> By mis-shaped prodigies beleaguered, such
> As Earth n'er bred, nor Air, nor the upper Sea:
> Where dwells *the Fury Form,* whose unheard name
> *With eager eye, pale cheek, suspended breath,*
> *And lips half-opening with the dread of sound,*
> Unsleeping Silence guards, worn out with fear
> Lest haply 'scaping on some treacherous blast
> The fateful word *let slip the Elements*
> And frenzy Nature.   (98–109)

All of this is, of course, by way of introduction to the subject of Joan's voices, the authenticity of which was presumably somewhat harder for the Englishmen and Protestants in the audience, indeed

[44] *Biographia Literaria,* II, 5–6.

for Coleridge himself, to accept, even on poetic faith, than the ecstasies of Lapland and Greenland wizards. In describing the particular "guardian Power" who appeared to Joan and the vision he presented her with, Coleridge introduces in one variant version images clearly related to the fountain of "Kubla Khan":

> And first a landscape rose
> More wild and waste and desolate, than where
> The white bear drifting on a field of ice
> Howls to her sunder'd cubs with piteous rage
> And savage agony. Mid the drear scene
> A craggy mass uprear'd its misty brow,
> Untouch'd by breath of Spring, unwont to know
> Red Summer's influence, or the cheerful face
> Of Autumn; yet its fragments many and huge
> Astounded ocean with the dreadful dance
> Of whirlpools numberless, absorbing oft
> The blameless fisher at his perilous toil. (123–147 of fragment) [45]

It may not be easy to determine precisely what topographical phenomena are in question here, but the combination of the natural dome, this time declared to be *un*touched by the sun, and fragments many and "huge," in dreadful "dance" forming whirlpools is familiar, and so is the moral ambiguity of the image, the grandeur, the beauty, and the terror.

There follows a more or less biographical account of the Maid's preparation for her divine vocation, then "fragments . . . intended to form part of the poem when finished," [46] concerned largely with her visions. At what may be the climax of her affirmation,

> She spoke, and instantly faint melody
> Melts on her ear, soothing and sad, and slow,
> Such measures, as at calmest midnight heard
> By agéd Hermit in his holy dream,
> Foretell and solace death; and now they rise

---

[45] *Poems*, p. 136 n. E. H. Coleridge attributes lines 141–43 to Southey.
[46] *Ibid.*, p. 142.

> Louder, as when with harp and mingled voice
> The white-robed multitude of slaughtered saints
> At Heaven's wide-open'd portals gratulant
> Receive some martyred patriot.   (328–36)

The melody is not in the same key as that of the Abyssinian maid, but its harmony induces a comparable ecstasy, and on awakening Joan sees a landscape strikingly similar to that of Xanadu:

>   The harmony
> Entranced the Maid, till each suspended sense
> Brief slumber seized, and confused ecstasy.
>   At length awakening slow, she gazed around:
> Still thinning as she gazed, an Isle appeared,
> Its high, o'er-hanging, white, broad-breasted cliffs,
> Glassed on the subject ocean.   (336–43)

In the original version lines 339–40 are even closer:

> But lo! no more was seen the ice-pil'd mount
> And meteor-lighted dome. —An Isle appear'd [47]

A "fair Form" is seen moving across an ancient battlefield "repairing all she might," making a garden out of pain and chaos, but she is interrupted by a sound as it were of ancestral voices:

> But soon a deep precursive sound moaned hollow:
> Black rose the clouds, and now, (as in a dream)
> Their reddening shapes, transformed to Warrior-hosts,
> Coursed o'er the sky, and battled in mid-air.

In the phantasmagoria that follows, Coleridge finds occasion to allude to certain primitive immortality myths (441–47), and appends the introduction to a Greek Prize Ode, with the following "literal translation":

Leaving the gates of Darkness, O Death! hasten thou to a Race yoked to Misery! Thou wilt not be received with lacerations of Cheeks, nor

[47] *Ibid.*, p. 143 n.

with funereal ululations, but with *circling Dances* and the joy of Songs. Thou art terrible indeed, yet thou dwellest with LIBERTY, stern GENIUS! Borne on thy dark pinions over the swelling Ocean they return to their native country. There by the side of *fountains beneath Citron groves,* the Lovers tell to their Beloved, what horrors, being Men, they had endured from Men.[48]

The last fragment but one echoes the beginning, and is given as Joan's reaction to the visions:

> 'Glory to Thee, Father of Earth and Heaven!
> All-conscious Presence of the Universe!
> Nature's vast ever-acting Energy!
> In will, in deed, Impulse of All to All!
> Whether thy love with unrefracted ray
> Beam of the Prophet's purgéd eye, or if
> Diseasing realms the Enthusiast, wild of thought,
> Scatter new frenzies on the infected throng,
> Thou both inspiring and predooming both,
> Fit instruments and best, of perfect end:
> Glory to Thee, Father of Earth and Heaven!   (459–69)

An undated manuscript note by Coleridge next to the first three of these lines repudiates the suggestion of pantheism contained in them,[49] but in 1796 he looked to necessitarianism and the "impersonality of the Deity" as philosophical sources of harmony between the ideal and the real, between the indispensable belief in ultimate order and the observed chaos of experience. In poems like "Religious Musings" and "The Destiny of Nations," he seems still to be groping for a directly theological myth that will reconcile these opposites in the Miltonic tradition, but neither the doctrines he sought to embody nor the images he found to embody them were sufficiently satisfactory to him to enable him to make of them successful or even complete poems. As we know from his remark in the *Biographia,*[50] Coleridge was not satisfied even with "The

---

[48] *Ibid.,* p. 147 n. GENIUS is Coleridge's translation of Τύραννε. See below, pp. 192–93.
[49] *Ibid.*   [50] Quoted above, p. 73.

Ancient Mariner" on this score, but, like the poems he links with it, and like "Kubla Khan," it escapes the Miltonic influence, employs a different and certainly, for Coleridge and his time, a more successful method. What remains constant, beneath the changes in philosophical doctrine and poetic method, is the problem—and the cluster of images we are following.

"To a Young Friend" (1796), like "To the Author of Poems," is a fully developed version of the poetic mount, described in a gentle key appropriate in view of the fact that the young friend in question is "proposing to domesticate with the author." One hesitates to suggest, for instance, that the woman wailing for her demon-lover appears in the form of a "fleecy dam," but she almost certainly does:

> A mount not wearisome and bare and steep,
>   But a *green mountain* variously up-piled,
> Where o'er the *jutting rocks* soft mosses creep,
> Or colour'd lichens with slow oozing weep;
>   Where *cypress and the darker yew* start wild;
> And, 'mid *the summer torrent's gentle dash*
> Dance brighten'd the red clusters of the ash;
>   Beneath whose boughs, *by those still sounds beguil'd,*
> Calm Pensiveness might muse herself to sleep;
>   Till haply startled by some fleecy dam,
> That rustling on the bushy cliff above
> *With melancholy bleat of anxious love,*
>   *Made meek enquiry for her wandering lamb:*
>   Such a *green mountain* 'twere most sweet to climb,
> E'en while the bosom ach'd with loneliness—
> How more than sweet, if some dear friend should bless
>   The adventurous toil, and up the *path sublime*
> Now lead, now follow: the glad landscape round,
> *Wide and more wide, increasing without bound!* (1–19)

The friends are to wander and pause, together or apart, as the "muse's witching charm" demands, listing the torrent's dash, up

to the topmost crag, where uprears "That shadowing Pine its old
romantic limbs," (32)

> And haply, bason'd *in some unsunn'd cleft*
> *A beauteous spring,* the rock's collected tears,
> Sleeps shelter'd there, scarce wrinkled by the gale!
>   Together thus, *the world's vain turmoil left,*
> Stretched on the *crag,* and shadow'd by the *pine,*
>   And bending o'er the clear *delicious fount,*
> Ah! dearest youth! it were a lot divine
> To cheat our noons in moralising mood,
> While west-winds fann'd our temples toil-bedew'd: (36–44)

Here, as in "Kubla Khan," the poetic experience is associated with
a sequestered spot, on a hill or mountain, close by a water-course,
and near ancient trees. The rest of the poem makes the "allegoric"
point explicit, though the note of peril is quite absent. The hill is a
"Hill of Knowledge":

> Thus rudely vers'd in allegoric lore,
> The Hill of Knowledge I essayed to trace;
> *That verdurous hill with many a resting-place,*
> *And many a stream,* whose warbling waters pour
>   To glad and *fertilize* the *subject* plains;

[The submerged metaphor in "subject" suggests the identification
of the mountain with a king.]

> That *hill with secret springs,* and *nooks untrod,*
> And *many a fancy-blest and holy sod*
>   Where Inspiration, his diviner strains
> Low-murmuring, lay; and starting from the rock's
> *Stiff evergreens,* (whose spreading foliage mocks
> Want's barren soil, and the bleak *frosts of age,*
> And Bigotry's mad *fire-invoking rage!*)
> O meek retiring spirit! we will climb
> Cheering and cheered, this lovely hill sublime;

The voices of the world do intrude, but gently, and as briefly as in
"Kubla Khan," then melt into the poetic reconciliation:

And from the stirring world up-lifted high
(Whose noises, faintly wafted on the wind,
To quiet musings shall attune the mind,
    And oft the melancholy *theme* supply),
    There while the prospect through the gazing eye
    Pours all its healthful greenness on the soul,
We'll smile at wealth, and learn to smile at fame,
Our hopes, our knowledge, and our joys the same,
    As *neighboring fountains image each the whole:*
Then when the mind hath drunk its fill of *truth*
    We'll discipline the heart to pure *delight,*
Rekindling sober joy's domestic flame.
They whom I love shall love thee, honour'd youth!
Now may Heaven realize *this vision bright!*
                    (49–76; "theme" italicized in text)

Only the Abyssinian maid seems to be missing, and her role is filled
by "Inspiration" in line 56.

The lines concerning "truth" and "delight" are a bit strange on
second glance and may bear some meditation. Apparently truth is
to be had for the asking; the mind has simply to drink its fill. But
we must discipline the heart to pure delight. Perhaps "pure" is the
key word, pure taken as opposed to impure, or less than pure, and
the delight in question a delight in truth, although the next line
suggests another interpretation: "Rekindling sober joy's domestic
flame." Earlier in the poem the two friends were to return

                    from the mount,
    To some lone mansion, in some woody dale,
    Where smiling with blue eye, Domestic Bliss
    Gives *this* the Husband's *that* the Brother's kiss!
                    (45–48; italics in text)

The relation between the poetry and the domestic life was for a
considerable period a vexed one for Coleridge, until he gave up
hope of combining them, and was able to admit to himself that he
had given up that hope. In any case, the two readings of "pure
delight" here are not mutually exclusive: it could at least be *hoped*

that delight in truth would rekindle the domestic flame. In "Kubla Khan" the problem has all but disappeared. One has the impression that the demon-lover will never return, and although the heart must still be "won" to delight, it has already drunk its fill of truth.

"To a Friend Who had Declared His Intention of Writing No More Poetry" (1796) is addressed to Lamb. The first section of the poem deals, by means of classical allusion, with the vocation of poetry. There is, however, a curious mixture of pagan and Christian metaphor, which no doubt reflects the confusion in Coleridge's mind concerning the final provenance of the poetic experience, a confusion not really to be wondered at. It is said that Genius had plunged Lamb

> in that wizard fount
> Hight Castalie: and (sureties of thy faith)
> That Pity and Simplicity stood by,
> And promis'd for thee, that thou shouldst renounce
> The world's low cares and lying vanities,
> Steadfast and rooted in the heavenly Muse,
> And wash'd and sanctified to Poesy.   (3–8)

But obviously the ceremony is a conventional christening, with godparents, baptism, and regeneration. And the ingenious confusion continues:

> Yes—thou wert plung'd, but with forgetful hand
> Held, as by Thetis erst her warrior son:
> And with those recreant unbaptizéd heels
> Thou'rt flying from thy bounden ministeries—
> So sore it seems and burthensome a task
> To weave unwithering flowers! But take thou heed:
> For thou art vulnerable, wild-eyed boy,
> And I have arrows mystically dipped
> Such as may stop thy speed.   (9–17)

There is something irresistibly amusing about the idea of Charles Lamb as the wild-eyed boy of "Kubla Khan," with flashing eyes and floating hair. When he objected to being called "gentle-hearted Charles" twice in "This Lime-Tree Bower," he might have bethought him that he had once been cast in a more romantic role.

In the second section of the poem, we find the poetic mount described in terms similar to those used in the poem addressed to Cottle ("The Author of Poems"), not expurgated as for Charles Lloyd (the "Young Friend"). In addition to the ancient tree and solemn music, we find deadly poisonous herbs to be plucked "with stopped nostril and glove-guarded hand" as a wreath for a dead poet's (Burns's) detractors. There is the "Kubla Khan" mixture of delicacy and danger:

> Oh! for shame return!
> On a bleak rock, midway the Aonian mount,
> There stands a lone and melancholy tree,
> Whose agéd branches to the midnight blast
> Make solemn music: pluck its darkest bough,
> Ere yet the unwholesome night-dew be exhaled,
> And weeping wreath it round thy Poet's tomb.
> Then in the outskirts, where pollutions grow,
> Pick the rank henbane and the dusky flowers
> Of night-shade, or its red and tempting fruit,
> These with stopped nostril and glove-guarded hand
> Knit in nice intertexture, so to twine,
> The illustrious brow of Scotch Nobility!   (25-37)

It might almost be possible to chart the topography of Coleridge's "mount." In any case a great many interesting things seem to occur "midway" the ascent. On second thought, Lamb might not have been pleased had he noticed that his recommended poetic activities were to be carried on at the same level with those of Joseph Cottle. The heights, the cloud-climb'd rock, are reserved for the giants of poetry—among whom Coleridge does not presume to number himself.

The first stanza of "Ode to the Departing Year" (1796) records strange music heard in a vision, played by the spirit of the depart-

ing year upon "the wild Harp of Time." The "harmony" is disturbing.

> Spirit who sweepest the wild Harp of Time!
>   It is most hard, with an untroubled ear
>   Thy dark inwoven harmonies to hear!
> Yet, mine eye fix'd on Heaven's unchanging clime
> Long had I listen'd, free from mortal fear,
>   With inward stillness, and a bowéd mind;
>   When lo! its folds far waving on the wind,
> I saw the train of the Departing Year!
>   Starting from my silent sadness
>   Then with no unholy madness,
> Ere yet the enter'd cloud foreclos'd my sight,
> I rais'd the impetuous song, and solemniz'd his flight.   (1–12)

This is not very close in terms of image to the damsel with a
dulcimer, but it does involve a personage seen in a vision playing
on a stringed instrument in such a way as to inspire the poet with
"no unholy madness" and cause him to raise "the impetuous song."
There is a problem, to be sure: it is hard not to be troubled by the
"dark inwoven harmonies," but there is no difficulty in *hearing*
them, and one has only to fix one's eye "on Heaven's unchanging
clime" to be caught up in the spirit of the occasion. The contrast
with "Kubla Khan"—"Could I revive within me . . ."—is clear.
And we should note in passing that genuine holiness is not quite
inconsistent with "madness," another word for the "enchantment"
of "Kubla Khan."

The impetuous song that follows is one of almost unrelieved
terror and bloodshed, though the Argument speaks of "the Divine
Providence that regulates into one vast harmony all the events of
time, however calamitous some of them may appear to mortals."
And in the second stanza personified Woes and Joys are called
upon to "Weep and rejoice!" In the earliest version,

> Seiz'd in sore travail and portentous birth
> (Her eyeballs flashing a pernicious glare)

Sick Nature struggles! Hark! her pangs increase!
Her groans are horrible! but O! most fair
The promis'd Twins she bears—Equality and Peace! [51]

Here, as in "Kubla Khan," we have the painful birth producing fair issue. The "flashing eyeballs" belong here to Nature rather than to the inspired poet.

Professor Harper's denomination of a number of Coleridge's poems, including "This Lime-Tree Bower My Prison" (1797), as "conversation poems," adapted from Coleridge's own subtitle to "The Nightingale," has a certain evident appropriateness. The poems in question certainly affect an informality of tone, at least to begin and end with. "This Lime-Tree Bower," for instance, begins "Well, they are gone, and here I must remain, / This lime-tree bower my prison!" But the term "conversation poem" is misleading if it is taken, as it might well be, to imply that the poems lack deliberate form. In fact, the repeated strategy is subtle and effective, and at its best succeeds in naturalizing the supernatural. The technique is different from that of "The Ancient Mariner" and "Christabel," but the end is the same.

The first section of "This Lime-Tree Bower" relates a kind of vision, in which the poet imagines the landscape his friends are traversing. He conjures up two scenes, the first of which seems to be a kind of "deep romantic chasm":

> They meanwhile,
> Friends, whom I never more may meet again,
> On springy heath, along the hill-top edge,
> Wander in gladness, and *wind down*, perchance,
> To that *still roaring dell,* of which I told;
> The roaring dell, *o'erwooded, narrow, deep,*
> And *only speckled by the mid-day sun;*
> Where its slim trunk the ash *from rock to rock*
> Flings *arching like a bridge;*—that branchless ash,
> *Unsunn'd and damp,* whose few poor yellow leaves

[51] *Poems,* p. 161 n.

> Ne'er tremble in the gale, yet tremble still,
> *Fann'd by the waterfall!* and there my friends
> Behold the dark green file of long lank weeds,
> That all at once (*a most fantastic sight*)
> Still nod and drip beneath the dripping edge
> Of the blue claystone.   (5–20)

The dell is isolated from outside influence, but instinct with a life of its own, by virtue of the stream. We know from the half-light and the strange substitute for a breeze that we are in a realm of poetic experience, and there is the suggestion of architecture, the ash arching like a bridge above the chasm. But there is hardly any suggestion of baleful influence—the chasm is perhaps in too close proximity to the domestic scene.

The friends are then imagined to emerge onto the height, and to view the setting sun, and the result is an ultimate vision:

> Ah! slowly sink
> Behind the western ridge, thou glorious Sun!
> Shine in the slant beams of the sinking orb,
> Ye purple heath-flowers! richlier burn, ye clouds!
> And kindle, thou blue Ocean! So my friend
> Struck with deep joy may stand, as I have stood,
> Silent with swimming sense; yea, gazing round
> On the wide landscape, gaze till all doth seem
> Less gross than bodily; and of such hues
> As veil the Almighty Spirit, when yet he makes
> Spirits perceive his presence.   (32–43)

We may suppose that, as in "Kubla Khan," it is somehow the combination of the two environments, of the unsunned dell and the blazing landscape seen from the heights, that induces the perception of the Almighty Spirit. As a result, Coleridge says, "A *delight* / Comes sudden on my heart," (43–44) and he is able to transform "This little lime-tree bower" into an equally eloquent habitation of the Almighty Spirit. This is perhaps the only case of vision and consequent creation without benefit of music.

Coleridge's early play *Osorio* (1797) may be said to have as its subject a woman wailing for her demon-lover, though her lover is really only a necromancer, not a demon, and his role as necromancer is assumed as a disguise. As the play opens Maria, whose betrothed is missing and possibly dead, is trying to justify her faithfulness to him to his father, who wants her to marry his brother. In her desperate effort she compares herself to a Moorish maiden:

> (As once I knew a crazy Moorish maid,
> Who dress'd her in her buried lover's cloaths,
> And o'er the smooth spring in the mountain cleft
> Hung with her lute, and play'd the selfsame tune
> He used to play, and listen'd to the shadow
> Herself had made);   (I, 30–35)

What we really seem to have here is a combination of the woman wailing for her demon-lover and the damsel with a dulcimer, a combination not infrequent in the poems, and appropriately enough she hangs o'er a spring in a mountain cleft. In this "fantastic mood" she thinks how it would be

> To be in Paradise, and with choice flowers
> Build up a bower where he and I might dwell,
> And there await his coming!   (I, 43–45)

The fact is she seems to combine all the persons in "Kubla Khan," except Kubla Himself, and we may be reminded of the situation in "The Eolian Harp." In these last lines she sees herself building the dome, the bower, under the inspiration of once-heard music that she herself reproduces. And what to her prospective father-in-law seems "crazy" is to her sublime.

We learn early in the play that the lover, Albert, is not dead at all. His brother Osorio, in love with Maria, had commissioned a Moor, Ferdinand, to murder him, under threat of reprisals deriving from the Inquisition, but Ferdinand had spared him at the last moment. After some years of slavery among the Moors he has now returned in disguise. His retreat has many familiar features:

> *Osorio.* Where does this wizard live?
> *Ferdinand.* You see that *brooklet?*
> Trace its course backward thro' a narrow opening
> It leads you to the place.
> *Osorio.*   How shall I know it?
> *Ferdinand.* You can't mistake. It is a *small green dale*
> *Built all around with high off-sloping hills,*
> And from its shape our peasants aptly call it
> The *Giant's Cradle.* There's a *lake in the midst,*
> And round its banks *tall wood,* that branches over
> And makes *a kind of faery forest* grow
> *Down in the water.* At the furthest end
> A puny *cataract* falls on the lake;
> And there (a curious sight) *you see its shadow*
> For ever curling, like a wreath of smoke,
> Up through the foliage of those *faery trees.*
> His *cot stands opposite*—you cannot miss it.
> Some *three yards up the hill a mountain ash*
> Stretches its lower boughs and scarlet clusters.   (II, 143–60)

This is obviously not one of Coleridge's more sensitive descriptions of natural scenery, certainly not one of his finer passages of verse—the "puny cataract" seems unforgivable, and it would not be easy to justify "His cot stands opposite—you cannot miss it" on grounds of dramatic propriety. But Albert has unmistakably found an encinctured paradise. It would be possible, and would work a great improvement, to substitute a version of lines 6 ff. of "Kubla Khan" —Osorio would not miss his destination.

Osorio engages Albert's services as a necromancer, charging him to communicate with Albert's soul, hoping thereby to convince Maria of her lover's death. After Albert's invocation to the spirit and a song sung behind the scenes, Osorio exclaims:

> *Osorio. This was too melancholy, father!*
> *Velez.*   Nay!
> My Albert lov'd sad music from a child.
> Once he was lost; and after weary search

We found him in *an open place of the wood,*
To which spot he had follow'd a blind boy
Who breathed into a pipe of sycamore
Some *strangely moving notes,* and these, he said
Were *taught him in a dream;* him we first saw
Stretched on the broad top of a sunny heath-bank;
And lower down, poor Albert fast asleep,
His head upon the blind boy's dog—   (III, 58–68)

Albert's soul is being called back from Paradise by means of music,
and the event that the father recalls in defense of the technique is,
curiously enough, a case of Albert's being *lost* as a result of following music, strangely moving notes, taught to the blind boy as the
Abyssinian maid's notes were taught to the poet, in a dream. As
usual, there is a wood and a hillside, the latter deliberately
graduated.

In the fourth act Osorio is plotting the death of his unwilling
accomplice, Ferdinand, and we have the description of a totally
negative "romantic chasm," exclusively redolent of evil, the place
in which Ferdinand is shortly to meet his death:

> *Ferdinand.* If every atom of a dead man's flesh
> Should move, each one with a particular life,
> Yet all as cold as ever—'twas just so!
> Or if it drizzled *needle-points of frost,*
> *Upon a feverish head* made suddenly bald—
> > *Osorio (interrupting him).* Why, Ferdinand, I blush
> > for thy cowardice.
> It would have startled any man, I grant thee.
> But such a panic.
> > *Ferdinand.*   When a boy, my lord!
> I could have sat whole hours beside that *chasm,*
> *Push'd in huge stones and heard them thump and rattle*
> Against its horrid sides; and hung my head
> Low down, and listen'd till the *heavy fragments*
> *Sunk, with faint crash,* in that still *groaning well*
> Which never thirsty pilgrim blest, *which never*

> *A living thing came near;* unless perchance,
> Some blind-worm battens on the ropy mould,
> Close at its edge. (IV, 32–48)

Here, it would seem, one aspect of a perennial image is being exploited for dramatic purposes. And even here, though its aspect is unrelievedly horrible, Ferdinand confesses to his early fascination with it. In "Kubla Khan" these sinister virtualities of the romantic chasm are suggested only briefly, but it is well to remember how far they can go in Coleridge's imagination.

CHAPTER THREE

The Annus Mirabilis and After

In approaching, for the particular purposes of this study, Coleridge's most impressive single work, the poems that he thought might have been improvements upon it, and others that followed it, it will be well to refocus attention upon some of the traits that Coleridge shared with the poets of his age. It has often been noticed that a remarkable number of romantic poems explicitly celebrate and analyze the poetic experience itself; but there must be one sense in which for all poets the experience itself, the sense of preternatural *contact,* is more deeply cherished than anything else, though most of them perform the pious cult of venerating the vessels of poetic grace. Being for whatever complicated reasons more explicitly aware than earlier poets of this experience as a psychological phenomenon distinguishable from its particular matrix or occasion, the romantic poets more often made what is perhaps the mistaken attempt to communicate it directly. But at their best they did what all poets do—they made poems out of it, myths, images, songs, commemorating its occurrence and, as well as might be, embodying it.

Some such myths or images must seem to the poet to be almost inseparable from the *contact* itself, to be therefore, for the original poem, inevitable, and thereafter an always available source. What was said at the beginning of Chapter Two about the sense in which most poets really write only one poem, or at the most two or three, might be considered in these terms. The reason may be not only that there are, after all, so few things to be said, but that most poets succeed in formulating only a few myths or integral clusters of images, and upon these, or fragments of them, they call on the most varied occasions. We might hazard an estimate that Coleridge elaborated three such master-myths, to be found in their most fully developed form in what posterity has, in spite of any critical opinion to the contrary, agreed to be his three greatest poems, "The Ancient Mariner," "Christabel," and "Kubla Khan." Without making the kind of investigation undertaken here in relation to "Kubla Khan," one can only guess, with the indirect aid of Lowes and Nethercot [1] and studies like Warren's interpretation of "The Ancient Mariner," [2] that the symbols of the other two poems also pervade Coleridge's poetry in some appreciable degree. What we are concerned with at the moment, of course, is the degree in which the symbols of "Kubla Khan" succeed in coalescing with those in the other "major" poems. In the probable nature of such things, one would expect the degree to be low, in terms of specific images, relatively high in terms of what we might momentarily permit ourselves to call Coleridgean archetypes.

The Ancient Mariner himself, as we learn in the early stanzas of the poem, is a person set off from the rest of his kind by the experiences he has lived through, the visions he has seen, and the sign of it is his "glittering eye." Fortunately, the wedding guest he stops, in spite of his dread and the urgency of his engagement, knows no spell so potent as that described at the end of "Kubla Khan," and so is forced to listen to the bright-eyed Mariner's whole story with almost uninterruptedly passive attention. Remembering the many poems in which opposition and only partially successful reconciliation between domestic bliss and exotic vision are recorded, we should not be surprised that the Mariner's tale interrupts a nuptial celebration. The sources in Coleridge's own life of his acute aware-

[1] John Livingston Lowes, *The Road to Xanadu* (Boston and New York: Houghton, Mifflin, 1927); Arthur Nethercot, *The Road to Tryermaine* (Chicago: University of Chicago Press, 1939).

[2] Robert Penn Warren, "A Poem of Pure Imagination, an Experiment in Reading," in *The Rime of the Ancient Mariner, with an Essay by Robert Penn Warren* (New York: Reynal & Hitchcock, 1946).

ness of this opposition between the domestic and the supernal are obvious, but of only incidental interest: the conflict is as old as Job and Oedipus, and in his more considerable poems Coleridge treats it in appropriately universal terms. Here in "The Ancient Mariner" the allusion seems vaguely biblical.

The Mariner's tale begins with a description of the beginning of the voyage:

> 'The ship was cheered, the harbour cleared,
> Merrily did we drop
> Below the kirk, below the hill,
> Below the lighthouse top.
>
> The Sun came up upon the left,
> Out of the sea came he!
> And he shone bright, and on the right
> Went down into the sea!'   (21–28)

The scene is thus set in elemental terms—hill, sun, and sea; and two man-made structures are associated with the hill, the kirk, and the lighthouse. Both are sources of light, both beacons, and the Mariner's voyage will be complete only when he returns to them, but it is not by their light that he is to be guided. Nor by that of the sun. In Part I, at least, the sun seems to be a good or at least a neutral symbol. At any rate nothing bad happens under its influence. But it is in the realm of *ice* that the Albatross appears, the ultimately ambiguous harbinger of good or evil. The scene almost amounts to caves of ice:

> 'And now there came both mist and snow,
> And it grew wondrous cold:
> And ice, mast-high, came floating by,
> As green as emerald.
>
> 'And through the drifts the snowy clifts
> Did send a dismal sheen:

> Nor shapes of men nor beasts we ken—
> The ice was all between.

> 'The ice was here, the ice was there,
> The ice was all around:
> It cracked and growled, and roared and howled,
> Like noises in a swound!'   (51–62)

We may take some instruction from the fact that the ice is here a cause of separation from the natural world, at least from the world of men and beasts, but it would seem to be a favorable separation, for it produces the Albatross, hailed in God's name like a Christian soul. The symbolism is at best difficult to follow and not obviously consistent, but at least it seems evident that we are as far from the customary world as possible. There is never any statement as to the purpose of the voyage, and so we may assume it to have been a voyage of discovery, like some of those in the accounts of which Lowes finds the sources of the poem's imagery. The voyagers have left the kirk and the lighthouse for unaccountable reasons, at the mercy of the winds—always associated for Coleridge with inspiration—and they arrive, at the first crisis of the poem, in a region of ice and snow, as green as emerald, where they "discover" not a new land, not anything remotely useful in the ordinary world, but the Albatross. His irrelevance to any practical concerns is made explicitly clear after his murder. At first the Mariner is accused by his empirically minded comrades of having killed the bird "That brought the fog and mist." (100) The killing of the bird, of this being that is not really "found" but that simply appears if in carelessness of practical concerns one voyages far enough into unknown realms, is as gratuitous as the voyage itself. There is no way of knowing in advance the rules of such a realm as this, and one may easily, in pure caprice or following some irrelevant impulse carried over from the everyday world, destroy the very treasure one has happened upon. Here we may think of Coleridge's response to Mrs. Barbauld's objection that the poem had not enough moral,

In suggesting that he thought perhaps it had too much he cited the story from the *Arabian Nights* "of the merchant's sitting down to eat dates by the side of a well, and throwing the shells aside, and lo! a genie starts up, and says he *must* kill the aforesaid merchant, *because* one of the date shells had, it seems, put out the eye of the genie's son." [3] The "moral" involved in the two instances would seem to be the same, and not one easy to explain to Mrs. Barbauld.

Though we need not be puzzled by the mariners' first condemning and then, when the wind continues, praising the crime, we may wonder how it happens that the wind does continue to blow after the crime is committed. Can it be that inspiration a little while outlasts its violation? Ordinarily it does. But surely enough, in this case, it does not last long:

> 'We were the first that ever burst
> Into that silent sea.
>
> 'Down dropt the breeze, the sails dropt down,
> 'Twas sad as sad could be;
> And we did speak only to break
> The silence of the sea!'   (105–10)

The possibility of exploring the "sunless sea," the "lifeless ocean," hardly occurs to one reading "Kubla Khan," but a good deal of "The Ancient Mariner" is taken up with the description of just such an exploration. To be sure, the sea here is not literally "sunless," but it is something worse:

> All in a hot and copper sky,
> The bloody Sun, at noon,
> Right up above the mast did stand,
> No bigger than the Moon.   (111–14)

And it is here, haunted by the outraged spirit of the land of mist and snow, the Albatross hung about his neck as a curse, that the

[3] *Table Talk*, pp. 86–87.

Mariner encounters the Night-mare LIFE-IN-DEATH, who arrives "Without a breeze, without a tide" (169). After the death of all his comrades, the Mariner finds himself

> Alone, alone, all, all alone,
> Alone on a wide wide sea!
> And never a saint took pity on
> My soul in agony.   (232–35)

No, this is not the "lifeless ocean" of "Kubla Khan." It is something as nearly unimaginable as possible, something that may be experienced but can only be defined by a contradiction—Life-in-Death. It is at this level that one may understand Professor Knight's denomination of "The Ancient Mariner" as the "purgatory" and "Kubla Khan" as the "paradise" of "Coleridge's Divine Comedy." [4]

In the scene of regeneration in Part V, after the Mariner has blessed the water-snakes (blessed them "unaware") and the Albatross has fallen from his neck, he describes a meteorological phenomenon in terms that recall, strangely enough, the landscape of "Kubla Khan":

> The thick black cloud was cleft, and still
> The Moon was at its side:
> Like waters shot from some high crag,
> The lightning fell with never a jag,
> A river steep and wide.   (322–26)

We have the mighty fountain in reverse, springing from a cleft on high (it is, after all, in the terms of "Kubla Khan," being viewed from below, from the lifeless ocean), and it is at this moment that the crew of dead men becomes reanimated, by a troop of spirits blest. At dawn the spirits leave the bodies:

> —they dropped their arms,
> And clustered round the mast;

[4] Knight, p. 83.

Sweet sounds rose slowly through their mouths,
And from their bodies passed.

Around, around flew each sweet sound,
Then darted to the Sun;   (350–55)

This association of the good spirits with the Sun suggests a
difficulty in the more or less rigid opposition between sun and
moon found in the poem by Robert Penn Warren. The relations
among the various lights here, as elsewhere in Coleridge's poetry,
are complex.

The evidence of salvation, of a whole world again inhabitable,
comes, predictably, in the form of music, natural, instrumental,
angelic:

Slowly the sounds came back again,
Now mixed, now one by one.

Sometimes a-dropping from the sky
I heard the sky-lark sing;
Sometimes all little birds that are,
How they seemed to fill the sea and air
With their sweet jargoning!

And now 'twas like all instruments,
Now like a lonely flute;
And now it is an angel's song,
That makes the heavens be mute.   (356–66)

In a swoon induced by a sudden movement of the ship, the Mariner
hears two spirits discussing his probable fate. One emphasizes the
affront his crime presents to the Polar Spirit, who "loved the bird
that loved the man / Who shot him with his bow."

The other was a softer voice,
As soft as honey-dew:
Quoth he, 'The man hath penance done,
And penance more will do.'   (406–9)

A hard thing to say, in a voice as soft as honey-dew. Could this be what it means to feed on honey-dew? In part, no doubt.

Near the end of Part VI the ship arrives miraculously in port on a moonlight night, and we are reminded of the earlier scene:

> The rock shone bright, the kirk no less,
> That stands above the rock:
> The moonlight steeped in silentness
> The steady weathercock.   (476–79)

The ship is met by the pilot and his boy and with them, providentially we must suppose, the Hermit good, who "lives in that wood / Which slopes down to the sea." They witness the appearance of the Seraphs as torches of light above the prostrate forms of the sailors and the miraculous sinking of the ship. When they pick the Mariner out of the bay, the effect he has upon them, even upon the Hermit, recalls the effect produced by the speaker in "Kubla Khan":

> I moved my lips—the Pilot shrieked
> And fell down in a fit;
> The holy Hermit raised his eyes,
> And prayed where he did sit.   (560–63)

The Pilot's boy goes mad, and takes the Mariner to be the Devil. There is no specific indication that the Hermit accedes to the Mariner's urgent request for shrift, but we know that the Mariner's penance goes on forever, and consists of a periodic compulsion to tell his tale and to compel others to listen—if only the curse of poetic inspiration always carried along with it the power to compel an audience! The sounds of the wedding feast impinge, and the sound of the vesper bell. The Mariner rejects the former for the latter:

> O Wedding-Guest! this soul hath been
> Alone on a wide wide sea:
> So lonely 'twas, that God himself
> Scarce seeméd there to be.

O sweeter than the marriage-feast,
'Tis sweeter far to me,
To walk together to the kirk
With a goodly company!—   (597–604)

The concluding twenty-one lines are no doubt the main source of Coleridge's feelings of undue "obstrusion of the moral sentiment."

There are not, it would appear, a great many close parallels between "The Ancient Mariner" and "Kubla Khan." Their number and character are nevertheless such as to give the impression that the two compositions have somehow to do with the same vast subject. They simply focus upon different parts or aspects of it, or see it from a different angle. We may again be reminded of Professor Knight's suggestion. If "The Ancient Mariner" is indeed a *purgatorio*, it should not be surprising that it is so much longer than "Kubla Khan." Only Dante has succeeded in describing paradise at the same length as hell and purgatory, and many readers have felt that his success was only relative.

"Christabel" (1797–1800), even in its unfinished state, is already somewhat longer than "The Ancient Mariner." The opening scene is at least in some important particulars similar to that of "Kubla Khan": there is a castle surrounded by a highly "romantic" grove, in which Christabel is praying, rather than wailing, for her own betrothéd knight rather than for a demon-lover. (The contrast between the betrothed knight and Geraldine may, among other things, be another of the many contrasts between the domestic and the supernal, the latter in this case in its most sinister guise.) Although the moon is not waning as in "Kubla Khan," its state amounts strangely to the same thing (and recalls the state of the sun in "The Ancient Mariner"):

The moon is behind, and at the full;
And yet she looks both small and dull.   (18–19)

One ancient tree in the grove is singled out for quintuple mention, an oak bare of leaves but covered with "moss and rarest mistletoe." (34) It is beneath this oak that Christabel kneels to pray, as the Hermit in "The Ancient Mariner" knelt to pray on the "rotted old oak-stump" covered with moss. (519–22) The oak is clearly associated with religious observance, though it is not so clear with just what kind. The mistletoe here, if it is not along with the moss simply a parasite affording a suggestion of the sinister, may point to the Druids, and through them in a general way to some pre-Christian religious rite. In the lines cited from "The Ancient Mariner," the Hermit's prayer cushion is "the moss that wholly hides / The rotted old oak-stump," which might conceivably be a very sophisticated allusion to religious evolution; and the second reference to the oak in "Christabel" hardly suggests a Christian context—"the huge, broad-breasted old oak tree." (42) In fact, one of the underlying sources of strangeness in "Christabel," as in "The Ancient Mariner," may be the juxtaposition of very specifically Christian with non-Christian elements. Coleridge seems to go out of what was certainly his ordinary way to make the Christian references Catholic, with repeated references to the Blessed Virgin. In "Christabel" this might be accounted for by appeal to the period in which the events are represented as taking place, but the events of "The Ancient Mariner" are quite timeless. It seems more likely that he employs this means, despite his theological objections to Catholicism, as a poetic device to enforce the contrast between orthodox and heterodox realms of experience. The precise nature of this contrast is not easy to determine, however.

The ambiguity is perhaps intentional, or at least inevitable, if, as I have suggested in other contexts, the distinction is between the poetic and the properly religious experience, a distinction that may become an opposition under certain circumstances. In this case, Christabel prays on one side of the oak, and then,

> The Lady sprang up suddenly,
> The lovely lady, Christabel!
> It moaned as near, as near can be,

But what it is she cannot tell.—
On the other side it seems to be,
Of the huge, broad-breasted, old oak tree.   (37–42)

The tree remains the center of attention in the lines that follow:

The night is chill; the forest bare;
Is it the wind that moaneth bleak?
There is not wind enough in the air
To move away the ringlet curl
From the lovely lady's cheek—
There is not wind enough to twirl
The one red leaf, the last of its clan,
That dances as often as dance it can,
Hanging so light, and hanging so high,
On the topmost twig that looks up at the sky.   (43–52)

And then we have the first crisis of the poem:

Hush, beating heart of Christabel!
Jesu, Maria, shield her well!
She folded her arms beneath her cloak,
And stole to the other side of the oak.
What sees she there?   (53–56)

Christabel is not wailing for a demon-lover, but a demon-lover is
what she finds, on the other side of the oak:

There she sees a damsel bright,
Drest in a silken robe of white,
That shadowy in the moonlight shone:
The neck that made her white robe wan,
Her stately neck, and arms were bare;
Her blue-veined feet unsandal'd were,
And wildly glittered here and there
The gems entangled in her hair.
I guess 'twas frightful there to see
A lady so richly clad as she—
Beautiful exceedingly!   (58–68)

Christabel's spontaneous reaction turns out, in the sequel, to be highly appropriate—

> Mary mother, save me now!
> (Said Christabel,) And who art thou?   (69–70)

—but readers of the poem cannot afford to gloss over the exceeding beauty of Geraldine. The poem "works" only if we, like Christabel, are genuinely seduced, and Coleridge repeatedly insists upon her beauty. It may help a little to notice that the gems entangled in her hair "glittered" like the eye of the Mariner, indeed like little Hartley Coleridge's eye in a poem to be treated later. In fact, Geraldine's own eyes "glitter" further on in the poem, when she drinks of the wild-flower wine made by Christabel's late mother— a demon-lover is nourished or stimulated only by the most sacred things one has to offer.

If one feels a certain weakness in the first part of the poem, it comes perhaps from the impression easily gathered that Christabel is an utterly innocent victim, that we are being presented with a picture of pure good as against pure evil, an easy allegory. But close attention to the critical scene dispels the impression. Christabel is good, surely enough, and it is important that she be so, but obviously Coleridge knew something about the complexities of apparent innocence. When Geraldine directs Christabel to unrobe herself, her alacrity begins to seem culpable, and calls for an exclamation mark:

> Quoth Christabel, So let it be!
> And as the lady bade, did she.
> Her gentle limbs did she undress,
> And lay down in her loveliness.   (235–38)

And she does not fall asleep, as an allegorically innocent maiden might be expected to do. She is at least complex enough to be curious:

> But through her brain of weal and woe
> So many thoughts moved to and fro,
> That it were vain her lids to close;
> So half-way from the bed she rose,
> And on her elbow did recline
> To look at the lady Geraldine.   (239–44)

What she sees Coleridge wisely does not say precisely:

> Behold! her bosom and half her side—
> A sight to dream of, not to tell!   (252–53)

Geraldine herself is dismayed, presumably by the effect the sight may have upon Christabel:

> Yet Geraldine nor speaks nor stirs;
> Ah! what a stricken look was hers!
> Deep from within she seems half-way
> To lift some weight with sick assay,
> And eyes the maid and seeks delay;

[But there is no cry of alarm from Christabel.]

> Then suddenly, as one defied,
> Collects herself in scorn and pride,
> And lay down by the Maiden's side!—
> And in her arms the maid she took,
>   Ah wel-a-day!   (255–64)

Ah wel-a-day indeed. Christabel is, surely enough, under a supernatural influence, but Coleridge obviously did not intend that this fact should eliminate all genuine moral conflict. Christabel is perhaps no more "guilty" than the Mariner who killed the Albatross, but she is guilty nevertheless. The beginning of "The Conclusion to Part I" makes the point clearly:

> It was a lovely sight to see
> The lady Christabel, when she
> Was praying at the old oak tree.
>   Amid the jagged shadows

Of mossy leafless boughs,
Kneeling in the moonlight,
To make her gentle vows;
Her slender palms together prest,
Heaving sometimes on her breast;
Her face resigned to bliss or bale—
Her face, oh call it fair not pale,
And both blue eyes more bright than clear,
Each about to have a tear.

With open eyes (ah woe is me!)
Asleep, and dreaming fearfully,
Fearfully dreaming, yet, I wis,
Dreaming that alone, which is—
O sorrow and shame! Can this be she,
The lady, who knelt at the old oak tree?

So much for Christabel.

And lo! the worker of these harms,

[Coleridge might have said "charms," but did not.]

That holds the maiden in her arms,
Seems to slumber still and mild,
As a mother with her child.   (298–301)

By the time we are well into Part II, the identity of both of the ladies has been called in doubt:

And Christabel awoke and spied
The same who lay down by her side—
O rather say, the same whom she
Raised up beneath the old oak tree!
Nay, fairer yet! and yet more fair!
For she belike hath drunken deep
Of all the blessedness of sleep!   (370–76)

The cadence of these last two lines is remarkably similar to that of the last two lines of "Kubla Khan":

For he on honey-dew hath fed,
And drunk the milk of Paradise.

And this is *Geraldine*. The similarity is not merely one of cadence, since there is the reference to drinking deep, as if of the milk of paradise, and in the lines that follow Christabel feels the sinister quality in her relation with Geraldine:

> 'Sure I have sinn'd!' said Christabel,
> 'Now heaven be praised if all be well!'
> And in low faltering tones, yet sweet,
> Did she the lofty lady greet
> With such perplexity of mind
> As dreams too lively leave behind.   (381–86)

Such perplexity might the speaker in "Kubla Khan" have felt, had he been able to recapture his vision of the Abyssinian maid, and then awaken. The poem, at any rate, informs us that all who heard his song would sense the danger. Coleridge knew as well as the next dramatist that there is no human drama in the confrontation of Good and Evil, that such a thing is indeed impossible, in this world at least, since things totally unlike cannot react upon each other. The drama and the human interest lie in establishing the ambiguous proportions. But in "Christabel," as elsewhere in Coleridge, we have something other than the confrontation of good and evil: we have the quest of the soul for *contact* with beauty, with its always attendant terrors. It is as if we had the story of the Garden of Eden retold with the poet as Adam and the forbidden tree the tree of Beauty (which is also, in its way, as Coleridge repeatedly makes clear, a tree of Knowledge).

In the case of "France: An Ode" (1798), we are clearly dealing with a different *kind* of poetry from that to be found in "The Ancient Mariner" and "Christabel." A cry of pain and disillusion, this poem is indeed "written with great energy," as the *Morning Post* commented on the occasion of its first publication.[5] At this

[5] *Poems,* p. 243 n.

distance it requires, perhaps, some knowledge of the occasional background and, more important, a reading aloud, fully to appreciate the fact. But with such knowledge, and a sensitive reading aloud, it emerges through the haze of now uncongenial rhetoric as a dignified statement of alarmingly personal passion. It reveals, as perhaps few poems do, the basis of the Romantic nexus between "communion with nature" and political aspiration, and that is not always an easy thing to understand. The poem as a whole may account in part for the delicacy of Shelley's attack, in the preface to *The Revolt of Islam,* upon those who had despaired too soon in the face of the degradations following upon the French Revolution. The first stanza is an invocation to all that Coleridge had found deeply moving in universal nature, which for him at this time included man:

> Ye Clouds! that far above me float and pause,
> Whose pathless march no mortal may controul!
> Ye Ocean-Waves! that, wheresoe'er ye roll,
> Yield homage only to eternal laws!
> Ye Woods! that listen to the night-birds singing,
> Midway the smooth and perilous slope reclined,
> Save when your own imperious branches swinging,
> Have made a solemn music of the wind!
> Where, like a man beloved of God,
> Through glooms, which never woodman trod,
> How oft, pursuing fancies holy,
> My moonlight way o'er flowering weeds I wound,
> Inspired beyond the guess of folly,
> By each rude shape and wild unconquerable sound!
> O ye loud Waves! and O ye Forests high!
> And O ye Clouds that far above me soared!
> Thou rising Sun! thou blue rejoicing Sky!
> Yea, every thing that is and will be free!
> Bear witness for me, wheresoe'er ye be,
> With what deep worship I have still adored
>   The spirit of divinest Liberty.   (1–21)

It is tempting, to the student of poetry, to take the Romantics' political enthusiasms as something ancillary, something that illuminates certain of their poems, but that is not to be considered seriously, since for the most part they seem to have been "visionary" in the pejorative sense of the word. Even very sympathetic readers often tend to be impatient with incursions of politics in their poetry—who, after all, can admire as poetry Coleridge's sonnets on Pantisocracy? And they do not, after all, sound like "Avenge, O Lord, thy slaughtered saints whose bones." But it is one thing to see that these poets were unable, for whatever complicated reasons, to make great poetry directly out of their political aspirations, and quite another to dismiss their attempts as genial prostitutions of their talents.[6] The fact is that they are still able to think of politics, quite simply, in terms of a network of institutions whose purpose is to aid human beings to fulfill their highest virtualities. Revolutionary as they were in many respects, they were still very close to an age-old political orthodoxy. (Their naïveté, and it is genuinely naïveté, stems most often, perhaps, from their tendency to overlook the Fall.) Since they seem to have found the sympathetic perception of natural objects the most immediate and dependable stimulus to the development of those highest virtualities of human nature, it was quite inevitable that nature and politics should be closely linked in their poetry.[7]

"France: An Ode" is as good an example of this linking as any to be found in Coleridge's poetry, and it is important for our understanding of "Kubla Khan" to note any symbolic analogues that exist between the two poems: "Kubla Khan" may very well be as much a political poem as anything else. There is, first, the ocean,

---

[6] For a surprising demonstration of the ubiquity of political concern in Coleridge's poetry, see Carl Woodring, *Politics in the Poetry of Coleridge* (Madison: University of Wisconsin Press, 1961).

[7] Can it be that our own Agrarians were the often announced "last of the Romantics"? (Though the individuals in question are very much alive, the past tense still seems appropriate in referring to them as "Agrarians.")

"Ocean-Waves" precisely, which are said to "Yield homage only to eternal laws." The association between the sea and eternity is commonplace enough, but it may serve to condition somewhat the "lifeless ocean" of "Kubla Khan." And there are the woods, associated as so often with singing, their "imperious branches" making music of the wind!" But one line in this passage is not easily comprehensible, line 6: presumably it is the *woods* that are "Midway the smooth and perilous slope reclined." What can it mean, literally, to say that the woods are "reclined" midway the slope? One suspects a lapse into a kind of automatic writing, since something very like the same image appears in half a dozen other places in Coleridge's poetry. In the first instance, the Pixies' Parlour is situated "half-way up a wood-covered hill," and is a place of moonlight, music, and "wildly-working dreams," similar to the "fancies holy" pursued here. In "The Eolian Harp" it is "on the midway slope / Of yonder hill" that the speaker, with half-closed eyelids, muses on tranquility, leaving his brain open to flitting phantasies "As wild and various as the random gales." The result is one of Coleridge's great ejaculations of poetic faith, or hope. In "To a Friend" the similarity is very striking:

> On a bleak rock, midway the Aonian mount,
> There stands a lone and melancholy tree,
> Whose aged branches to the midnight blast
> Make solemn music . . . .

Here the location is identified as the proper place of the most serious poetry. In "Love," written about the same time as "Kubla Khan," and having, as we shall see, striking resemblances to it in other respects, we find the poet saying that

> Oft in my waking dreams do I
> Live o'er again that happy hour,
> When midway on the mount I lay,
> Beside the ruined tower.

The scene is again moonlit, and calls forth musical and poetic inspiration—a soft and doleful air, an old and moving story.

And so when, in "France: An Ode," we find the somehow misplaced line, it is not hard to see how it slipped in: all of its usual accompaniments are present, and the subject is the poetico-political inspiration to be received from nature. The name of this perilous slope may be Mount Abora.

The poem continues with an account of Coleridge's enthusiasm at the first strokes of the French Revolution, and his opposition, in spite of patriotic qualms, to England's alliance against the new republic. He was prepared even for certain excesses on the part of the revolutionaries:

> 'And what,' I said, 'though Blasphemy's loud scream
>   With that sweet music of deliverance strove!
>   Though all the fierce and drunken passions wove
> A dance more wild than e'er was maniac's dream!
>   Ye storms, that round the dawning East assembled,
> The Sun was rising, though ye hid his light!   (43–48)

One cannot but wonder if Coleridge was explicitly conscious of the irony involved in his use here of an image so close to the one that appears in the Pantisocracy sonnet and the "Monody on the Death of Chatterton":

> And dancing to the moonlight roundelay,
> The wizard Passions weave an holy spell.

In these former cases the wizard passions were deliberately invited to weave their spell in the cottag'd dell, and there was no apparent awareness of potential conflict. At the later stage the passions are drunken and maniacal, and though they are somehow inextricably bound up with the advance of liberty, it is still possible in spite of this fact to foresee the nations freed by the compelling example of France, "Till Love and Joy look round, and call the Earth their own." (63)

The French invasion of Switzerland dispelled all such hope, caused him for the moment at least to despair of politics as a means of salvation, and permanently changed his attitude toward revolution as a political means.[8]

> Forgive me, Freedom! O forgive those dreams!
> I hear thy voice, I hear thy loud lament,
> From bleak Helvetia's icy caverns sent—
> I hear thy groans upon her blood-stained streams!   (64–67)

I have been unable to determine whether Coleridge was alluding here to a particular reported event, or whether, as seems possible, it was simply that no defilement could be more dire in his mind than the defilement of an "icy cavern." Certainly it is shocking to think of bloody rapine in those caves of ice! There one hears only the echoes of far distant wars.

Coleridge's temporary renouncement of political effort itself is contained in the final stanza:

> The Sensual and the Dark rebel in vain,
> Slaves by their own compulsion! In mad game
> They burst their manacles and wear the name
>   Of Freedom, graven on a heavier chain!
> O Liberty! with profitless endeavor
> Have I pursued thee, many a weary hour;
> But thou nor swell'st the victor's strain, nor ever
> Didst breathe thy soul in forms of human power.
> Alike from all, howe'er they praise thee,
> (Nor prayer, nor boastful name delays thee)
>   Alike from Priestcraft's harpy minions,

[8] An "Argument" furnished with one newspaper version of the poem characterizes the fifth stanza as "An address to Liberty, in which the Poet expresses his conviction that those feelings and that grand *ideal* of Freedom which the mind attains by its contemplation of its individual nature, and of the sublime surrounding objects . . . do not belong to men, as a society, nor can possibly be either gratified or realized, under any form of human government; but belong to the individual man, so far as he is pure, and inflamed with the love and adoration of God in Nature." *Poems*, p. 244 n.

And factious Blasphemy's obscener slaves,
    Thou speedest on thy subtle pinions,
The guide of homeless winds, and playmate of the waves!
And there I felt thee!—on that sea-cliff's verge,
    Whose pines, scarce travelled by the breeze above,
Had made one murmur with the distant surge!
Yes, while I stood and gazed, my temples bare,
And shot my being through earth, sea, and air,
    Possessing all things with intensest love,
        O Liberty! my spirit felt thee there.   (85–105)

Here the appeal is from politics to direct communion with nature. Though there is a faint resemblance to the landscape of "Kubla Khan," there is none of its machinery. Nevertheless, we may consider that one obstacle in the way toward it has been removed.

In "The Old Man of the Alps" (1798) we have a pastoral version of the woman wailing for her demon-lover. She lives "Beside the torrent and beneath a wood, / High in these Alps," (7–8) and her story is told by her bereaved father, an old shepherd. In her carefree days, when she still expected her lover to return from the wars, she went "Singing in the woods or bounding o'er the lawn." (17) When the old man, like an ancestral voice, told tales of pain and oppression,

> *She* play'd with fancies of a gayer hue,
> Enamour'd of the scenes her *wishes* drew;
> And oft she prattled with an eager tongue
> Of promised joys that would not loiter long,
> Till with her tearless eyes so bright and fair,
> She seem'd to see them realis'd in air!
> In fancy oft, within some sunny dell,
> Where never wolf should howl or tempest yell,
> She built a little home of joy and rest,
> And fill'd it with the friends whom she lov'd best:
> (27–36; italics in text)

Having realized her sunny home in air, within a kind of garden,

> Her thoughts were wild, her soul was in her eye,
> She wept and laugh'd as if she knew not why;
> And she had made a song about the wars,
> And sang it to the sun and to the stars!   (59–62)

Intoxicated by her own music, rather like Maria in *Osorio*, she dares to sing of the wars within the very precincts of the imagined paradise. When she learns of her lover's death, her anguish leaves her mind imperfect.

> *No delight*
> Thenceforth she found in any cheerful sight,
> Not ev'n in *those time-haunted wells and groves*
> Scenes of past joy, and birth-place of her loves.
> If to her spirit any sound was dear,
> 'Twas the deep moan that spoke the tempest near:
> Or *sighs which chasms of icy vales outbreathe,*
> *Sent from the dark imprison'd floods beneath.*   (75–82)

And so we have a house of joy (realized in air) within a sunny dell, and we have also the haunted groves, breathing chasms, icy vales, and dark imprisoned floods. If it is to be remarked that the lover in the case is not a demon-lover but, in the father's words, "a valiant boy," we must also consider that all absent lovers, certainly all dead lovers who maintain their hold, are demon-lovers, lovers who belong to a realm we cannot know.

> She wander'd up the crag and down the slope,
> But not as in her happy days of hope,
> To seek the churning-plant of sovereign power,
> That grew in clefts and bore a scarlet flower!
> She roam'd, without a purpose, all alone,
> Thro' high grey vales unknowing and unknown.   (83–88)

If we find the rhetoric somewhat cloying, it may be in part because, as in some of Wordsworth's poems of which this is reminiscent, it seems inappropriate to the person presented as employing it. But at least the psychology is good—the old shepherd who cannot forbear telling us that the churning-plant grew in clefts and bore a scarlet flower! And he is alluding to the time-honored cure for cases of this kind, at least among the poor—steady occupation.

The maddened girl haunts only one human habitation, a "towering convent," where she seeks "To ease her soul by penitence and prayer," (98) another interjection of the orthodox Christian element, but she nevertheless dies outside in a night of storm.

In "Fears in Solitude" (1798) it is as if Coleridge had learned the lesson set out two months before in "France: An Ode," that true liberty is not to be realized under any form of human government but to be achieved by the individual through "adoration of God in Nature." Like the earlier poem, this is a more or less poetic reflection upon the political situation, now in the crisis of an expected invasion from France. The poet finds himself in

> *A green and silent spot, amid the hills,*
> A small and silent dell! O'er stiller place
> No *singing* sky-lark ever poised himself.
> The hills are *heathy, save that swelling slope,*
> Which hath a gay and gorgeous covering on,
> All *golden* with the never-bloomless furze,
> Which now blooms most profusely: (1–7)

It is one of those sunny spots of greenery, in a naturally sequestered garden furnished with a golden dome, and music.

> but the dell,
> Bathed by the mist, is fresh and delicate
> As vernal corn-field, or the unripe flax,
> The level sunshine glimmers with green light
> Oh! 'tis a quiet spirit-healing nook!   (7–12)

As always, beneath the shining dome, the cool protected grot. And, as always, it produces vision:

> And he, with many feelings, many thoughts,
> Made up a meditative joy, and found

Religious meanings in the forms of Nature!
And so, his senses gradually wrapt
In a half sleep, he dreams of better worlds,
And dreaming hears thee still, O singing lark,
That singest like an angel in the clouds!   (22–28)

Here are only the benign elements, in this natural vision seen to the accompaniment of angelic music, but the world of violence breaks in upon it nonetheless. The poet himself assumes the role of an ancestral voice prophesying war:

My God! it is a melancholy thing
For such a man, who would full fain preserve
His soul in calmness, yet perforce must feel
For all his human brethren—O my God!

It is still for his *brethren* that he must feel, not yet for himself. As we saw, the violence is in no way intrinsic to the vision.

It weighs upon the heart, that he must think
What uproar and what strife may now be stirring
This way or that way o'er these silent hills—
Invasion, and the thunder and the shout,
And all the crash of onset; fear and rage,
And undetermined conflict—even now.
Even now, perchance, and in his native isle:
Carnage and groans beneath this blessed sun!   (29–40)

Most of the two hundred lines that follow constitute a kind of prophetic sermon addressed to the English people, calling upon them to be worthy of victory. Some of it is very moving, though Coleridge himself remarked that it "is perhaps not Poetry,—but rather a sort of middle thing between Poetry and Oratory— sermoni propriora. —Some parts are, I am conscious, too tame even for animated prose." [9] It might be read as an expansion of lines 29–30 of "Kubla Khan." At the end, he is able with comparative

[9] *Ibid.,* p. 257 n.

ease to transfer his thoughts back to the "green and silent dell," and no magic results, certainly no necessity for exorcism, no flashing eyes and floating hair.

"The Nightingale" (1798) is another effort, as it were, to separate the joyous from the melancholy or sinister. With apologies to Milton, he denies that the nightingale is a melancholy bird, attributing the conventional idea to

> some night-wandering man whose heart was pierced
> With remembrance of a grievous wrong,
> Or slow distemper, or neglected love,
> (And so, poor wretch! filled all things with himself,
> And made all gentle sounds tell back the tale
> Of his own sorrow).   (16–21)

Later on the recognition of a melancholy element in nature is associated with dissipation:

> And youths and maidens most poetical,
> Who lose the deepening twilights of the spring
> In ball-rooms and hot theatres, they still
> Full of meek sympathy must heave their sighs
> O'er Philomela's pity-pleading strains.   (35–39)

Those on the other hand who know "Nature's sweet voices, always full of love / And joyance," (42–43) surrendering their whole spirit "to the influxes / Of shapes and sounds and shifting elements," (27–29) find the nightingale a merry bird. And he then proceeds to imagine a scene like that in Xanadu, without the romantic chasm:

> And I know a grove
> Of *large extent,* hard *by a castle huge,*
> Which the *great lord* inhabits not; and so
> This grove is wild with tangling underwood,
> And the *trim walks* are broken up, and grass,
> Thin grass and king-cups grow within the paths.   (49–54)

A deserted pleasure-dome! And here the nightingales are

> Stirring the air with such a harmony,
> That should you close your eyes, you might almost
> Forget it was not day! On moonlight bushes,
> Whose dewy leaflets are but half-disclosed,
> You may perchance behold them on the twigs,
> *Their bright, bright eyes, their eyes both bright and full,*
> *Glistening,* while many a glow-worm in the shade
> Lights up her love-torch.   (62–69)

It is almost as if *we* know what all this means, having read "Kubla Khan," but that Coleridge does not yet. A familiar figure is to be found wandering in the castle grounds:

>   A most gentle Maid,
> Who dwelleth in her hospitable home
> Hard by the castle, and at latest eve
> (Even like *a Lady vowed and dedicate*
> *To something more than Nature in the grove*)
> Glides through the pathways; she knows all their notes,
> That gentle Maid! and oft, a moment's space,
> What time the moon was lost behind a cloud,
> Hath heard a pause of silence; till the moon
> Emerging, hath awakened earth and sky
> With one sensation, and those wakeful birds
> Have all burst forth in choral minstrelsy,
> As if some sudden gale had swept at once
> *A hundred airy harps!* And she hath watched
> Many a nightingale perch giddily
> On blossomy twig still swinging from the breeze,
> And to that motion tune his *wanton song*
> *Like tipsy Joy that reels with tossing head.*   (69–86)

It is as if "Kubla Khan" were about to burst forth. It is at the end of this poem that Coleridge tells of taking his son Hartley out into the moonlight when he had been frightened by a dream:

> And he beheld the moon, and, hushed at once,
> Suspends his sobs, and laughs most silently,

>   While his fair eyes, that swam with undropped tears,
>   Did *glitter* in the yellow moon-beam!   (102–5)

The first thing to be noted about "The Wanderings of Cain" (1798) is that Coleridge published this work with the same kind of explanation or apology as that with which he published "Kubla Khan," depreciating its poetic value and pleading the insistence of others. In the case of "Kubla Khan," Lord Byron is said to have been responsible. Also, like "Kubla Khan," it is presented as a fragment, of which Coleridge says, "I have in vain tried to recover the lines from the palimpsest of my memory: and I can only offer the introductory stanza, which had been committed to writing for the purpose of procuring a friend's judgment on the metre, as a specimen." [10] In this case, however, he was able to recall the substance of at least a large part of the forgotten lines, although it would seem, to judge by the unpublished fragments among his papers,[11] that he "recalled" it at different times in different versions. What we now have of it consists of eighteen lines of verse and a prose version of "Canto II," a kind of textured summary.

It is a little surprising that the composition, fragmentary though it be, has not received more attention from critics, in view of its declared connection with "The Ancient Mariner." As Coleridge tells the story in his prefatory note, the poem was planned as a joint production with Wordsworth, who was to write the first canto while Coleridge wrote the second. But the original idea was Coleridge's, and Wordsworth failed to produce, a failure for which Coleridge suggests two reasons:

Almost thirty years have passed by; yet at this moment I cannot without something more than a smile moot the question which of the two things was the more impracticable, for a mind so eminently original to compose another man's thoughts and fancies, or for a taste so austerely pure and simple to imitate the Death of Abel? [12]

---

[10] *Ibid.*, p. 287.   [11] *Ibid.*, p. 285.   [12] *Ibid.*, p. 286.

Coleridge's implication that his own taste was not "so austerely pure and simple" might be offered as evidence in support of morally ambiguous and complex interpretations of poems like "The Ancient Mariner" and "Kubla Khan." He tells us that, when it became apparent that Wordsworth could not finish his canto, they both realized "the exceeding ridiculousness of the whole scheme—which broke up in a laugh: and the Ancient Mariner was written instead."[13] On the basis of this passage and his investigation of the sources, Lowes declares "Cain" to be "broadly synchronous with 'The Ancient Mariner' and 'Kubla Khan,' " saying that all three of them "in the diversity and multitudinousness of their elements . . . are of a piece."[14] The kinship of "The Wanderings of Cain" with "The Ancient Mariner" might be suggested by the very titles, along with a little knowledge of the latter poem, but the relation to "Kubla Khan" is perhaps not so obvious.

At the beginning of the "Second Canto," we find Cain and his son making their way through "a forest of fir-trees":

at its entrance the trees stood at distances from each other, and the path was broad, and the moonlight and the moonlight shadows reposed upon it, and appeared quietly to inhabit that solitude. But soon the path winded and became narrow; and the sun at high noon sometimes speckled, but never illumined it, and now it was dark as a cavern.
(3–9)

We should note here that though we are presumably in a wild "forest," there *is* a path, the trees are spaced, and the forest is, in the most diaphanous way, "inhabited." A region touched only by moonlight, or speckled by the noonday sun (cf. "This Lime-Tree Bower," line 11), we recognize as being in the realm of the poetic experience, but at the moment Cain and his son enter, it is "dark as a cavern." They are in the realm of inspiration, but under unfavorable circumstances. Cain asks the child to guide him, "And the innocent little child clasped a finger of the hand which had

[13] *Ibid.*, p. 287.   [14] Lowes, p. 588.

murdered the righteous Abel, and he guided his father." (14–16)
The inextricable juxtaposition of innocence and guilt is reinforced
when the child tells his father that he tried the day before to play
with the squirrels in the trees, but that they fled from him, though
he would be as good to them as his father is to him. In answer to
the child's demand for an explanation, Cain falls groaning to the
ground and calls out:

'The Mighty One that persecuteth me is on this side and on that; he
pursueth my soul like the wind, like the sand-blast he passeth through
me; he is around me even as the air!'   (33–35)

Here we have a reversal of Coleridge's many paeans to the omnipresence of God in Nature,[15] and the wind of inspiration has
become a sandblast. Like the Ancient Mariner after he killed the
albatross, Cain has forfeited his connection with God through
Nature, and God's presence is a source of anguish:

'O that I might be utterly no more! I desire to die—yes, the things that
never had life, neither move upon the earth—behold! they seem
precious to mine eyes. O that man might live without the breath of life
in his nostrils.'   (36–39)

That a man might live, that is, without contact, without the ability
or the impulse, both precarious and dangerous, to experience the
world, safe from the poetic experience, having somehow violated it.

'So I might abide in darkness, and blackness, and an empty space! Yea,
I would lie down, I would not rise, neither would I stir my limbs till I
became as the rock in the den of the lion, on which the young lion
resteth his head whilst he sleepeth. *For the torrent that roareth far off
hath a voice:* and the clouds in heaven look terribly on me; the Mighty
One who is against me speaketh in *the wind of the cedar grove;* and in
silence I am dried up.'   (39–47)

[15] See "Fears in Solitude," 17–28; "This Lime-Tree Bower," 37–43; "The
Destiny of Nations," 15 ff.; "Religious Musings," 45–58, 105–16; "The
Eolian Harp," 26–33, 44–48.

Here is a man to whom all the solicitations of nature are as a curse, because, as we learn from the alternative manuscript version,[16] "he neglected to make proper use of his senses." The wind of the cedar grove, instead of inspiring him to utterance, strikes him dumb. The voices of nature are voices of condemnation and threat. Paradoxically, he wants to become "one" with nature in order to escape her. (A passage like this might well receive properly cautious biographical consideration in discussions of the much-vexed matter of Coleridge's laziness.)

Enos leads his father onward through the wood:

The path was dark till within three strides' [17] length of its termination, when it turned suddenly; the *thick black trees* formed *a low arch,* and the moonlight appeared for a moment like a dazzling portal.

(57–60)

The boy runs ahead into the moonlight and is affrighted when his father emerges with his ravaged countenance and figure. Through the dazzling portal they have entered not a pleasure-dome but an utterly desolate wasteland, in the midst of which the child had previously discovered a pitcher and cake, toward which he has been leading his father. With all the biblical language Coleridge employs in his "summary," one is reminded here of things like the valley of the shadow of death. It is in this desert that sustenance has been found, and that salvation is evidently to be found also. And a little child shall lead them. . . .

Here they come upon the ghost of Abel, who, surprisingly, is in as great torment as Cain. The Shape cries out in lamentation, in a voice the boy recognizes:

[16] *Poems,* p. 285 n.

[17] The attention of psychoanalytically minded critics might be directed to Coleridge's evident compulsion to irrelevantly accurate measurement. Cf. David Beres's diagnosis of Coleridge as an oral character, "A Dream, A Vision, and A Poem; a Psychoanalytic Study of the Origins of *The Rime of the Ancient Mariner,*" *International Journal of Psycho-Analysis,* XXXII, No. 2 (1951), 97–116.

'Ere yet I could speak, I am sure, O my Father, that I heard that voice. Have I not often said that I *remembered a sweet voice?* O my father! this is it':   (101–4)

To the innocent boy, the voice is like that of the damsel with the dulcimer, but to Cain it is more like that of the woman wailing for her demon lover:

and Cain trembled exceedingly. The voice was sweet indeed, but it was thin and querulous, like that of a feeble slave in misery, who despairs altogether, yet can not refrain himself from weeping and lamentation.
(104–7)

It is possible to see Cain and Enos here as two aspects of the same personality, the damned and the redeemable. In "Frost at Midnight" Coleridge thinks of his own son, Hartley, in something like this way, contrasting his own youth with that which he foresees for his son. Over and over it is Enos who makes the gesture of contact, and in the alternative version there is question of his being sacrificed. Here it is he who is able to go around and look upon the stranger's face.

And the Shape shrieked, and turned round, and Cain beheld him, that his limbs and his face were those of his brother Abel whom he had killed! And Cain stood like one who struggles in his sleep because of *the excessive terribleness of a dream.*   (110–14)

Whatever else is involved, this is a confrontation between good and evil, in their most ancient human embodiments, but like others we have encountered it is strangely ambiguous. The Cain we have seen is touchingly good to his own son, who loves him in complete confidence; and Abel, instead of having been gathered to the reward of his own innocence, as we should expect, is feeble, miserable, and querulous, and it is to *Cain* that he looks for *his* salvation. One might expect Cain to be haunted by the ghost of Abel, but, like a suppliant, the Shape fell at his feet, and embraced his knees, and cried out with a bitter outcry, 'Thou eldest born of Adam, whom Eve, my mother, brought forth, cease to torment me! I was feeding my flocks in green pastures by the side of quiet waters, and thou killedst me; and now I am in misery.' (115-20)

Now one is tempted to see Cain and *Abel* as two aspects of the same personality. The Abel in him, who has made acceptable sacrifices to God (cf. "The Eolian Harp," 49-64), has been slain by the Cain in him—really slain, and the Abel cannot be resurrected without the rehabilitation of the Cain as well, through what is left of Abel in him, represented here by Enos.

Cain himself, understandably puzzled by Abel's statement, raises him up and asks him:

'The Creator of our father, who had respect unto thee, and unto thy offering, wherefore hath he forsaken thee?' (126-29)

We may be reminded of Asia's questions to Demogorgon in *Prometheus Unbound*—Cain is asking the ultimate questions, e.g., how does God allow the good to be overcome? The scene that follows has echoes of the Crucifixion:

Then the Shape shrieked a second time, and rent his garment, and his naked skin was like the white sands beneath their feet; and he shrieked yet a third time, and threw himself on his face upon the sand that was black with the shadow of the rock, and Cain and Enos sat beside him [like the two thieves, the good and the bad?]; the child by his right hand, and Cain by his left. *They were all three together under the rock, and within the shadow.* (128-35)

This moment would seem to be the crisis of the fable. If we suppose the three figures to represent three aspects of the one personality, they are at this moment at the maximum of conscious dissociation and, at the same time, are shown as identical in their plight, all three lost or saved together. And it is at this point, perhaps, that we have a glimpse of what a remarkable poem this might have been, had Coleridge succeeded in poetically realizing, in embodying, the issues involved. It would surely have made a fourth to add to the great three.

Before attempting to answer Cain's impossible question, Abel speaks to the child:

'I know where the cold waters are, but I may not drink, wherefore didst thou then take away my pitcher?' (136–38)

The child, the vestige of Abel still alive in Cain, deprives Abel of the possibility of nourishment. It is as if Abel could reassert himself in his own integrity if he were quite absent in Cain— and so Cain could achieve his ambition of annihilation into stone. As it is, Enos, the remnant of Abel in Cain, has appropriated the *means* of obtaining water, the living water, without knowing where the water is. Only Abel knows, and he is dead, has no command over means. If these interpretations are valid, we have here a remarkably complex effort at analysis of the psychological process involved in the disintegration of the poetic personality, when, without grace, it touches the boundaries of religious experience. It is, of course, misleading here to speak of the "poetic personality"—we have to do at this level with the generic human personality, with a generic human predicament of which the poet is merely an acute example.

Cain interposes before Enos can answer Abel's question:

'Didst thou not find favour in the sight of the Lord thy God?' The Shape answered, 'The Lord is God of the living only, the dead have another God.' Then the child Enos lifted up his eyes and prayed; but Cain rejoiced secretly in his heart. 'Wretched shall they be all the days of their mortal life,' exclaimed the Shape, 'who sacrifice worthy and acceptable sacrifices to the God of the dead; but after death their toil ceaseth [as indeed would Cain's, could he become as a rock, were the Abel in him totally dead]. Woe is me, for I was well beloved by the God of the living, and cruel wert thou, O my brother, who didst snatch me away from his power and his dominion.' (138–48)

So there is for each of us a sense in which if it were possible to set free the good that is in us, at the price of our utter damnation, that good might be imagined as realizing its own autonymous nature. But it is inconceivable that we should let it go. We can do everything to *kill* it, deliberately or accidentally, but we cannot let it go. Tied to Cain, dead through his agency, deprived of all means, his only possibility of sustenance usurped, paradoxically, by the element of himself, Enos, that unaccountably survives in Cain, Abel is life exiled in the realm of death, while Cain is death condemned to life. We remember the nightmare of "The Ancient Mariner." It should be obvious that in all this Coleridge is not concentrating upon the invention of a novel theology—as theology this would surely at any time have been abhorrent to him—but upon a psychological elaboration.

It turns out that Cain, though he knows he has offended the God of the living, knows no more than the child Enos who the God of the dead is to whom he has offered worthy and acceptable sacrifices, and has no assurance of having pleased him even so. It must be remembered that in the biblical account Cain had brought an offering "of the fruit of the ground" (Gen. 4:3), something purely and simply natural. He had, as it were, depended upon nature for his salvation, whereas Abel had offered "of the firstlings of his flock and of the fat thereof," something that in the sequel turned out to be a prescribed, liturgical sacrifice, something involving the shedding of blood, prefiguring redemption by the Crucifixion. (We may suppose that in Eden, before the Fall, Cain's natural offering would have been acceptable.) And so, as the Shape fled over the sands, "Cain said in his heart, 'The curse of the Lord [the God of the living, presumably] is on me; but who is the God of the dead?' " And he pursues Abel in order to find out.

Abel outruns him, but wheels back again to the rock, "and the child caught hold of his garment as he passed by, and he fell upon the ground." (155–56) Again it is the child who maintains contact with Abel, or the phantom of Abel, and Cain can again address him, in words that perfectly describe the state of degradation in which one is prevented by the destruction of a capacity from even *longing* for that capacity except in an abstract way:

'Abel, my brother, I would lament for thee, but that the spirit within me is withered, and burnt up with extreme agony.[18] Now, I pray thee, by thy flocks, and by thy pastures, and by the quiet rivers which thou lovedst, that thou tell me all that thou knowest.' (164–68)

What he asks for in fact turns out to be not all that Abel knows, but only what he knows about the "God of the dead." The implication is that there is really no hope of salvation, of the reintegration of Cain and Abel, but only of finding a way in which to render the fallen state bearable by making it *complete:*

'Who is the God of the dead? where doth he make his dwelling? what sacrifices are acceptable unto him? for I have offered, but have not been heard; and how can I be afflicted more than I already am?' (168–72)

Abel's answer leaves us, and doubtless Cain, in the dark, although it is possible that Abel knows some answer that Cain in his fallen state cannot yet imagine:

'O that thou hadst had pity on me as I will have pity on thee. Follow me, Son of Adam! and bring thy child with thee!'
    And they three passed over the white sands between the rocks, silent as shadows. (172–76)

The expression "Son of Adam" tends to confirm Cain as the prototype of "Man." But that is the end of the fragment as published, and Coleridge evidently never felt equal even to sketching out the Paradise Regained that would seem to be its logical sequel. Yet after even so cursory an examination of this curious composition, it does indeed seem ridiculous to suppose that Wordsworth

---

[18] Here we may be reminded of the "grief without a pang, void, dark, and drear" of "Dejection."

might have written its first canto—and not at all ridiculous to imagine that we have here the skeleton of what might have become one of the great poems of the language. Lacking that poem, we must simply content ourselves with "The Ancient Mariner," the leading symbols of which are perhaps less intrinsically rich, though they have the corresponding advantage of being less heavily freighted with possibly intrusive conventional associations.

The "rough draft of a continuation or alternative version . . . found among Coleridge's papers" is dated 1798 by E. H. Coleridge, from internal evidence, and he remarks that "Mr. Hutchinson, who reprints (*Lyrical Ballads of 1798*, Notes, pp. 259–60) a selected passage from the MS. fragment, points out 'that Coleridge had for a time thought of shaping the poem as a narrative addressed by Cain to his wife.'" [19] If this projected poem is in fact concerned primarily with the disintegration of the poetic personality, such a format is not surprising. When, in 1802, he finally wrote his definitive statement on the subject, in "Dejection: An Ode," he addressed it to Sara Hutchinson, the person to whom he felt the closest affinity. Indeed, what poet, what person, would not find it easier, might not find it indispensable, to address an analysis of the inmost struggles and failures of his being to someone he utterly loved and who, he might believe, utterly loved him? By 1798 this person could no longer conceivably be Sara Coleridge, and he did not find Sara Hutchinson until 1799. When we come to consider the intent of "Kubla Khan," and the place that poem holds in Coleridge's work, it will be important to remember that it falls between "The Wanderings of Cain" and "Dejection," if we accept one of Miss Schneider's alternative dates for it.

The rough draft or alternative version, like the published one, contains a number of images strikingly suggestive of "Kubla Khan." At the beginning of the fragment, Cain "falls down in a trance—when he awakes he sees a luminous body coming before him" in the form of an orb of fire. Reluctantly he follows it "to near

[19] *Poems*, p. 285 n.

the bottom of the wild woods, brooks, forests, etc. etc." Taking the shape of a man, the being tries to persuade Cain to burn out his eyes in expiation of his enormous guilt, but Cain argues that his original punishment was due to the fact that "he neglected to make a proper use of his senses, etc." What surely contributes to our difficulty in interpreting a number of Coleridge's major poems is our modern difficulty in understanding the association he apparently assumes between theological guilt, or *sin,* with all its biblical implications, and the vagaries of the poetic experience. Great efforts, deliberate or otherwise, have been made in the last hundred years to divorce these two areas of experience from each other, perhaps as a reaction against the Romantic tendency to confuse them. As a result, it seems strange to us that the poetic experience should be conceived as involving any "religious" perils, if indeed we can conceive of religious perils at all. But Coleridge was near the beginning of this effort to distinguish between the two realms, tempted as he was to erase the distinction, to substitute the poetic for the religious experience. For him the temptation had disastrous results, because he was still able to appreciate the idolatry involved—later the substitution seems to have been made with at least temporary success by many poets, beginning with the second generation of Romantics. It may be that "Kubla Khan" is the record of a moment when success seemed possible to Coleridge—the last moment when it did, the last moment when he was able to record the expectation of a "beatific" vision, a poetic contact with reality substitutable for a mystical contact, and even here it is described as hedged about with perils. We can see the difference when we come to Shelley, Keats, and Byron, each of whom, in his own individual way, struggled with the problem, with the disasters attendant upon the effort to make an ultimate of the poetic experience, and each left the records of that struggle in his poems; but these later poets, perhaps with the exception of Byron, seem to have succeeded in making the substitution of poetry for religious experience without entirely awaking to its perils, and being silenced by them. In this state of more or less invincible ignorance, very great poetry can be produced, but it is a long time before we can again have poets like Shakespeare or Pope, who carry poetry as far in some direction as it can possibly go, make it carry unbelievable weights of human concern, without ever dreaming that it is anything other than, anything more than poetry; or, on the other hand, poets like Milton or Hopkins, "religious poets," whose poetry never breaks down under the weight of its religious subject matter, precisely because it is "religious *poetry*," not poetic religion.

It is in some such context as this, perhaps, that we must try to understand how the failure "to make a proper use of the senses" can be somehow seriously equated with the sin of Cain, how, for that matter, throughout the Romantic period and after, poems about poetry come to be written in terms of the most august of theological myths.

It develops that the spirit who urges upon Cain the sacrifice of his eyes in expiation for his misuse of the senses is an evil spirit. He answers Cain's protest with an argument that reminds one immediately of the last section of "Kubla Khan"; he says that

God is indeed a God of mercy, and that an example must be given to mankind, that this end will be answered by *his terrible appearance,* at the same time he will be gratified with *the most delicious* sights and feelings.[20]

It is as if he promised the vision of the Abyssinian maid, in return for perpetual blindness. Cain is tempted, "over-persuaded," but having climbed the rocks for a farewell look at nature, he relents,

and turning to declare this to the being, he sees him dancing from rock to rock in his former shape *down those interminable precipices.*[21]

In what must be another scene, or even a second alternative version, we find Cain at

[20] *Ibid.,* p. 285 n.   [21] *Ibid.,* pp. 285–86 n.

Midnight on the banks of the Euphrates. Cedars, palms, pines. Cain discovered sitting on the upper part of *the ragged rock,* where is *cavern overlooking the Euphrates,* the *moon rising* on the horizon. . . . The Beasts are out on the ramp—he hears *the screams of a woman* and children surrounded by tigers.[22]

Here we have a woman wailing in the most savage of places. She turns out to be Cain's wife, and it is a demon-beset lover who answers her call. In telling her his story, Cain employs something like a combination of the published version and the previously recounted vision in the draft. This time a pseudo-Abel leads him into "an immense gulph filled with water, whither they descend followed by alligators, etc." (The "etc." is an eloquent touch!) "They go till they come to an immense meadow so surrounded as to be inaccessible." In this combination of Kubla's garden and the romantic chasm, the false Abel offers sacrifice of the blood of his own arm to what seems to be "the God of the dead." He undergoes a kind of transfiguration, and urges Cain to offer sacrifice of blood from the arm of his son Enoch. We know that the temptation for Cain must be great, since this would seem to be a replica of Abel's original, successful sacrifice of blood, and in fact it requires the miraculous appearance of the real Abel from heaven, accompanied by the archangel Michael, to deter him from making this ultimate sacrifice to the God of the dead, to deter him from killing the remnant of Abel left to him. "And Abel carries off the child." Again no paradise regained, for here the fragment ends.

If, in dealing with the published version, we were right in supposing that the child somehow represents the Abel element in Cain, this variant is consistent with it. Somehow Cain has killed the Abel in him, cut himself off from a right relationship with God, through misuse of his senses associated with making a natural, vegetable offering to God instead of a liturgical blood

[22] *Ibid.,* p. 286 n.

offering. But something of Abel is left in him, represented by the child. If only he will sacrifice *that,* the evil spirit suggests, he will be happy—in other words, he will be all Cain. The real Abel "addresses Cain with terror, warning him not to offer up his innocent child." We can hardly presume to be surprised that Coleridge failed to write this poem, and it is not hard to imagine why he felt impelled, with whatever apologies, to publish an outline of it. We can certainly appreciate his warning to the reader that "the less he attributes its appearance to the author's will, choice, or judgment, the nearer to the truth he will be." [23] Some close attention to the remains may constitute an appropriate tribute to its possibilities.

Like "The Wanderings of Cain," "The Ballad of the Dark Ladié" (1798) is also a fragment, but in this case there is evidence as to its intended length, 190 lines, of which we have sixty.[24] There is, of course, a notorious number of fragments among Coleridge's poems, but this one shares the distinction with "Christabel" of having been singled out as a potential improvement upon "The Ancient Mariner," and that is a sufficient call upon our attention. The Dark Ladié, by her very cognomen, immediately suggests the woman wailing for her demon-lover, and in fact she has a good deal in common with her. The first stanza of the poem sets an at least vaguely familiar scene:

> Beneath yon birch with silver bark,
> And boughs so pendulous and fair,
> The brook falls scatter'd down the rock:
> And all is mossy there!   (1–4)

The similarity of the brook falling scattered down the rock in wooded terrain to the landscape of "Kubla Khan" is obvious. Less so, perhaps, is the suggestion of "sunny spots of greenery" in the line "And all is mossy there." In the second stanza we come upon the Ladié:

[23] *Ibid.,* p. 287.   [24] *Ibid.,* p. 293 n.

And there upon the moss she sits,
The Dark Ladié in silent pain;
The heavy tear is in her eye,
    And drops and swells again.   (5–8)

She is weeping, rather than wailing, perhaps because she is a "ladié" rather than a "woman," a lady with a page, whom she sends "Up the castled mountain's breast" in search of her lover, in whom there is as yet no suggestion of any demonic quality. She has been waiting for him all day, and when he finally comes to her, over the brook, she casts off all ladylike restraint:

She springs, she clasps him around the neck,
She sobs a thousand hopes and fears,
Her kisses glowing on his cheeks
    She quenches with her tears.   (21–24)

And so we have a woman sitting by a rocky brook beneath a castled mount, weeping for her absent lover. In this case he arrives, and provokes what might be called hysterical manifestations.

The poem continues, after a hiatus, with the woman's appealing passionately to the knight for "shelter," on the ground that she has given him all and has been spurned by her friends, who presumably find the match for some reason unacceptable. His answer introduces the sinister, if not precisely demonic, note in his character, as judged by the Ladié's reaction to it. He begins by informing her that

'Nine *castles* hath my noble sire,
    None *statlier* in the land.'   (35–36)

He might be inviting her into Kubla's stately pleasure-dome: the fairest of the nine is to be hers. But there is a disturbing condition to the invitation:

'Wait only till the stars peep out,
    The fairest shall be thine:

> 'Wait only till the hand of eve
> Hath wholly closed yon western bars,
> And through the dark we two will steal
>   Beneath the twinkling stars!'—   (39–40)

She has, as it were, spent all day in a sunny spot of greenery, and now he is asking her to pass through the deep romantic chasm under the light of the stars before she may enter the pleasure-dome. Her reaction is one of panic:

> 'The dark? the dark? No! not the dark?
> The twinkling stars? How, Henry? How?'
> O God! 'twas in the eye of noon
>   He pledged his sacred vow!
> And in the eye of noon my love
> Shall lead me from my mother's door, . . .   (49–50)

And she proceeds, in the three stanzas that remain of the poem, to describe the most conventional of noontime weddings, complete with bridesmaids, flower girls, and music.

Here, at any rate, there can surely be no doubt as to the "fragmentary" character of the poem, and it is hard to see, judging by what exists of it, what Coleridge might have meant by suggesting that it should have more nearly realized his ideal than "The Ancient Mariner." Yet we should not suppose that he made such a statement carelessly, and the "Kubla Khan" elements in it suggest, at least, the depth at which it was conceived.

A poem like "The Snow-Drop" (1798) [25] is fascinating. How is it possible that the man we know Coleridge to have been, the man who had written "The Ancient Mariner" and "Christabel," who was to write *The Friend* and *The Statesman's Manual,* how is it possible that such a man can at the age of twenty-eight have written "The Snow-Drop," with two opening stanzas like these?

---

[25] For the date (E. H. Coleridge gives 1800), see Woodring, *Politics in the Poetry of Coleridge,* pp. 123–24.

Fear no more, thou timid Flower!
Fear thou no more the winter's might,
The whelming thaw, the ponderous shower,
The silence of the freezing night!
Since Laura murmur'd o'er thy leaves
The potent sorceries of song,
To thee, meek Flowret! gentler gales
      And cloudless skies belong.

Her eye with tearful meanings fraught,
She gaz'd till all the body mov'd
Interpreting the Spirit's thought—
The Spirit's eager sympathy
Now trembled with thy trembling stem,
And while thou droopedst o'er thy bed,
With sweet unconscious sympathy
      Inclin'd the drooping head.

It is possible, no doubt, to extract a prose paraphrase that, in the light of a certain sympathetic historical interest in the Romantic movement, is not really too embarrassing; but so much of Coleridge requires no such special allowance, and even with it the rhetoric seems inexcusable. The best thing we can do, I think, is momentarily to relax all standards of aesthetic judgment and to rest puzzled, amazed, wonderstruck, and even a little envious, in the face of the mere coexistence of such ingenuousness and such sophistication (the poem alludes to Mrs. Robinson). Any other reaction might lead us to the idea that there is hope for all of us, and surely there isn't.

In the third stanza we come upon an allusion to the "witching rhymes" of "Perdita," and may be alerted to the possibility of relevance of "Kubla Khan" (a relevance even more sharply evident, as we shall see, in a later poem to Mrs. Robinson, "A Stranger Minstrel").

All of them whom Love and Fancy grace,
When grosser eyes are clos'd in sleep,
The gentle spirits of the place
Waft up the insuperable steep,
On whose vast summit broad and smooth
Her nest the Phoenix Bird conceals,
And where *by cypresses o'erhung*
      The heavenly Lethe steals.

A sea-like sound the branches breathe,
Stirred by the Breeze that loiters there;
And all that stretch their limbs beneath,
Forget the coil of mortal care.
Strange mists along the margins rise,
To heal the guests who thither come,
And fit the soul to re-endure
      Its earthly martyrdom.

This is hardly the language one expects in a poem on the snow-drop, or on Perdita's "Ode to the Snow-drop." In one way of look-ing at "Kubla Khan," its two subjects are Love and Fancy, and the exact relation between them is no clearer there than here, or in "Love." But somehow those who are graced by both are wafted up the insuperable steep and in their immortality are brooded over by that symbol of death the cypress, in a realm where recollection and oblivion are equivalent. A sea-like sound the branches breathe, and the breeze that loiters there seems at the same time to come from Parnassus and from the lifeless ocean. Surely nothing is more treacherous in the reading of poetry than the interpretation of sound as sense, but it may be harmless, at least, to point out a similarity between

> And all that stretch their limbs beneath
> Forget the coil of mortal care.

[and]

> And all who heard should see them there,
> And all should cry, Beware! Beware!

Certainly all must beware of those who by whatever means forget the coil of mortal care, their flashing eyes, their floating hair, and it is well if some Lethe fits them to endure their earthly martyrdom.

The last two stanzas, omitted by J. D. Campbell in his edition of 1893 as "too imperfect to print,"[26] may be repeated here on the ground that they offer a unique account of the damsel dismissed so abruptly in "Kubla Khan":

> The margin dear to moonlight elves
> Where Zephyr-trembling Lilies grow,
> And bend to kiss their softer selves
> That tremble in the stream below:—
> There nightly borne does Laura lie
> *A magic Slumber* heaves her breast:
> *Her arm, white wanderer of the Harp,*
> Beneath her cheek is prest.
>
> The Harp uphung by golden chains
> Of that low wind which whispers round,
> With coy reproachfulness complains,
> In snatches of reluctant sound:
> And music hovers half-perceiv'd,
> And only *moulds the slumberer's dreams;*
> *Remember'd LOVES* relume her cheek
> With Youth's returning gleams.

If this is indeed the damsel with the dulcimer, we are evidently embarked upon an infinite regress, for she too is inspired in dreams by music that recalls remembered loves, and the situation is complicated by the fact that her harp, uphung in golden chains, is obviously the Eolian Harp, that coy maid half yielding to her lover, and we know that maiden, that simplest lute, to have been the poet himself.

[26] *Poems,* p. 356 n.

CHAPTER FOUR

Echoes in a Minor Key

Chronological divisions in the works of poets are at best indispensable conveniences, and ought not to be allowed to create serious problems. The year 1797–98 has for a long time been recognized as a kind of climax in Coleridge's poetic career, for the very good reason that it accounts for "The Ancient Mariner," "Christabel," and, according to most computations, "Kubla Khan." Although Miss Schneider's arguments for dating "Kubla Khan" as late as the spring of 1800 are very persuasive, it still does seem true that that poem must be looked upon as an unaccountable late flowering of poetic mastery if we suppose it to have been written very long after the *annus mirabilis*. But much stranger things have happened in the lives of poets. In any case, the poems of 1799 and after, though far from homogeneous in character, do seem to have a certain nostalgic quality that is distinguishable from the quality of the poems that precede them. If indeed "Kubla Khan" falls within this period, that very fact must be a consideration in reading it.

In the case of images as nearly ubiquitous as those we are following through Coleridge's poems, their presence in poems or fragments he chose to translate is not surprising, and suggests one of the possible reasons for his translating them. The very title of one of the poems Coleridge chose to translate from Stolberg suggests the reason for his interest in the poem: "On a Cataract, from a Cavern Near the Summit of a Mountain Precipice" (1799?).[1] The entire poem might serve as a gloss on lines 16–25 of "Kubla

[1] The poem is "Der Felsenstrom," not "Unsterblicher Jüngling," as E. H. Coleridge gives the title, and may be found in *Gedichte der Brüder Christian und Friedrich Leopold Grafen zu Stolberg*, ed. Heinrich Christian Boie (Leipzig: Weygandschen Buchhandlung, 1779), pp. 124–27.

Khan," the fountain section, since here the significance of the
fountain is made quite explicit.

> Unperishing youth!
> Thou *leapest from forth*
> *The cell of thy hidden nativity;*   (1–3)

The locale is holy if not enchanted:

> Never mortal saw
> The cradle of the strong one;
> Never mortal heard
> The gathering of his voices;
> The deep-murmured charm of the son of the rock,
> That is lisp'd evermore at his *slumberless fountain*.[2]   (4–9)

This is obviously a version of the mighty fountain of Xanadu, and
two lines later there is a verbal echo—

> There's a cloud at the portal, a spray-woven veil
> At the shrine of his *ceaseless* renewing;   (10–11)

The birth of the fountain is ceaselessly renewed and the place of
its birth a "shrine," a "holy twilight" in line 17: surely the resulting
river will be a "sacred" one. The lines that follow develop the image
of the cloud, absent from "Kubla Khan":

[2] Coleridge follows Stolberg closely in his first nine lines (a translation of
Stolberg's first seven), although "The cell of thy hidden nativity" is hardly
a translation of "Aus Felsenkluft":

> Unsterblicher Jüngling!
> Du stromest hervor
> Aus Felsenkluft.
> Kein Sterblicher sah
> Die Wiege des Starken;
> Es hörte kein Ohr
> Das Lassen des Edlen im Spondelnden Quell!

What follows in Coleridge's "translation" is only in the vaguest way related
to Stolberg's poem, which is just under twice as long as Coleridge's but contains no "shrine," no "holy twilight," no "Visions of Dawn," no "Life
invulnerable."

> It embosoms the roses of dawn,
> It entangles the shafts of the noon,
> And into the bed of its stillness
> The moonshine sinks down as in slumber,
> That the son of the rock, that the nursling of heaven
> May be born in a holy twilight!   (12–17)

In a manuscript version, instead of "It embosoms the roses of dawn," we find "It embodies the Visions of Dawn,"[3] less consistent perhaps as metaphor, but closer to Coleridge's real preoccupation. The lights in these lines are the half-lights that he associates with the poetic experience. The implied equivalence of unperishing youth and poetic vitality is not for him a strained one.

The poem closes with an "antistrophe":

> The wild goat in awe
> Looks up and beholds
> Above thee the cliff inaccessible;—
> Thou at once full-born
> Madd'nest in thy joyance,
> Whirlest, shatter'st, splitt'st,
> Life invulnerable.   (18–24)

In conjunction with an eminence awesomely overlooking a chasm, the last four lines here are close in image, if not language, to lines 21–24 of "Kubla Khan":

> Huge fragments vaulted like rebounding hail,
> Or chaffy grain beneath the thresher's flail:
> And 'mid these dancing rocks at once and ever
> It flung up momently the sacred river.

It would probably be stretching a point to dwell upon the paradox of line 22—"Madd'nest in thy joyance"—but that is, in a way, the whole paradox of "Kubla Khan."

Coleridge's homesickness while he was in Germany produced

[3] *Ibid.*, p. 308 n.

several undistinguished poems, one of which, "Home-Sick" (1799),
he himself characterized as a "hobbling Ditty." [4] The term would
not fit the "Lines Written in the Album at Elbingrode, in the Harz
Forest" (1799), though they are hardly in his best vein. It might
not be unjust to say of them that they have Wordsworth's weaknesses without his virtues. The descriptive opening of the poem
includes several items suggestive of the landscape of "Kubla Khan,"
but nothing comes of them in what follows, nothing, that is, bearing any similarity to the development of "Kubla Khan." What the
poem does is to forecast "Dejection" in a very explicit way, and
such a poem has no place for the sacred river or the Abyssinian
maid, certainly not for the poet who on honey-dew hath fed.

> I stood on Brocken's *sovran height,* and saw
> *Woods crowding upon woods, hills over hills,*
> *A surging scene,* and only limited
> By the blue distance.　　　　　　(1–4)

Though far from the sea, Coleridge spontaneously finds a way of
limiting the landscape, as if he were in England. We are already
warned: there is no "garden" here.

> 　　　　　　Heavily my way
> Downward I dragged through *fir groves* evermore,
> Where *bright green moss* heaves in sepulchral forms
> *Speckled with sunshine;* and, but seldom heard,
> The sweet bird's *song* became a hollow sound;
> And the breeze, murmuring indivisibly,
> Preserved its solemn murmur most distinct
> From many a note of many a *waterfall,*
> And the *brook's chatter;* 'mid whose islet stones
> The dingy kidling with its tinkling bell
> Leaped frolicsome, or old romantic goat
> Sat, his white beard waving.　　　　(4–15)

In these lines beauty is not juxtaposed with terror but deadened
by ennui. The very multitudinousness, the extent of the scene is

[4] *Collected Letters,* I, 493.

burdensome. The sovran height, the woods, the hills, the fir groves and the spots of greenery, the song and the moving water are all there, Coleridge notes them as it were by reflex, but the country is far from Xanadu, a fact that becomes obvious with the "dingy kidlet" and the "old romantic goat." [5] We are, simply enough, in Germany, and that is ostensibly at least the trouble, as Coleridge goes on to explain:

> I moved on
> In low and languid mood: for I had found
> That outward forms, the loftiest, still receive
> Their finer influence from the Life within;—
> Fair cyphers else: fair but of import vague
> Or unconcerning, where the heart not finds

[no native of Xanadu would expect what follows]

> History or prophecy of friend, or child
> Or gentle maid, our first and early love,
> Or father, or the venerable name
> Of our adoréd country! O thou Queen,
> Thou delegated Deity of Earth,
> O dear, dear England!   (15–26)

The poem concludes with a paean to "My native Land," but as we learn later in "Dejection," only absence made it possible for Coleridge to believe that the native land from which he was beginning to feel exiled was England. He finally settled for British nationality, but his native land was Xanadu.[6]

---

[5] Are we to picture this goat sitting amid the rocks in the stream? Perhaps.

[6] This is to say something as extravagant as but no more extravagant than G. Wilson Knight says of Byron in *Lord Byron; Christian Virtues* (New York: Oxford University Press, 1953). In many respects Byron and Coleridge stand together as Romantic poets, if one employs that somewhat unfortunate term in the most unlimiting sense possible. It is to be remarked at the very least that among Romantic poets they share the distinction of being at the same time the most vicious and the most perennially religious.

Without being explicit, the birth image in "Kubla Khan" is fairly obvious, and earth is the mother:

> And from this chasm, with ceaseless turmoil seething,
> As if this earth in fast thick pants were breathing,
> A mighty fountain momently is forced:

We have seen that in "On a Cataract," imitated from Stolberg, the offspring of the birth is "Unperishing youth," "Life invulnerable." And so it is not surprising that Coleridge was attracted to Stolberg's expansion of the mother image in *Hymne an die Erde,* of which his "Hymn to the Earth" (1799) is a "free translation." [7]

> Earth! thou mother of numberless children, the nurse and the mother,
> Hail! O Goddess, thrice hail! Blest be thou! and, blessing, I hymn thee!
> Forth, ye sweet sounds! *from my harp, and my voice shall float on your surges—*
> Soar thou aloft, O my soul! and bear up my song on thy pinions.
> Travelling the vale with mine eyes—*green meadows* and lake with green island,
> *Dark in its basin of rock,* and *the bare stream flowing in brightness,*
> Thrilled with thy beauty and love *in the wooded slope of the mountain,*
> Here, great mother, I lie, thy child, with his head on thy bosom!
> Playful the spirits of *noon, that rushing soft through thy tresses,*
> Green-haired goddess! refresh me; and hark! as they hurry or linger,
> Fill the pause of *my harp,* or sustain it with musical murmurs.
> *Into my being thou murmurest joy,* and tenderest sadness
> Shedd'st thou, like dew, on my heart, till *the joy and the heavenly sadness*
> Pour themselves forth from my heart in tears, and the hymn of thanksgiving.   (1–14)

Here is a song that might be sung by the damsel with a dulcimer singing in praise of Mount Abora. And we must think back to the

---

[7] *Ibid.,* p. 327 n. The translation, very free indeed, is based upon the first 36 lines or so of Stolberg's 167-line poem. See Christian und Friedrich Leopold Grafen zu Stolberg, *Gesammelte Werke* (Hamburg: Friedrich Perthes, 1827), pp. 201–13.

ambiguities of role reflected in "The Eolian Harp," [8] where the
poet *was* the harp, played upon by the breezes, and the harp was a
maiden, half yielding to her lover. The third section of the "Hymn
to the Earth" includes a variant description of these nuptials, as
they proceed to parturition:

Say mysterious Earth! O say, great mother and goddess,
Was it not well with thee then, when first thy lap was ungirdled,
Thy lap to the genial Heaven, the day that he wooed thee and won
      thee!
Fair was thy blush, the fairest and first of the blushes of morning!
Deep was the shudder, O Earth! the throe of thy self-retention:
Inly thou strovest to flee, and didst seek thyself at thy centre!
Mightier far was the joy of thy sudden resilience; and forthwith
Myriad myriads of lives teemed forth from the mighty embracement.
Thousand-fold tribes of dwellers, impelled by thousand-fold instincts,
Filled, as a dream, the wide waters; the rivers sang on their channels;
Laughed on their shores the hoarse seas; the yearning ocean swelled
      upward;
Young life lowed through the *meadows,* the *woods,* and the *echoing
      mountains,*
Wandered bleating in valleys, and *warbled on blossoming branches.*
                                                    (20–33) [9]

Earth, under the embrace of Heaven, brings forth the mighty
fountain and constitutes herself a garden; but without Kubla
there is no pleasure-dome. The whole mystery reflected in "Kubla
Khan" may be primarily concerned just with this relation between
the decreeing monarch and the intrinsic force and beauty of
nature.[10] The "Hymn to the Earth," like so many of the poems we
have read, would seem to be a fragment of the whole that is "Kubla
Khan."

[8] See above, pp. 51 ff.
[9] Lines 24–26, "Deep was the shudder . . ." have no counterpart in the
original.
[10] On the necessity of the artist, see "On Poesy and Art," *Biographia
Literaria* II, 257–58, a passage to which we shall have occasion to allude
later on.

As the poem "Love" (1799) now stands (minus four preliminary and three concluding stanzas of the original version published in the *Morning Post*), the first stanza may strike one as only vaguely related to the matter of the poem:

> All thoughts, all passions, all delights,
> Whatever stirs this mortal frame,
> All are but ministers of Love,
> And feed his sacred flame.

There follows immediately the recollection of a particular event, but the rest of the poem is in effect an illustration of this very general statement, showing how in one instance a doleful story produced a happy reaction, through the agency of love. Presumably the "all" in "All are but ministers of Love" really means "all," including the "wild," the "savage," even the demon-haunted.[11] "Kubla Khan" is as full of love as of poetry, and this statement might serve as reassurance for those, like Howard Parsons,[12] who are disturbed by the apparent logical contradictions involved in Coleridge's description of the "romantic chasm" or, like Lane Cooper,[13] by his "unworthy, acquiescent admission of demoniac love within the so-called 'holy precincts.'" Of course neither in this poem nor in "Kubla Khan" is there any "explanation" of how the reconciliation of such opposites is possible, but that is hardly something we ought to ask of the poems. It should be noted also that here is another linking of "thought" and "delight"—and "passion."

The setting of the frame story of "Love" has a certain remote similarity to that of "Kubla Khan":

[11] We may be reminded here of Wordsworth's habit of telling sad, even gory tales to naïve listeners by the family fireside or in the summer shade, and drawing from them by means not always quite clear the most reassuring lessons (e.g., in *Excursion*, Book I, "Michael," "Peter Bell").

[12] "A New Interpretation of Coleridge's 'Kubla Khan,'" *Poetry Review*, XXXIV (1943), 112–14.

[13] "The Abyssinian Paradise in Coleridge and Milton," *Modern Philology*, III (1905–06), 327–32.

> Oft in my waking dreams do I
> Live o'er again that happy hour,
> When *midway on the mount I lay,*
> *Beside the ruined tower.*   (5–8)

There is also moonlight, "blended with the lights of eve." In this case the speaker is able to recover the song of that happy hour, but the situation seems to be related to that of "Kubla Khan," if at all, by opposition: here the *maiden* is inspired by the doleful song of the *lover.* As for the songs themselves, there is no way of knowing whether they are similar. In spite of a great deal of careful research and ingenious conjecture on the part of many readers concerning the provenance of "Mount Abora," it still does not seem possible to decide with any confidence what might be the tenor of a song about that much-disputed mountain, whether doleful or merry, or both.

In the tale within the tale, however, the parallel is more interesting. Here we have a lover moaning for his Lady-love and being visited instead by a demon-love (cf. Christabel). Having been scorned by the Lady of the Land, "he crossed the *mountain-woods,* / Nor rested day or night"; and we are told

> That sometimes from the *savage den,*
> And sometimes from the *darksome shade,*
> And sometimes starting up at once
>   In *green and sunny glade,*—
>
> There came and looked him in the face
> *An angel beautiful and bright;*
> And that *he knew it was a Fiend,*
>   This miserable Knight!

Clearly these are events that might take place in Xanadu, or in the wilderness of Cain, where the distinction between angels and fiends was so difficult to make. Inspired, it would seem, by the vision of this angel-fiend, the Knight in his crazed state unwittingly rescues the Lady of the Land from an "outrage worse than death" (the story recalls Geraldine's fabrication). We are told that as a result she relents,

> And that she nursed him in a *cave;*
> And how his madness went away,
> When on the yellow forest-leaves
> A dying man he lay;— (61–64)

We are spared his last words, for Genevieve, the listening loved one of the frame story, interrupts with tears, a meek embrace, and a declaration of love that is to be consummated in marriage. And so the doleful tale produces the happy result. In the original version, the three additional concluding stanzas introduce another "woeful tale of love," the story of the Dark Ladié, to which the whole of the poem "Love" was at first announced as an "Introduction." The two stories do seem to be roughly complementary, as nearly as we can judge from the fragmentary "Ballad of the Dark Ladié," but it is hard to think under what formal concept one might constitute an "introduction" to the other. Possibly this difficulty explains in part Coleridge's failure to achieve the total composition, and since in his mind, as we have seen, it was, along with "Christabel," to be superior to "The Ancient Mariner," the failure is an important one. It amounts, in Coleridge's opinion, to his having failed to write his greatest poem. The thematic element common to both the Dark Ladié poems and "Christabel" and absent from "The Ancient Mariner" and "Cain" is what might be described as the exploration of the positive and negative virtualities of sexual love. For whatever reasons, Coleridge was unable to complete a narrative poem with this as a major theme. It would seem to be fully integrated into "Kubla Khan," but there, of course, it is by way of allusion, as befits a lyric poem.

Beginning with *Sibylline Leaves* in 1817, "Love" was printed as the first of a group of "love poems," and prefaced by a motto from

Petrarch expressing the aging man's philosophic nostalgia in recalling the passions of his youth, and concluding thus:

For I shall not seem the same man when I gather all these thoughts
　　together:
My brow is altered, I have another way of life, a different frame of
　　mind,
And another voice sounds out—
Now let us pity those lovers who burn with passion while we keep cold
　　our heart—
Now let us be ashamed that we did so love.
My mind, now calm, looks back in horror at those old turmoils,
And as I look at them again, it seems some other must have said these
　　things.[14]

If "Kubla Khan" dated from 1817, we might be certain that "Could I revive within me . . ." is to be read "Even if I could, but I can't." But evidently Coleridge felt that the poems of roughly the period of "Kubla Khan" did not express such a sentiment, and so he affixed the motto.[15]

Coleridge called "Thought Suggested by a View of Saddle-back in Cumberland" (1800) a "versified reflection":

[14] Trans. by T. G. Dumarae. The Latin follows (from the beginning):

> Quas humilia tenero stylus olim effudit in aevo,
> Perlegis hic lacrymas, et quod pharetratus acuta
> Ille puer puero fecit mihi cuspide vulnus.
> Omnia paulatim consumit longior aetas,
> Vivendoque simul morimur, rapimurque manendo.
> Ipse mihi collatus enim non ille videbor:
> Frons alia est, moresque alii, nova mentis imago,
> Voxque aliud sonat—
> Pectore nunc gelido calidos miseremur amantes,
> Jamque arsisse pudet. Veteres tranquilla tumultus
> Mens horret, relegensque alium putat ista locutum.

See *Poems,* p. 332 n.
[15] For a discussion of the import of the line "Could I revive within me," see House, pp. 115–16.

On stern Blencartha's perilous height
    The winds are tyrannous and strong; [16]
And flashing forth unsteady light
From stern Blencartha's skiey height,
    As loud the torrents throng!
Beneath the moon, in gentle weather,
They bind the earth and sky together.
But oh! the sky and all its forms, how quiet!
The things that seek the earth, how full of noise and riot!

The view of Saddle-back with its waterfalls in the moonlight only very vaguely suggests the landscape of "Kubla Khan"— there is the mountain, there are the thronging torrents, and there is moonlight. But the thought suggested by the view concerns what may be called one of the major themes of "Kubla Khan"—the possibility of reconciliation between violence and order, between the temporal and the eternal. As we shall see, he returns to this kind of image for it later on in the "Hymn Before Sunrise." It is worth noting also that the mountain is "stern," the winds that sweep it "tyrannous," a fact to be kept in mind in considering the significance of Kubla's being a tyrannical monarch.

Like "Love," "The Mad Monk" (1800) employs the strategy of the tale within a tale. The setting of the frame story places us within a familiar environment:

I heard a *voice from Etna's side;*
    Where o'er *a cavern's mouth*
    That fronted to the south
A chestnut spread its umbrage wide:

A hermit or a monk the man might be;
    But him I could not see:
And thus the *music* flowed along,
    In melody like to old Sicilian Song: (1–8)

[16] For a discussion of the relation of these two lines to a poem by Isaac Ritson, and of other matters related to them, see Lowes, pp. 604 j–41. The word "tyrannous" is Coleridge's.

The story that follows may be summarized as that of a man whose vision of the maid destroys him instead of delighting him as in "Kubla Khan," because, having unsuccessfully aspired to her love, he took her by force, through murder. This is a cruel twist to the "Kubla Khan" story, but even so the monk is inspired to sing, from his cavern in Etna's side. The beginning of his song is strikingly similar in language and meter, not to "Kubla Khan" but to the Intimations Ode, begun two years after the publication of "The Mad Monk":

> 'There was a time when earth, and sea, and skies,
>   The bright green vale, and forest's dark recess,
> With all things, lay before mine eyes
>   In steady loveliness:
> But now I feel, on earth's uneasy scene,
>   Such sorrows as will never cease;—'   (9–14)

In addition to the anticipation of the more famous and better poem, we have here also suggestions of the landscape of "Kubla Khan," the "bright green vale," "the forest's dark recesses," and the "steady loveliness" contrasted with sorrow. If we take this, like the Intimations Ode, to be an attempted explication of a crisis of poetic sensibility, still the two causes assigned for the lapse of pristine inspiration are quite different. Instead of attributing the lapse to a kind of gradual evolution under natural influences, as Wordsworth does, this poem tells of one who has forfeited his inspiration by his own act of violence, by trying to seize in the act of murder that which was not really his. There are undertones of Cain. And what follows is appropriately different in tone from the sequel in the Intimations Ode:

> 'I only ask for peace;
> If I must live to know that such a time has been!   (14–15)

One feels that this poem must have been written *after* "Kubla Khan."

Like the speaker in "Kubla Khan," the Mad Monk also has a
vision of past inspiration, in the form of a nightmare:

> 'Last night, as o'er the *sloping turf* I trod,
>   The *smooth green turf,* to me a vision gave
> Beneath mine eyes, the sod—
>   The roof of Rosa's grave!

The vision is one to be quelled:

> My heart has need with dreams like these to strive,
>   For, when I woke, beneath mine eyes I found
>   *The mossy plot of ground,*
> On which we oft have sat when Rosa was alive.—
>   Why must *the rock, and margin of the flood,*
>   Why must *the hill so many flow'rets bear,*
> Whose colours to a *murder'd* maiden's blood
>   Such sad resemblance wear?—
>   (25–32); "murder'd" italicized in text)

It is in the next stanza that we come upon the clue to the mystery:

> '*I struck the wound,*— this hand of mine!
> For oh, thou maid divine,
>   I lov'd to agony!
> The youth whom thou call'd'st thine
>   Did never love like me!'   (33–37; italics in text)

This is, to be sure, in Coleridge's most embarrassing manner—one
cannot help thinking of a real or imagined rival for the love of
Sara Hutchinson; but one cannot help thinking at the same time—
and this is less embarrassing—of the poet whose vision is slipping
away, or for whom what had seemed to be his vision has become
paralyzingly painful, painful to the point of eliciting feelings of
guilt that permeate all he sees:

> 'Is it the stormy clouds above
>   That flash'd so red a gleam?
>   On yonder downward trickling stream?—

'Tis not the blood of her I love.—
The sun torments me from his western bed,

(This is more painful but less hopeless than the lines of "Dejection": "Though I should gaze forever / On that green light that lingers in the west: . . .")

Oh, let him cease for ever to diffuse
Those crimson spectre hues!
Oh, let me lie in peace, and be for ever dead!'   (38–44)

We may be reminded of Cain's wish to "be utterly no more." Nothing even in "Dejection" goes so far as this and the concluding couplet, spoken by the narrator:

Here ceas'd the voice. In deep dismay,
Down thro' the forest I pursu'd my way.

In the original version there are four more lines:

The twilight fays came forth in dewy shoon
Ere I within the Cabin had withdrawn
The goatherd's tent upon the open lawn—
That night there was no moon.[17]

The revised ending is no doubt more effective—the twilight fays seem quite superfluous—but if one has followed the significance of moonlight in Coleridge's poetry, the last line might betray the intent of the whole poem.

Among all those who have puzzled over the identity of the Abyssinian maid, I think it has occurred to no one to link her with Mrs. Mary Robinson, and the effort would seem offhand a thankless one, but the six opening lines of "A Stranger Minstrel" (1800) might serve as an alert:

As late on Skiddaw's mount I lay supine,
Midway th'ascent, in that repose divine

[17] *Poems*, p 349 n.

> When the soul centred in the heart's recess
> Hath quaff'd its fill of Nature's loveliness,
> Yet still beside the fountain's marge will stay
> And fain would thirst again, again to quaff;   (1–6)

We may suspect, if Coleridge is lying supine on a mount, especially "Midway th'ascent," that we shall have to do with the poetic experience, and the lines that immediately follow make it clear that that is in question. Coming from one who is, among other things, a "Romantic poet of nature," the lines may seem strange. We might not expect that the soul "in that repose divine," "centred in the heart's recess," could ever have "quaff'd its *fill* of Nature's loveliness," but by 1800 Coleridge was beginning to know very well that that was possible, because it does not fill full enough. And he could still be philosophical about it:

> Then when the tear, slow travelling on its way,
>   Fills up the wrinkles of a silent laugh—
> In that sweet mood of sad and humorous thought
> A form within me rose, ...   (7–10)

How else make consequent sense in the context of the tear and laughter, the "sweet mood of sad and humorous thought?" The twenty-eight-year-old poet is recognizing, with a smile and a tear, that "nature" is not enough. (One thinks of Wordsworth on Mount Snowden.) As a matter of fact, it was already apparent by this time that even an ordinary maid, like Sara Fricker, was not enough to make nature answer the requirements made of her. But perhaps some maid might, a maid like Mary Evans, whom one had hardly known at all really, or like Sara Hutchinson, whom one might still hope to know, or, best of all, a maid of magical song—like Mrs. Robinson:

> A form within me rose, *within me wrought*
> *With such strong magic, that I cried aloud,* . . .   (10–11)

And he cries aloud to a mountain, one significantly like the mountain in "Kubla Khan":

'Thou ancient Skiddaw by thy helm of cloud,
And by thy many-colour'd *chasms* deep.
And by their *shadows* that forever sleep,
By yon small flaky mists that love to creep
Along the edges of those *spots of light,*
Those *sunny islands* on thy *smooth green height,*   (12–17)

Shepherds, dogs, and boys fill out the picture.

And by this laugh, and by this tear,
I would, old Skiddaw, she were here!
A lady of sweet song is she,
Her soft blue eyes were made for thee!
O ancient Skiddaw, by this tear,
I would, I would that she were here!'   (22–27)

But she is *not* here, and Skiddaw counsels the stoicism of despair
(the poem is not conceived in Coleridge's happiest vein):

Then ancient Skiddaw, stern and proud,
    In sullen majesty replying,
Thus spake from out his helm of cloud
    (His voice was like an echo dying!):—
'She dwells belike in scenes more fair,
And scorns a mount so bleak and bare.'   (28–33)

She dwells belike in Abyssinia, singing of Mount Abora. But to the
poet such sullen pride in despair is not yet possible:

I only sigh'd when this I heard,
Such mornful thoughts within me stirr'd
That all my heart was faint and weak,
    So sorely was I troubled!
No laughter wrinkled on my cheek,
    But O the tears were doubled!   (34–39)

In a passage in which the dome, the mountain, and the king
coalesce in heralding the maid and her song, Skiddaw, the bare but
proud domestic version of Helicon, relents "(His voice was like
a *monarch* wooing)":

'Nay, but thou dost not know her might,
　The pinions of her soul how strong!
But many a stranger in my height
Hath sung to me *her magic song,*
　Sending forth *his ecstasy*
　In her divinest melody,
And hence I know her soul is free,
She is where'er she wills to be,
Unfetter'd by mortality!　　(46–54)

Having first seemed to say "If only you could but you can't revive
within you," Skiddaw now seems to be saying something like "If
you could, and perhaps you can"—

　　She is where'er she wills to be,
　　Unfetter'd by mortality!
Now to the *"haunted beach"* can fly,
　Beside the *threshold scourged with waves,*
　Now *where the maniac wildly raves,*
"Pale moon, thou spectre of the sky!"
No wind that hurries o'er my height
Can travel with so swift a flight.
　I too, methinks, might merit
　The presence of her spirit!
　To me too might belong
The honour of her song and *witching melody,*
　Which most resembles me,
　Soft, various, and sublime,
　Exempt from wrongs of Time!'
　　　(53–67; line 58 italicized in text)

Here is a melody that actually "resembles" a mount. If a melody
can resemble a mountain, there is no reason why it cannot resemble
a dome, especially since mountains and domes seem to be roughly
interchangeable in Coleridge's imagery. If only we understood the
resemblance, we might have some idea just how the revival of the
Abyssinian maid's song would enable the poet to build that dome
in the air. The mountain in this poem is curious, if one examines

the series of adjectives attentively, "Soft, various, and sublime."
Few mountains outside Xanadu are both soft and sublime, and
even Xanadu is not quite "Exempt from wrongs of Time!" It may
be simply that the song of the maid, at the same time that it is
like the mountain in being soft, various, and sublime, serves to
make those qualities of the natural object more available by bringing an easily recognizable personality into nature. Under the influence of something at once most appealingly human (the maid)
and producing (in song) an artistic expression of the humanly
intelligible qualities of the mountain (that symbol of the relation
between the natural and the supernatural), it might be possible
to create an object like the mountain in its intrinsic intelligibility,
but rendered *available*—"The object of art is to give the whole
ad hominem." [18]

The poem ends with two couplets that hardly require comment:

> Thus spake the mighty Mount, and I
> Made answer, with a deep-drawn sigh:—
> 'Thou ancient Skiddaw, by this tear,
> I would, I would that she were here!'

How could one in all conscience decide when "Kubla Khan" was
written? It may be that "A Stranger Minstrel" was written on one
day and "Kubla Khan" on the next. At least we know that within
the confines of the same poem "Could I" can bear opposite
meanings.

The evidence is that Coleridge's fragmentary drama, "The Triumph of Loyalty" was written in the autumn of 1800,[19] and that its
genesis is to be traced to Lessing's *Hamburgische Dramaturgie,* in
which Lessing called attention to the lack of any adequate treatment of the story of Elizabeth and Essex in English, at the same
time extolling and summarizing a Spanish treatment of the sub-

---

[18] "On Poesy and Art," reprinted in *Biographia Literaria*, II, 262.
[19] *Poems*, II, p. 1061 n.

ject by Antonio Coëllo (died 1652).[20] Lessing's implied challenge might alone account for Coleridge's undertaking to remedy the defect in English dramatic literature, but as we read what he produced we discover more personal reasons for his attraction to the subject.

The scene of this historical drama, written only a few months after the latest date suggested for "Kubla Khan," is described as "A cultivated Plain, skirted on the Left by a Wood. The Pyrenees are visible in the distance. Small knots of Soldiers all in the military Dress of the middle Ages are seen passing across the Stage." This "delightful plain," as it is called in the first line of the play, is only in the vaguest way reminiscent of the landscape of "Kubla Khan," but not many lines later we come upon a much closer analogue. Earl Henry is arriving in his native Navarre, recalled from the command of a victorious campaign through the chicanery of the Chancellor. To his friend Sandoval he admits that his depression is due not simply or even primarily to this public wrong, but to "causes of less public import." In the fragment that survives, these latter causes receive by far the most attention.

Sandoval. Connected, I presume, with that *Mansion,* the spacious *pleasure grounds* of which we noticed as we were descending from the mountain. *Lawn and Grove, River and Hillock*—it looked *within these high walls, like a World of itself.*   (25–29)

Here we have most of the features of Kubla's establishment, with the explicit commentary that it constitutes "a World of itself." It should be remarked that these "pleasure grounds" are associated in the sequel with highly ambiguous events, but that the connotation of the term can by no means be taken to be derogatory. We know nothing of the original builder of this mansion, but its one-time tenant was a traitor, an unsuccessful pretender to the throne of Navarre, Don Manrique, who with his sons, was executed in

[20] *Notebooks,* Vol. I, 869   21.83 and 871   1.11, n's.

secret, at the instance of the same unsavory Chancellor. The cause of Earl Henry's depression on seeing the mansion again lies in his relationship with Don Manrique's surviving daughter, Oropeza, whom he had wooed under the most unfavorable of circumstances —her father's strong disapproval, and the fact that he was himself really in love with the queen (we do not, after all, have enough of the drama to justify criticism of things like motivation). Earl Henry's attitudes are so far from clear in the passages that reveal them that one is led to cast him in the role of demon-lover, and Oropeza in that of the woman wailing:

> *Sandoval.* You lov'd the daughter of Don Manrique?
> *Earl Henry.*   Loved?
> *Sandoval.* Did you not say, you woo'd her?
> *Earl Henry.*   Once I loved
> Her whom I dar'd not woo!—
> *Sandoval.*   And woo'd perchance
> One whom you lov'd not!
> *Earl Henry.*   O I were most base
> Not loving Oropeza. True, I woo'd her
> Hoping to heal a deeper wound: but she
> Met my advances with an empassion'd Pride
> That kindled Love with Love.   (263–70)

This all seems transparently autobiographical, a version of Coleridge's courtship of Sara Fricker, not having dared to woo Mary Evans. To be sure, Mary Evans was already far in the past by 1800, and he was already in love with Sara Hutchinson, but new loves, especially if they are unrealizable, tend to give rise to nostalgic retrospection. In any case, there is surely a sense in which it is true to say that *all* of Coleridge's wooing was in hope "to heal a deeper wound."

At this point in the conversation, Earl Henry is understandably defensive. He protests to Sandoval:

> But thou art stern, and with unkindling Countenance
> Art inly reasoning whilst thou listenest to me.   (276–77)

Little wonder, we may think, if we have ever had the fascinating chore of being a lover's confidant, but Sandoval is equal to the role, and adroitly parries the reproach:

> *Sandoval.* Anxiously, Henry! reasoning anxiously.
> But Oropeza—
> *Earl Henry.* Blessings gather round her!
> *Within this wood there winds a secret passage,*
> *Beneath the walls,* which open out at length
> Into *the gloomiest cover of the Garden.*—
> The night ere my departure to the Army,
> She, nothing trembling, led me through that gloom,

[Again one is tempted to hear the autobiographical echo of Coleridge the reluctant bridegroom.]

> And to the covert by a silent stream,
> Which, with one star reflected near its marge,
> Was the sole object visible around me,
> The night so dark, so close, the umbrage o'er us!
> No leaflet stirr'd;—yet pleasure hung upon us,
> The gloom and stillness of the balmy night-air.
> A little further on *an arbor stood,*
> *Fragrant with flowering Trees*—I well remember
> What an uncertain glimmer in the Darkness
> Their snow-white Blossoms made—thither she led me,
> To that sweet bower! Then Oropeza trembled—
> I heard her heart beat—if 'twere not my own.
> *Sandoval.* A rude and scaring note, my friend!   (278–97)

It is impossible not to remark in passing how excessively implausible this conversation is, how totally lacking in any kind of verisimilitude—this is a general and a comrade-at-arms, a Spanish general and comrade-at-arms, returning from a campaign. It is no wonder that the drama remained a fragment.[21] The Earl replies:

---

[21] Lines 277–344, the only portion of the poem that bore any personal meaning for Coleridge, were published in 1817 as "The Night-Scene; A Dramatic Fragment," *Poems,* pp. 421–23.

> *Earl Henry.*   Oh! no!
> I have small memory of aught but pleasure.
> The inquietudes of fear, like lesser Streams
> Still flowing, still were lost in those of Love:
> So love grew mightier from the Fear, and Nature,
> Fleeing from Pain, shelter'd herself in Joy.

[The cynicism is surely unintentional.]

> The stars above our heads were dim and steady,
> Like eyes suffus'd with rapture. Life was in us:
> We were all life, each atom of our Frames
> A living soul—I vow'd to die for her
> With the faint voice of one who, having spoken,
> Relapses into blessedness, I vow'd it:
> That solemn Vow, a whisper scarcely heard,
> A murmur breath'd against a lady's Cheek.
> Oh! there is Joy above the name of Pleasure,
> Deep self-possession, an intense Repose.
> No other than as Eastern sages feign,
> The God, who floats upon a Lotos Leaf,
> Dreams for a thousand ages; then awaking,
> Creates a world, and smiling at the bubble,
> Relapses into bliss.   (298–317)

Here is indeed a demon-lover, from the point of view of a woman looking for a husband and protector. She is caught here in the early stage, before she has been deserted and left wailing, but already she has a premonition of trouble:

> Ah! was that *bliss*
> *Fear'd as an alien, and too vast for man?*
> For suddenly, intolerant of its silence,
> Did Oropeza, starting, grasp my forehead.
> I caught her arms; the veins were swelling on them.
> *Thro' the dark Bower she sent a hollow voice;—*
> 'Oh! what if all betray me? what if thou?'
> I swore, and with an inward thought that seemed
> The unity and substance of my Being,

I swore to her, that were she red with guilt,
I would exchange my unblench'd state with hers.— (317–27)

Fortified by this vivid recounting of his past moment of resolution, Earl Henry professes himself ready to go and face Oropeza, but the wily Sandoval is still skeptical:

> Friend! by that winding passage, to the Bower
> I now will go—all objects there will teach me
> Unwavering Love, and singleness of Heart.
> Go, Sandoval! I am prepared to meet her—
> Say nothing of me—I myself will seek her—
> Nay, leave me, friend! I cannot bear the torment
> And Inquisition of that scanning eye.— (328–34)

Earl Henry retires to the wood and Sandoval—his alter ego—[22] is left to reflect upon the probability of his fulfilling his mission:

> *Sandoval* (alone). O Henry! always striv'st thou to be great
> By thine own act—yet art thou never great
> But by the Inspiration of great Passion.
> The Whirl-blast comes, the desert-sands rise up
> And shape themselves; from Heaven to Earth they stand
> As though they were *the Pillars of a Temple,*
> *Built by Omnipotence in its own honour!*
> *But the Blast pauses, and their shaping spirit*
> *Is fled:* the mighty columns were but sand,
> And lazy Snakes trail o'er the level ruins!
> I know, he loves the Queen. I know she is
> His Soul's first love, and this is ever his nature—
> To his first purpose, his soul toiling back
> Like the poor storm-wreck'd [sailor] to his Boat,
> Still swept away, still struggling to regain it. (335–49)

The analysis is complex, and not very easy to follow. Since Earl Henry seems at the moment to be attempting to accomplish something "by his own act," in the absence of great Passion, the

---

[22] (or his friend Robert Southey)

Whirl-blast image would seem to allude not to his coming rapprochement with Oropeza but to his love for the Queen; yet Earl Henry's own description of his previous meeting with Oropeza most closely corresponds to this temple of sand, and Sandoval goes on to oppose to it Earl Henry's undying love for the Queen. And the Whirl-blast image itself is ambiguous in its connotations. Various readers have heard in it an echo of "Kubla Khan," and some have taken the "Temple, / Built by Omnipotence in its own honour" as evidence of the negative character of Kubla's decree. It sounds tyrannical and selfish, and certainly Sandoval seems to be employing the image in a derogatory fashion. But then it is hard to believe that in a poem by Coleridge the wind of Inspiration can be an intrinsically "bad" thing, and we have run across a good many indications that "Omnipotence" does not necessarily bear a negative value for Coleridge. But the decisive note is offered by the "shaping spirit," looking forward as it does to his "shaping spirit of Imagination" in "Dejection," which constitutes another more extensive but perhaps equally puzzling account of its having fled. Sandoval, as a friendly outsider, has presumably observed successive storms of passion in Earl Henry, and seen the temples they produced, lordly but evanescent because in some inexplicable way the passion has not been met, at least not by an all-fulfilling object. "His Soul's first love" is forever beyond his grasp, and as a result he leaves ruins, not palaces, behind. Certainly Kubla's dome is one that the poet has dreamed, under the Inspiration of great Passion, dreamed as possible of existence, but always the Blast, the wind of inspiration, pauses, something "Suspends what nature gave [him] at [his] birth, / [His] shaping spirit of Imagination," and he is left struggling to regain it.

In what remains of the fragment, it turns out that not Oropeza but the Queen is in the arbor, pursued by conspirators who plan to murder her. Earl Henry is in some rather confusing way instrumental in saving her and he comes upon her as the fragment ends.

Again, we may conjecture that something other than laziness prevented the completion of the work. It was not given to Coleridge to figure forth a meeting with the Abyssinian maid.

"Dejection: An Ode" (1802) is the first of the poems being considered here that we know, by all computations, to have been written later than "Kubla Khan," at least two years later, possibly three or four. Its imagery belongs to an entirely different family from that of "Kubla Khan," and the rhetorical strategy of the two poems could hardly be more different; yet the poems are related as two widely divergent treatments of the same problem, the relation between the poet and whatever it is that confirms his being to the extent of making it fruitful *ad extra*. I think we read the following lines more knowingly if we have the Abyssinian maid in the back of our minds:

> And would we aught behold, of higher worth,
> Than that inanimate cold world allowed
> To the poor loveless ever-anxious crowd,

[Here, of course, is a kind of class distinction not foreign in spirit to Xanadu.]

> Ah! from the soul itself must issue forth
> A light, a glory, a fair luminous cloud
>   Enveloping the Earth—
> And from the soul itself must there be sent
>   A sweet and potent voice of its own birth,
> Of all sweet sounds the life and element!

> O pure of heart! thou need'st not ask of me
> What this strong music in the soul may be!
> What, and wherein it doth exist,
> This light, this glory, this fair luminous mist,
> This beautiful and beauty-making power.
>   Joy, virtuous Lady! Joy that ne'er was given,
> Save to the pure, and in their purest hour,
> Life, and Life's effluence, cloud at once and shower,

> Joy, Lady! is the spirit and the power,
> Which wedding Nature to us gives in dower
> A new Earth and new Heaven,
> Undreamt of by the sensual and the proud—

[What a thin line there is between accurate self-esteem, even grate-
fulness for gifts received, and sinful "pride"!]

> Joy is the sweet voice, Joy the luminous cloud—
> We in ourselves rejoice!
> And thence flows all that charms or ear or sight,
> All melodies the echoes of that voice,
> All colours a suffusion from that light.   (50–75)

I have discussed elsewhere at some length the ambiguities of this
very curious marriage ceremony, in which it is hardly possible even
to identify the principals, and which, on one plausible interpretation, represents a sharp reversal or recantation of Coleridge's faith
in poetry, in the poetic experience of nature. All here comes from
within, and "clothes" nature. The situation requires that the poet
be capable of decreeing the garden, the new Earth and new
Heaven, like Kubla Khan, without the aid of any inspirational
music, any granted vision. All melodies are echoes of that voice,
but the voice comes wholly from within. Already in "Kubla Khan,"
it came not directly from the "influxes of nature," as in "The Nightingale" and some earlier poems, but through the medium of a
"vision." In "Dejection" Coleridge seems to be quite sure that he
cannot revive within him the symphony and song, and, if one likes,
there is a kind of heroism in his taking all the blame upon himself.
Yet in fact throughout the poems there would seem to be a con-
tinually fluctuating ambiguity as to the primary source of the
miracle of inspiration, and how could it be otherwise? We may in
this connection recall the cases in which avatars of the Abyssinian
maid are identified with the poet himself.

In "Dejection" the "strong music of the soul" is "Joy," apparently having its origin in the soul itself, a generative force that makes of the earth a kind of paradise, clothing it as a light, a glory, a fair luminous mist. It is a "beautiful and beauty-making power." And here, where it is definitively absent, there is no suggestion of its ominous implications. Only its positive aspects are insisted upon. When the wished-for storm, the onetime source of inspiration, actually comes, late in the poem, it presents itself as the very contrary of the desired inspiring force, the inspiration that might make possible the building of a dome in air; but it is still unmistakably the storm of inspiration, and it does exhibit the ominous characteristics. The poet turns from his "viper thoughts," from "Reality's dark dream," to listen to it, as if above the ceaseless turmoil seething a stately dome might be erected, but

> What a scream
> Of agony by torture lengthened out
> That lute sent forth! Thou Wind, that *rav'st* without,
>   Bare *crag,* or *mountain-tairn,* or *blasted tree,*
> Or *pine-grove* whither woodman never clomb,
> Or *lonely house, long held the witches' home,*
>   Methinks were fitter instruments for thee,
> *Mad Lutanist!*
>
> *   *   *
>
>   What tell'st thou now about?
>   'Tis of the rushing of an host in rout,
> With groans, of trampled men, with smarting wounds—
> At once they groan with pain, and shudder with the cold!
>   (97–104; 110–13)

Here the voices prophesying war are no longer "heard from far"; they have invaded the very site of the possible garden, the Abyssinian maid is a mad lutanist, and we find a pathetic version of the woman wailing:

> It tells another tale, with wounds less deep and loud!
>   A tale of less affright,

And tempered with delight,
As Otway's self had framed the tender lay,—
　　'Tis of a little child
　　Upon a lonesome wild,
Not far from home, but she hath lost her way:
And now moans low in bitter grief and fear,
And now screams loud, and hopes to make her mother hear.

　　　　　　　　　　　　　　　　　(117–25)

It may be that even the woman wailing for her demon-lover is an aspect of the poet.

The poem ends with his hoping for his friend that she may find the whole world a joy-filled garden, that she will be so at one with things that it will be as if she had made them:

To her may all things live, from pole to pole,
Their life the eddying of her living soul!
　　O simple spirit, guided from above,
Dear Lady! friend devoutest of my choice,
Thus mayest thou ever, evermore rejoice.　(135–39)

He would seem to have forgotten the theory expounded in stanza 4, where the sweet and potent voice must issue from the soul itself. It is a strange contradiction that the "simple spirit" should be "guided from above," but the creative spirit, the poet, must furnish his own inspiration. "Confusion" would be a more accurate term than contradiction, since the injunctions of stanza 4 are addressed to people in general, including both the poet and the Lady, and the condition of "Joy" for all of them is the kind of purity attributed by implication to the Lady in the last stanza. In the *Morning Post* version, the contradiction is patent, since the lines in stanza 7 are addressed to Edmund, "lofty Poet." He is to live in innocent oneness with a wholly beneficent nature, and all the problems that furnish the subject matter of the rest of the poem are dismissed, not solved—unless he is conceived to be living in Xanadu, where nature is art, art nature, and the ancestral voices have been stilled.

Coleridge himself makes the explicit connection between "The Picture; or the Lover's Resolution" (1802) and "Kubla Khan," quoting in the preface to the latter lines 91–100 of "The Picture" as presenting an analogue of the arrival of the man from Porlock, which prevented the recollection of the remainder of the dream of Xanadu, the dream that could be recreated "Could I revive within me / Her symphony and song." Although the lines Coleridge quotes in his preface do not suggest it, there is in "The Picture" a maid closely analogous to the damsel with the dulcimer:

> Daughter of genius! stateliest of our maids!
> More beautiful than whom Alcaeus wooed,
> The Lesbian woman of immortal song!   (170–72)

More beautiful she is than the tenth muse herself, and the whole poem has to do with the necessity or non-necessity of the intervention of such a being, such an influence, into the poetic experience of nature, if that experience is to be satisfying and fruitful, if it is to result in artistic creation. As George Whalley has suggested,[23] the poem doubtless arose out of current circumstances in Coleridge's life, out of the vicissitudes of his relationship with Sara Hutchinson, who came as near as any human being could to providing what he required from the Abyssinian maid. The occasion would seem to have been the not uncommon one in which the lover, rebellious against partial captivity when what he imperiously longs for is total captivity, which would argue total concern on the part of the beloved, indulges in a fantasy of escape, as if it were possible to recover the bliss of ignorance:

> Through weeds and thorns, and matted underwood
> I force my way;

[At these junctures, a resistant not an idyllic nature is required,

---

[23] George Whalley, *Coleridge and Sara Hutchinson and the Asra Poems* (London: Routledge & Kegan Paul, 1955), pp. 31 n., 129.

allowing one to express one's hostility at the same time that one
weds nature in revenge.]

> now climb, and now descend
> O'er rocks, or bare or mossy, with wild foot
> Crushing the purple whorts; while oft unseen,
> Hurrying along the drifted forest-leaves
> The scared snake rustles.

[There is no denying that Coleridge is a tempting subject for the
Freudian analyst.]

> Onward still I toil,
> I know not, ask not whither! A new joy,
> Lovely as light, sudden as summer gust,
> And gladsome as the first-born of the spring,
> Beckons me on or follows from behind,
> Playmate or guide! The master-passion quelled
> I feel that I am free.   (1–11)

But emerging into this state of illusory freedom from the "master-
passion," from the very necessity for the master-passion, into this
state of innocent communion with nature, what the lover no-
tices, apparently unconsciously, is a landscape with overtones of
"Kubla Khan," and the forewarned reader may suspect a trap:

> With dun-red bark
> The fir-trees, and the unfrequent slender oak,
> Forth from this tangle wild of bush and brake
> Soar up, and form a melancholy vault
> High o'er me, murmuring like a distant sea.   (12–16)

If we are inclined to take this as a remote version of the romantic
chasm, we may be surprised to learn (line 17) that "Here Wisdom
might resort, and here Remorse"; but in the next line we find that
in addition to Wisdom and Remorse, neither of them readily associated with the woman wailing for her demon-lover, "Here too the

love-lorn man" might come. But if he does so it is not to wail for
his demon-love. He rather,

> sick in soul
> And of this human heart aweary,
> Worships the spirit of unconscious life
> In tree or wild-flower.—Gentle lunatic!   (18–21)

Poor fool, he thinks himself to be in Eden, and an Eden without
the snake (one thinks of those who interpret the first part of
"Kubla Khan" as a version of Eden).

> If so he might not wholly cease to be,
> He would far rather not be that he is;
> But would be something that he knows not of,
> In winds or waters, or among the rocks!   (22–25)

If there were any doubt, after "Gentle lunatic," that this is a portrait
of illusion, one would have only to remember that these were the
thoughts of Cain:

Yea, I would lie down, I would not rise, neither would I stir my limbs
till I became as the rock in the den of the lion, on which the young lion
resteth his head while he sleepeth.

To ask in this sense to be "one with nature" is to desire abdication
from the human condition.

The next twenty lines embark upon an exorcism of love, couched
in pastoral terms, after which we find the lover patently inviting
Nemesis:

> This is my hour of triumph! I can now
> With my own fancies play the merry fool,
> And laugh away worse folly, being free.
> Here will I seat myself, beside this old,
> Hollow, and weedy oak, which ivy-twine
> Clothes as with net-work: here will I couch my limbs,
> *Close by this river,* in this silent shade,
> As *safe and sacred* from the step of man
> As an invisible world—   (46–54)

The poet who has written "Kubla Khan" can hardly write "safe and sacred" together without irony. And he may also remember the oak in "Christabel," on the other side of which Geraldine was found. The maid appears, but in the guise of not appearing!

> The breeze that visits me,
> Was never Love's accomplice, never raised
> The tendril ringlets from the maiden's brow,
> And the blue, delicate veins above her cheek;
> Ne'er played the wanton—never half disclosed
> The maiden snowy bosom, scattering thence
> Eye-poisons for some love-distempered youth,   (58–64)

One is tempted to ask just how present an absent maiden can be, and the answer is, probably, more present than a present one.

> And thou too, desert stream! no pool of thine
> Though clear as lake in latest summer-eve,
> Did e'er reflect the stately virgin's robe,
> The face, the form divine, the downcast look
> Contemplative! Behold! her open palm
> Presses her cheek and brow! her elbow rests
> On the bare branch of half-uprooted tree,
> That leans towards its mirror!   (72–79)

It is some measure of the excellence of "Kubla Khan" that it has no need of forms divine or downcast looks contemplative. Yet even in this respect the maiden is reminiscent of Christabel, who had a "stricken look" at the moment of crisis, and who is described on her first appearance as having a "ringlet curl," a "stately neck," and "blue-veined feet." But Christabel made the mistake of disclosing *all* her bosom "and half her side."

The maid of "The Picture" is surely the most elusive of maids: in the first place, she emphatically does not exist in the "plot" of the poem; then, within the rhetorical device that she does inhabit, only her image, not herself, is to be looked upon; and finally, she destroys the image. If she is an avatar of the damsel with a dul-

cimer, it would seem by this time quite impossible that the vision
of her be revived.

> Who erewhile
> Had from her countenance turned, or looked by stealth,
> (For Fear is true-love's cruel nurse), he now
> With steadfast gaze and unoffending eye,
> Worships the watery idol, dreaming hopes
> Delicious to the soul, but fleeting, vain,
> E'en as that phantom-world on which he gazed,
> But not unheeded gazed: for see, ah! see,
> The sportive tyrant with her left hand plucks
> The heads of tall flowers that behind her grow,
> Lychnis, and willow-herb, and fox-glove bells:
> And suddenly, as one that toys with time,
> Scatters them on the pool! (79-91)

In any case it seems obvious that we are in a different dispensation
from that of "Kubla Khan," if the maid deliberately destroys the
vision. There follows the passage that Coleridge quotes in the
preface of "Kubla Khan":

> Then all the charm
> Is broken—all that phantom world so fair
> Vanishes, and a thousand circlets spread,
> And each mis-shape the other. Stay awhile,
> Poor youth, who scarcely dar'st lift up thine eyes!
> The stream will soon renew its smoothness, soon
> The visions will return! And lo! he stays:
> And soon the fragments dim of lovely forms
> Come trembling back, unite, and now once more
> The pool becomes a mirror; (91-100)

We might expect the poem to continue, He built that dome in air,
that sunny dome, but

> behold
> Each wildflower on the marge inverted there,

And there the half-uprooted tree—but where,
O where the virgin's snowy arm, that leaned
On its bare branch? He turns and she is gone!
Homeward she steals *through many a woodland maze*
Which he shall seek in vain. Ill-fated youth!   (100–106)

It is almost as if the speaker of "Kubla Khan," frustrated by the wantonly cruel disappearance of the vision, went wandering like the wailing woman through the paths of Kubla's garden in search of the Abyssinian maid.

Go day by day, and waste thy manly prime
In mad love-yearning by the vacant brook,
Till sickly thoughts bewitch thine eyes, and thou
Behold'st her shadow still abiding there,
The Naiad of the mirror!   (107–11)

But, as a reader might by now have forgotten, the speaker in this poem is still enjoying his "hour of triumph," and this is all an account of what is not happening:

Not to thee,
O wild and desert stream! belongs this tale:
Gloomy and dark art thou—*the crowded firs*
Spire from thy shores, and stretch across thy bed,
Making thee *doleful as a cavern-well:*
Save when the shy king-fishers build their nest
On thy steep banks, no loves hast thou, wild stream!   (111–17)

Again the paradox, apparent at least to the reader of "Kubla Khan": this wild, unhaunted Nature bears a haunting resemblance to the romantic chasm, to the whole landscape of "Kubla Khan." Hence an element of suspense, and the lines that follow intensify it:

This be my chosen haunt—emancipate
From Passion's dreams, a freeman, and alone,
I rise and trace *its devious course.* O lead,
Lead me to deeper shades and lonelier glooms.

Lo! stealing through the *canopy of firs,*
How fair the sunshine spots that mossy rock,
Isle of *the river, whose disparted waves*
Dart off asunder with an angry sound,
How soon they re-unite! And see! they meet,
Each in the other lost and found: and see
Placeless, as spirits, *one soft water-sun*
Throbbing within them, heart at once and eye!
With its soft neighborhood of filmy clouds,
The stains and shadings of forgotten tears,
Dimness o'erswum with lustre! Such the hour
Of deep enjoyment, following after love's brief feuds
And hark, *the noise of a near waterfall!* (118–34)

It is a dangerous comparison for one who wants to consider himself
"emancipate / From Passion's dreams," but he continues:

> I pass forth into light—I find myself
> Beneath a weeping birch (most beautiful
> Of forest trees, the Lady of the Woods),
> *Hard by the brink of a tall weedy rock*
> *That overbrows the cataract.* How bursts
> The landscape on my sight! (135–40)

And the landscape in question turns out to be a version of the
garden:

> Two crescent hills
> Fold in behind each other, and so make
> *A circular vale, and land-locked,* as might seem,
> With brook and bridge, and grey stone cottages,
> Half hid by *rocks and fruit-trees.* At my feet,
> The whortle-berries are bedewed with spray,
> Dashed upward by the *furious waterfall.* (140–46)

As the speaker penetrates into this natural garden, which he describes in lines about which perhaps nothing can any longer be
said (there is, for instance, "a sleeping child, / His dear head pil-

lowed on a sleeping dog"), he rather surprisingly finds a picture painted on birch bark:

> A curious picture, with a master's haste
> Sketched on a strip of pinky-silver skin,
> Peeled from the birchen bark! Divinest maid!
> Yon bark her canvas, and those purple berries
> Her pencil! See, the juice is scarcely dried
> On the fine skin! She has been newly here;
> And lo! yon patch of heath has been her couch—
> The pressure still remains! O blesséd couch!   (159–66)

It is perhaps unnecessary to go on to the end of this remarkably disjointed poem. The maid who was previously described as, precisely, not existing in the actual situation—her nonexistence was a testimony to the speaker's emancipation—now not only exists but has a name that he knows, Isabel, and she is the "Daughter of genius! stateliest of our maids!" As the poem ends, the speaker is on his way to find her. Like the Abyssinian, she is eminently fitted to be a source of inspiration, and Coleridge has forgotten her nonexistence!

Matilda Betham is perhaps no less likely than Mrs. Robinson as an exemplar of the Abyssinian maid. "To Matilda Betham from a Stranger" (1802) opens with a highly conventional and not in the least moving panegyric upon Miss Betham's verse. In the second paragraph, in addition to an allusion to Sappho, recalling the tribute to Mrs. Robinson, we find an abstract statement of the principle involved in the final section of "Kubla Khan":

> The Almighty, having first composed a Man,
> Set him to music, framing Woman for him,
> And fitted each to each, and made them one!
> *And 'tis my faith that there's a natural bond*
> *Between the female mind and measured sounds,*
> Nor do I know a sweeter Hope than this,
>   That [24] this sweet Hope, by judgment unreproved,

[24] "That" here must be a misprint for "Than."

That our own Britain, our dear mother Isle,
May boast one Maid, a poetess *indeed*,
Great as th'impassioned Lesbian, in sweet song,
And O! of holier mind, and happier fate.
                (18–28; "indeed" italicized in text)

Coleridge is never at his best as a metaphysical poet, and often at
his worst as a patriotic one, but there is good reason to take seriously
his profession of faith in the mysterious connection between the
female mind and measured sound: as we have seen, it pervades his
poetry to a remarkable degree, and he shares it with a large number of poets, none of whom, I suppose, has ever given a satisfactory
account of it.

It has been known at least since 1844 that Coleridge's "Hymn
Before Sunrise, in the Vale of Chamouni" (1802) is an expansion
of Frederika Brun's "Ode to Chamouny." [25] The note he prefixed
to it on its first publication in the *Morning Post* suggests to the
attentive reader the reason for his fixing upon the poem as congenial in subject matter and likely to stimulate his flagging poetic
impulses:

Chamouni is *one of the highest mountain valleys* of the Barony of
Faucigny in the Savoy Alps; and *exhibits a kind of fairy world*, in
which *the wildest appearances (I had almost said horrors) of Nature
alternate with the softest and most beautiful.* The chain of Mont Blanc
is its *boundary;* and besides the Arve *it is filled with sounds from the
Arveiron, which rushes from the melted glaciers, like a giant, mad with
joy, from a dungeon,* and forms *other torrents* of snow-water, having
their rise in the glaciers which *slope down into the valley.*

Here are most of the primary images of "Kubla Khan"—height
and depth, the delicate and the horrible, the wild and the bounded,
joy and vitality issuing from one abyss and flowing into another.
The note goes on to draw a lesson somewhat different from what

[25] *Poems*, pp. 376–77 n.

one would prefer to call the import of "Kubla Khan," but clearly related to it:

> The beautiful *Gentiana major,* or greater gentian, with blossoms of the brightest blue, grows in large companies a few steps from the never-melted ice of the glaciers. I thought it an affecting emblem of the bold-ness of human hope, venturing near, and, as it were, leaning over the brink of the grave. Indeed, the whole vale, its every light, its every thought— Who *would* be, who *could* be an Atheist in this valley of wonders! [26]

It seems more and more evident that there is no cause to be surprised that Coleridge admitted an image of demonic love to subsist on the fringes of Paradise, that he was capable of calling something at once "holy" and "enchanted."

In the first section of the poem Coleridge does what we have seen him do so often: he *sees* the garden of Xanadu in looking at a natural scene. It was the ability to do this that he believed to characterize the poet, and that he so admired in Wordsworth, "the fine balance of truth in observing, with the imaginative faculty in modifying the objects observed; and above all the original gift of spreading the tone, the atmosphere, and with it the depth and height of the ideal world around forms, incidents, and situations." [27] Later on he speaks of "poetic" objects as not merely beautiful and accurately described, but "modified by a predominant passion; or by associated thoughts or images awakened by that passion; or when they have the effect of reducing multitude to unity, or succession to an instant; or lastly, when a human and intellectual life is transferred to them from the poet's own spirit." [28] In these passages he is concentrating upon the artistic, the making, side of the process, how the artist renders what he "sees." Elsewhere he conceives the process in the other direction, from nature to man, with art as a term for the point of juncture:

[26] *Ibid.,* p. 377 n. (italics in latter section in text).
[27] *Biographia Literaria,* I, 59.   [28] *Ibid.,* II, 16.

As soon as the human mind is *intelligibly addressed by* an outward image exclusively of articulate speech, so soon does art commence. . . . In this sense nature itself is to a religious observer the art of God; and for the same cause art itself might be defined as of a middle quality between a thought and a thing, or, as I said before, the union and reconciliation of that which is nature with that which is exclusively human. It is the figured language of thought, and is distinguished from nature by the unity of all the parts in one thought or idea. Hence nature itself would give us the impression of a work of art, if we could see the thought which is present at once in the whole and in every part; . . .[29]

These opening lines of "Hymn Before Sunrise" are one of Coleridge's many efforts, this time with the aid of Fredericke Brun, to perform this function, to see and render what is humanly intelligible in the art of God:

> Hast thou a charm to stay the morning-star
> In his steep course? So long he seems to pause
> On thy bald awful head, O sovran BLANC,
> The Arve and Arveiron at thy base
> Rave *ceaselessly;* but thou, most awful Form!
> Risest from forth thy silent sea of pines,
> How silently!   (1-7)

Mont Blanc is apostrophized as a potentate, rising in his own supernal calm out of turbulence and darkness, and we cannot but

---

[29] "On Poesy and Art," *Biographia Literaria*, II, 254–55 (italics added). Here we touch on a matter that Ernest Tuveson has discussed in great detail in *The Imagination as a Means of Grace* (Berkeley & Los Angeles: University of California Press, 1960). At one point (p. 145) he observes that for the Romantic poet "the ideal is absorbed into the material. Where the Platonist ascends a ladder from images to idea, the romanticist perceived, in the images of sense, the full spiritual reality which corruption and bigotry, delusion and superstition, rather than the veil of the material, have long hidden from mankind. We can hardly say that such thinking is this-worldly, as opposed to other-worldly. Rather, the terms lose their significance, for this attitude attempts to be *both*: it sees in this world all that had been perceived in both. The imagination is a means of reconciliation, for through it mere sense is infused with ideal meaning. Through the imagination is nature supernaturalized." It might be more accurate to speak in terms of aspiration.

think of the pleasure-dome overlooking the romantic chasm. There are even the evergreens.

> Around thee and above
> Deep is the air and dark, substantial, black,
> An ebon mass: methinks thou piercest it,
> As with a wedge! But when I look again,
> It is thine own calm home, *thy crystal shrine,*
> Thy habitation from eternity!
> O dread and silent Mount! I gazed upon thee,
> Till thou, still present to the bodily sense,
> Didst vanish from my thought: entranced in prayer
> I worshipped the Invisible alone.   (7–16)

Since, in contrast to "Kubla Khan," this poem is in what Coleridge characterized as the Wordsworthian genre, it is not surprising that it should recall a poem like "This Lime-Tree Bower." In a version sent to Southey, these lines occur, with the notation, "You remember I am a Berkleyan": [30]

> Struck with joy's deepest calm, and gazing round
> On the wide view may gaze till all doth seem
> Less gross than bodily; a living thing
> That acts upon the mind, and with such hues
> As clothe th'Almighty Spirit, when he makes
> Spirits perceive his presence.

Five years later he is no longer a Berkleyan, but the effect, and the cadence, are the same. Studies of Coleridge's philosophical development tend naturally to emphasize the revolutions he underwent— if he had gone on having sons, we should have a complete record [31] —but a survey of his images gives evidence of remarkable stability on another level, a level that some psychologists at least would consider more profound.

[30] *Poems,* p. 180 n.
[31] Would the youngest have been named Immanuel or Aristocles, that is the question.

In this poem no separate image is introduced, like the Abyssinian maid in "Kubla Khan," to carry the melody,

> Yet, like *some sweet beguiling melody,*
> So sweet, we know not we are listening to it,
> Thou, the meanwhile, was blending with my Thought,
> Yea, with my Life and *Life's own secret joy:*
> Till *the dilating Soul, enrapt, transfused,*
> Into the mighty vision passing—there
> As in her natural form, swelled vast to Heaven!   (17–23)

If we understood the exact import of line 20, "Yea, with my Life and Life's own secret joy," we should perhaps know all there is to know about Coleridge—and a good many other things. *Here* is what would happen could he revive within him the symphony and song, his soul would assume "her natural form," he would *become* the dome, "swelled vast to Heaven!" It is not difficult to imagine the result being such that the ignorant might weave a circle round him thrice, and close their eyes in holy dread.

With a certain frenetic desperation, he proceeds, as the poem continues, to build, as it were, that dome in air, or at least to exhort himself to do so:

> Awake, my soul! not only passive praise
> Thou owest! not alone these swelling tears,
> Mute thanks and secret ecstasy! Awake!
> Voice of sweet song! Awake, my heart, awake!
> *Green vales and icy cliffs,* all join my Hymn.   (24–27)

One hears an echo of the urgent cry in "Religious Musings," "Believe thou, O my soul, / Life is a vision shadowy of Truth!" And of Wordsworth's pathetic insistence in the Intimations Ode, "I hear, I hear," "I feel, I feel." But here there is, as there is not in "Kubla Khan," an explicit reference to a Power above both the potentate and the poet:

Thou first and chief, sole sovereign of the Vale!
O struggling with the darkness all the night,
And visited all night by troops of stars,
Or when they climb the sky or when they sink:
Companion of the morning-star at dawn,
Thyself Earth's rosy star, and of the dawn
Co-herald: wake, O wake, and utter praise!   (29–35)

And here are questions that would be surprising indeed if addressed to Kubla:

Who sank thy *sunless pillars deep in Earth?*
Who filled thy countenance with *rosy light?*
Who made thee *parent of perpetual streams?*   (36–38)

They are, as a matter of fact, the questions we all ask concerning that miraculous garden, and they amount to the one question: what is the ultimate source of that sunny dome, those caves of ice, and those perpetual streams?

And you, ye five *wild torrents fiercely glad!*
Who called you forth from night and utter death,
From *dark and icy caverns* called you forth,
Down those precipitous, black, jaggéd rocks,
Forever shattered and the same forever?
Who gave you your *invulnerable life,*
Your strength, your speed, your *fury,* and your *joy,*
Unceasing thunder and eternal foam?

And then the sunless sea, the lifeless ocean:

And who commanded (and the silence came)
Here let the billows stiffen, and have rest?   (39–48)

There follow addresses to the ice-falls (that "Adown enormous ravines slope amain"), to the flowers ("Ye living flowers that skirt the eternal frost"), and finally again to the Mount:

Rise, O ever rise,
Rise like a cloud of *incense* from the Earth!

Thou kingly Spirit throned among the hills,
Thou dread ambassador from Earth to Heaven,
Great Hierarch! tell thou the silent sky,
And tell the stars, and tell yon rising sun
Earth, with her thousand voices, praises GOD.   (79–85)

Perhaps nowhere else are the relations among Poet, Monarch, and Mountain made so explicit, but the maid is present only by implication, and the wailing woman is forgotten altogether, though the environment is such that nothing could be less surprising than her sudden appearance.

If the Abyssinian maid is not explicitly mentioned in the "Hymn," "The Blossoming of the Solitary Date-Tree" (1805) supplies the deficiency. The theme of the poem has to do with the necessity for a relationship of love if the individual's own possibilities are to be realized, and a few particular images reinforce the echo of "Kubla Khan." The poem is a fragment, and this time Coleridge accounts for its fragmentary state by pleading the loss of a manuscript page containing the first two stanzas. He supplies the gist of them in a prose summary, which begins with a highly familiar juxtaposition of images:

Beneath the blaze of a tropical sun the mountain peaks are the Thrones of Frost,

and in this case there follows a scientific explanation of the co-existence of sun and ice: "through the absence of objects to reflect the rays." But this is, after all, a love poem, in the most usual sense of the term, and there is no place in it for frost.

Beneath the blaze of a tropical sun the mountain peaks are the Thrones of Frost, through the absence of objects to reflect the rays. 'What no one with us shares, seems scarce our own.' The presence of ONE,
The best belov'd who loveth me the best, is for the heart, what the supporting air from within is for the hollow globe with its suspended

car. Deprive it of this, and all without, that would have buoyed it aloft even to the seat of the gods, becomes a burthen and crushes it to flatness.

One can hardly refrain from questioning Coleridge's story about the lost manuscript page, so difficult is it to imagine how this mixture could ever have been turned into poetry.

If the second summarized stanza were read as a gloss upon the "Could I" of "Kubla Khan," it might reinforce a feeling that House pushes things too far in interpreting that statement as analogous to "Could you make it Wednesday instead of Thursday, it would be easier for me." These expressions seem to issue from one who means by "Could I," "If only I could, but I can't":

The finer the sense for the beautiful and the lovely, and the fairer and lovelier the object presented to the sense; the more exquisite the individual's capacity for joy, and the more ample his means and opportunities of enjoyment, the more heavily will he feel the ache of solitariness, the more unsubstantial becomes the feast spread around him.

Up to this point he might seem to be saying simply that without the veritable presence of the Abyssinian maid all solicitations are in vain, but he goes on,

What matters it, whether in fact the viands and the ministering graces are shadowy or real, to him who has not hand to grasp nor arms to embrace them?

But we must remember that at least five years have passed since "Kubla Khan." As time went on Coleridge seems to have become increasingly uncertain whether his ideal was "shadowy or real." Later in this poem he compares himself to a "blind Arab" in a lonesome tent, listening for a voice. When it comes, it is not the right one, "Then melts the bubble into idle air." Long afterward, a year before his death, in "Love's Apparition and Evanishment" (1833), he is again "Like a lone Arab, old and blind . . . Who sits beside a ruin'd well, . . . and listens for a human sound—in vain!"[32] Was there a connection in Coleridge's mind between Arabs and Abyssinians? It does not seem impossible.[33]

The third stanza of "The Solitary Date-Tree" is an impressive confession in the midst of a not very impressive poem. The language is measured and eloquent (modern readers ought perhaps to be less disdainful of "O's"), the thought just:

> Imagination; honourable aims;
> Free commune with the choir that cannot die;
> Science and song; delight in little things,
> The buoyant child surviving in the man;
> Fields, forests, ancient mountains, ocean, sky,
> With all their voices—O dare I accuse
> My earthly lot as guilty of my spleen,
> Or call my destiny niggard! O no! no!
> It is her largeness, and her overflow,
> Which being incomplete, disquieteth me so!

If only he had never seen that fatal vision! It is in the fourth stanza that he compares himself to the blind Arab, describing as it were the momentary or illusory reappearance of the Abyssinian maid, and her final vanishing:

> For never touch of gladness stirs my heart,
> But tim'rously beginning to rejoice
> Like a blind Arab, that from sleep doth start
> In lonesome tent, I listen for thy voice.
> Belovéd! 'tis not thine; thou art not there!
> Then melts the bubble into idle air,
> And wishing without hope I restlessly despair.

Here is surely a distant echo of "that dome in air," lost past all hope of recall. The poem ends with one of Coleridge's most pathetic cries: "Why was I made for Love and Love denied to me?" He

---

[32] See also "Phantom or Fact" (1830?).
[33] For an exhaustive account of Coleridge's interest in *The Arabian Nights,* see Lowes, pp. 459–61.

means Sara Hutchinson, no doubt—but what does Sara Hutchinson mean?

In most of the contexts we have examined so far, it is difficult to see the analogues of the garden and the pleasure-dome as symbols of a *false* paradise. In the analogues, as well as in "Kubla Khan" itself, it would seem simplest, and therefore, unless something prevents, best, to see the dome and garden of Kubla as prototypes that the poet may hope, under the most favorable circumstances, to reproduce "in air." But in "Separation" (1805) we have a close verbal analogue of the dome presented in an explicitly unfavorable light:

> A sworded man whose trade is blood,
>   In grief, in anger, and in fear,
> Thro' jungle, swamp, and torrent flood,
>   I seek the wealth you hold so dear!
>
> The dazzling charm of outward form,
>   The power of gold, the pride of birth,
> Have taken Woman's heart by storm—
>   Usurp'd the place of inward worth.

The dichotomy is all too clear, and in the third stanza the dome is unmistakably associated with the negative side of it:

> Is not true Love of higher price
>   Than outward Form, though fair to see,
> *Wealth's glittering fairy-dome of ice,*
>   *Or echo of proud ancestry?*

There is hardly a closer verbal equivalent anywhere among the poems, and there is even the accompaniment of ancestral voices.

At this point one becomes acutely aware that one is engaged in a very delicate and uncertain enterprise. The object of the enterprise, held in common by all those who find it impossible to rest in what may, very questionably, be called "pure experience" of poetry, is to find more or less rationally comprehensible patterns in the use of imagery. But it may suddenly occur to one that the *poet* need not, and most probably does not, feel any such compulsion. His project is to create poems, or rather, one poem after another, and, like other human beings, although he is subject to subconscious tendencies toward consistency, he is quite capable of knowingly, even deliberately, indulging in *in*consistency. It is we his readers who strive to find consistent patterns of imagery to aid us in our interpretations, not he who deliberately strives to create an interpoem consistency of imagery. We have also to keep in mind the inevitable intricacy of images, and to remember that, subject to his own compulsions, the poet is free at each moment to choose among their virtualities. There must be cases, for instance, in which he falls into the use of an habitual image because he feels subconsciously comfortable with it, because it fits in with needs that lie deep in his psyche, but in which he uses it to voice explicit feelings other than those that are responsible for its being habitual with him.

It would seem easiest to argue that in "Separation" we have to do with a directly autobiographical situation, that Coleridge is writing a love poem on a highly emotional plane, and that in such a context one can expect that no image is too sacred to be sacrificed. The argument would be plausible, perhaps, but not really very convincing. The proposition underlying this whole discussion is that rationally comprehensible patterns *can* be found, do exist, and it will hardly do to argue in a difficult instance that one must not ask that such patterns be consistent (although in fact one must not, in the last analysis, ask it). If, granting the obvious inconsistency, we can with reasonable conviction see an underlying consistency, we shall all be more comfortable, and possibly really better informed.

The contrast presented in this poem is between outward form and inward reality, the "glittering fairy-dome of ice" representing the former, while the latter is a feeling in "the bottom of my heart."

Of course, in almost any scale of values, the motive is more important than its visible result if one looks at things from a certain perspective; and one is most likely to be conscious of this way of looking at things where all one can claim is the motive, not the "outward Form." In such instances the best of us are tempted to denigrate the "outward form." In this interpretation, Coleridge's use of the "fairy-dome of ice" here would be a measure of the depth of his despair. In "Kubla Khan," he is envisaging the possibility of achieving both, the inner reality and the outward form. We ought none of us to have too great difficulty in appreciating how a cherished symbol of fulfillment can become an object of bitter disdain in a moment of frustration.

By 1828, even the provisional possibility of recreating the domain of Kubla Khan is out of the question—nearly thirty years have passed, and Coleridge is fifty-six years old, the sage of Highgate, the protégé of the Gillmans. And yet in a moment of revery it is still possible for him to recognize and insinuate himself into the garden of another, the garden of Boccaccio. The poem that results is the last in which we can trace some vestige of his perennial dream, and the last real poem he wrote. The first section of the poem tells how, as the poet sat in a mood of "vacancy," the kind of mood he had known at least since the time of "Dejection," the watchful Mrs. Gillman slipped into his hand a drawing:

> Boccaccio's Garden and its faery,
> The love, the joyaunce, and the gallantry!
> An Idyll, with Boccaccio's spirit warm,
> Framed in the silent poesy of form.   (15–18)

In describing the effect of the picture upon him, he compares its silent "poesy" to music:

> Like flocks adown a newly-bathéd steep
> Emerging from a mist: or like a stream
> Of music soft that not dispels the sleep,

But casts in happier moulds the slumberer's dreams,
Gazed by an idle eye with silent might
The picture stole upon my inward sight.   (19–24)

Music is, among other things, *form,* immediately graspable (lova-
ble), translatable into one's own emotion. The picture sets off a
long train of recollections, starting with his boyhood:

And one by one (I know not whence) were brought
All spirits of power that most had stirr'd my thought
In selfless boyhood . . .
Or charmed my youth, that, kindled from above,
Loved ere it loved, and sought a form for love;   (27–29; 31–32)

Here, in two lines, we have an adequate diagnosis of the role of love
in Coleridge's life. Doubtless all love that is worthy of the name is
somehow "kindled from above," but happily not all lovers are so
exigent in seeking out a form for love. One wonders if Mary or
either of the two Sara's read this poem. And we learn also, in very
few words, the relation of poetry to philosophy for Coleridge, that
much-debated problem:

And last, a matron now, of sober mien,
Yet radiant still and with no earthly sheen,
Whom as a fairy child my childhood woo'd
Even in my dawn of thought—Philosophy;
Though then unconscious of herself, pardie,
She bore no other name than Poesy;
And like a gift from heaven, in lifeful glee,
That had but newly left a mother's knee,
Prattled and play'd with bird and flower, and stone,
As if with elfin playfellows well known,
And life reveal'd to innocence alone.   (46–56)

Here we ought to recall the many references in the early poems to
the poetic mount as a mount of Knowledge, and his felicitous
coupling of "Science and song" in "The Solitary Date-Tree." It is

hardly to be wondered at that Coleridge does not try to give us the words to the song about Mount Abora, sung by the fairy child from Abyssinia.

Provided with this ready-made pictorial paradise, he glides into it without effort, wide awake, no longer as in a dream within a dream:

> Thanks, gentle artist! now I can descry
> Thy fair creation with a mastering eye,
> And all awake! and now in fix'd gaze stand,
> Now wander through the Eden of thy hand;   (57–60)

(Those who find subtle notes indicating a false paradise in "Kubla Khan" would do well to ponder these lines: if Boccaccio's garden is an "Eden," it would seem evident that this was not one of the biblical symbols that Coleridge felt to be particularly sensitive, and his biblical sensitivities were highly developed by 1828.)

> Praise the green arches, on the fountain clear
> See fragment shadows of the crossing deer;

(still the preoccupation with reflections in water)

> And with that serviceable nymph I stoop
> The crystal, from its restless pool, to scoop.
> I see no longer! I myself am there,
> Sit on the ground-sward, and the banquet share.   (61–66)

In this privileged imaginary garden, the vision is finally revived, in the most remarkable way:

> 'Tis I, that sweep that lute's love-echoing strings,
> And gaze upon the maid who gazing sings:
> Or pause and listen to the tinkling bells
> From the high tower, and think that there she dwells.   (67–70)

All lovers of Coleridge must share his debt to Dr. and Mrs. Gillman. I think we must add to it Mrs. Gillman's handing to him at a crucial moment Stothard's illustration of Boccaccio—as a result, in his old age, he found himself accompanying the Abyssinian maid upon the lute and receiving gaze for gaze. And the nice thing is that Coleridge knew as well as we just what kind of experience it was:

> With old Boccaccio's soul I stand possest,
> *And breathe an air like life,* that swells my chest.　(71–72)

We may very well end this survey with the remaining lines of Coleridge's "last" poem:

> The brightness of the world, O thou once free,
> And always fair, rare land of courtesy!
> O Florence! with the Tuscan fields and hills
> And famous Arno, fed with all their rills;
> Thou brightest star of star-bright Italy!
> Rich, ornate, populous,—all treasures thine,
> The golden corn, the olive, and the vine.
> Fair cities, gallant mansions, castles old,
> And forests, where beside his leafy hold
> The sullen boar hath heard the distant horn,
> And whets his tusks against the gnarléd thorn;
> Palladian palace with its storied halls;
> Fountains, where Love lies listening to their falls;
> Gardens, where flings the bridge its airy span,
> And Nature makes her happy home with man;
> Where many a gorgeous flower is duly fed
> With its own rill, on its own spangled bed,
> And wreathes the marble urn, or leans its head,
> A mimic mourner, that with veil withdrawn
> Weeps liquid gems, the presents of the dawn;—
> Thine all delights, and every muse is thine;
> And more than all, the embrace and intertwine
> Of all with all in gay and twinkling dance!
> Mid gods of Greece and warriors of romance,
> See! Boccace sits, unfolding on his knees
> The new-found roll of old Maieonides;

But from his mantle's fold, and near the heart,
Peers Ovid's Holy Book of Love's sweet smart!
O all-enjoying and all-blending sage,
Long be it mine to con thy mazy page,
Where, half conceal'd, the eye of fancy views
Fauns, nymphs, and wingéd saints, all gracious to thy muse!

Still in thy garden let me watch their pranks,
And see in Dian's vest between the ranks
Of the trim vines, some maid that half believes
The vestal fires, of which her lover grieves,
With that sly satyr peeping through the leaves!

CHAPTER FIVE

Toward an Interpretation

The preceding chapters represent the merest adumbration of the significant complexity of Coleridge's poetry, considered as a body, as in some way a whole work. Certainly many of the individual poems do not seem to justify by their intrinsic excellence the kind of attention that their place in this survey might suggest. But two observations occur. One is that a number of the individual poems may deserve more attention than our current taste easily allows us to give them. The other is that, in a sense regardless of his poems, we have few *poets* in our literature who have revealed themselves to us as completely as Coleridge, if only we cultivate an ear for his echoes. And we need as much to know about poets and poetry as about poems.

It will have become obvious in the course of these chapters that, although the survey of the poems was undertaken with a view to facilitating the reading of "Kubla Khan," in reality a kind of circular argument has been at work all along, in a far from orderly way. After noticing apparent versions of "Kubla Khan" images in a few poems and registering their import as well as one provisionally can, one begins willy-nilly to employ a virtual and fragmentary "interpretation" of "Kubla Khan" itself in reading the other poems. If one's understanding is enriched at all, not obfuscated, it is enriched gradually in both directions, toward and away from "Kubla Khan," and it would probably be impossible, and surely unprofitable, to try to trace the logic of the process. The aim, after all, is attentive reading, not the extraction of a system. And if there are sufficient reasons for approaching the interpretation of even so

provocative a poem as "Kubla Khan" by so circuitous a route as the
one we have been following, one of them must be that the process
renders evident the impossibility of arriving at a neat "solution" to
the "problem." If the exercise "proves" anything at all, it is that
the poem in question is one reflection, one product, of a lifetime
of exploration, suffering, and discovery on the part of a man with
a keen sensibility and profound intelligence who was enough of a
maker to render both evident.

At this point it is perhaps sufficient simply to read the poem,
allowing the echoes to do whatever work they will, and they will,
of course, do something different for each reader. What follow are
one reader's reactions, aided in as many points as possible by some
others who have recorded their own readings.

It might be well to begin by considering the title of the poem:
"Kubla Khan" (ignoring for the moment its subtitle: "Or, A
Vision in a Dream. A Fragment"). Perhaps no aspect of the poem
has been more sharply disputed than the role of Kubla himself,
and it is most obviously a crux in the interpretation of the poem. At
one extreme we find the interpretation of J. B. Beer, who sees
Kubla as the Tartar king of tradition, fierce, cruel, bearing the
brand of Cain, a symbol of the eighteenth-century man of understanding, trying to impose rational order on the universe, a personage with whom Coleridge cannot be supposed to be identified.[1]
In essential agreement, Carl Woodring feels that Kubla is not the
type of the poet, but the type of the tyrant.[2] Lowes's convincing
association of Kubla with Aloadine, who, with however laudable
motives from a Mohammedan point of view, created an artificial
paradise to seduce young men to his service,[3] tends to support this
interpretation. At the other extreme there is G. Wilson Knight,
who finds in Kubla a symbol of "God: or at least one of those
'huge and mighty forms,' or other similar intuitions of gigantic

[1] Beer, pp. 222, 251, 267–68.
[2] Woodring, "Coleridge and the Khan," *Essays in Criticism*, IX (1959)
362. See also, Woodring, *Politics in the Poetry of Coleridge*, pp. 49 ff.
[3] Lowes, pp. 360 ff.

mountainous power, in Wordsworth." [4] He compares him, and the comparison is very persuasive, to the Emperor in "Sailing to Byzantium." [5] Between these two extremes there are the interpretations of Humphry House, who thinks Kubla may be "Representative Man" or "Mankind in General," [6] and Dorothy F. Mercer, who sees in him "man generically," but a "prince of men, hence a man able to . . . dissolve, diffuse, dissipate the facts of experience and to recreate them so all may participate in his insight." [7] And so we have a scale ranging from God to an agent, at least, of the Devil.

What, then, can we find in Coleridge's own usages to help us narrow the scale? For one thing, we can examine his practice in the matter of titles. Very few of his poems use the name of a personage as the main element of their titles, and among those that do are certainly the most interesting ones for our purpose: "The Rime of the Ancient Mariner," "Christabel," "The Ballad of the Dark Ladié, A Fragment," and that other fragment, "The Wanderings of Cain." In each of these four works, the personage of the title is the protagonist, who undergoes an ordeal resulting in part from his own deficiencies, and leading toward an ambiguous kind of salvation, as we know from the only finished work among them and from suggestions in the others. Even Cain is the protagonist, not the villain. All of these are narrative poems, however, and "Kubla Khan" is not. No action at all takes place within the poem: everything mentioned either has taken place in the past or may take place in the future. Therefore the poem has, properly speaking, no protagonist. But if Coleridge's choice of a title in this case is at all consistent with his usual practice, it is very unlikely that Kubla is the "villain" of the piece.

[4] Knight, p. 93.

[5] For other similarities between Coleridge and Yeats, see my *Dark Night of Samuel Taylor Coleridge*, pp. 59–61.

[6] House, p. 120.

[7] Mercer, "The Symbolism of 'Kubla Khan,' " *The Journal of Aesthetics and Art Criticism*, XII (1953), 60.

Several entries in Coleridge's notebooks may also give some hint as to the quality of the associations Kubla had for him. Twice his name actually occurs. In 1802 the following entry was made: "Kublaikhan ordered letters to be invented for his people—"[8] Miss Coburn suggests that this is an echo from *Purchas his Pilgrimage,* where Kubla's predecessor Genghis is said to have received letters from a conquered Nestorian sect.[9] If so, the transfer to Kubla is interesting, and even more so the transformation of the event: Coleridge sees Kubla as *decreeing* that letters be *invented* for his people (something very nearly impossible in the normal course of events). Miss Coburn also suggests that Kubla may have occurred to Coleridge at this point in "a context of tyrants" (Alexander is described in an uncomplimentary way in the next entry). But if he is a despot he would seem to be a benevolent one, acting for his people, and in order to bring them *knowledge.* Only a few months earlier, Coleridge had noted of himself: "Bear witness for me, what thoughts I wandered about with—if I ever imagined myself a conqueror, it was always to bring peace—but mostly turned away from these thoughts to more humane & peaceable Dreams."[10] And though here he speaks of Alexander as "talkative & fond of Flattery—obstinate—,"[11] two years before he had noted, "Alexander's Feast—a noble subject still for a bold fellow."[12]

Miss Coburn traces the other explicit Kubla reference to Purchas also, and dates it January, 1804: "Cublai Chan began to reign, 1256 the greatest Prince in Peoples, Cities & Kingdoms that ever was in the World."[13] At this late date, in any case, Coleridge was not thinking of the Khan simply as an obscure Eastern tyrant. There is also an entry of 1799, the source of which Miss Coburn does not suggest, having to do with a later Khan:

In the year 1783 The Tarter Chan, Schapin Gueray, who had been driven out of his dominions by his Subjects, & reinstated by the Russian

---

[8] *Notebooks,* Vol. I, 1281   8.30.   [9] *Ibid.,* n.
[10] *Ibid.,* Vol. I, 1214   2.10 f14.   [11] *Ibid.,* Vol. I, 1282   8.31.
[12] *Ibid.,* Vol. I, 759   5½.15.   [13] *Ibid.,* Vol. I, 1840   16.223 f68.

Court, set on foot a Translation of the Great French Encyclopaedie into the Tartar Language /.[14]

Though this most recent Khan must surely have been something of a tyrant to get himself driven out by his people, he too is concerned with improving the minds of his subjects. In 1799 Coleridge could probably still consider the translation of the *Encyclopedia* a laudable gesture. The general import of these scattered references might lead us to eliminate the negative end of our scale. Kubla clearly does not appear as the Devil, or even one of his agents. He is a king with virtually unlimited powers, which he is specifically mentioned as using only to increase the spread of knowledge. Before leaving the *Notebooks*, we should examine one other entry, which concerns a figure whom Coleridge certainly came to think of as one of the worst of tyrants:

A Throne the Δος που στα of Archimedes—Poet Bonaparte—Layer out of a World-garden—[15]

It is hard to think that in 1802 (the year Miss Coburn assigns to the entry), Coleridge could have spoken of a "Layer out of a World-garden" without thinking of Kubla Khan. If the note read only "Bonaparte . . ." it might be a fairly good indication that in Coleridge's mind Kubla was simply a tyrant, and that his having him lay out what almost all readers feel to be a superlatively beautiful garden as the illustration of his tyranny is simply maladroit. But what he says is "Poet Bonaparte," and that makes all the difference.[16]

As we turn to the poems for further enlightenment, it becomes apparent that in this enterprise we are faced with one of the eternal problems of criticism. It is necessary, in the nature of things, to

[14] *Ibid.*, Vol. I, 424   3½.32.   [15] *Ibid.*, Vol. I, 1166   6.94.

[16] We may be reminded that Coleridge once thought of one of his great heroes, Martin Luther, as general and as poet, a general fighting against an army of evil beings, a poet who did not write but *acted* poems. (See *The Friend, Complete Works*, II, 131.)

consider one item at a time, to begin somewhere, for instance with Kubla, as we are doing. But even if what we found in the background of Coleridge's reading and writing amounted to the most clear-out portrait of that monarch, his weight *in the poem* could still only be guessed at when the weight of everything else in the poem had been equally well determined and the relations among them established. A little reflection leads to the conclusion that it is probably impossible to read poems at all, certainly impossible to read about them, without being necessarily *wrong* at every moment. Yet some people do read them, perhaps even more read about them, and it seems necessary only that we be fully aware of our constant momentary error, and hold fast to the strange belief that an accumulation of errors can somehow lead us closer to the truth.

References in the poems considered in previous chapters can help us in at least two ways in our effort to come to a more precise sense of the import of Kubla in the poem that bears his name. In the first place, he is, inescapably, a king, if not precisely a tyrant still a great and powerful king, an absolute monarch. Knowing Coleridge's lifelong antipathy toward absolute monarchy as a political system, one may be tempted to suppose that it is this aspect of Kubla, as found in Purchas and elsewhere, that is primarily operative in the poem, and therefore that Kubla must in some way be a villain. But when we go back to the poems we find that as early as 1795, in "To the Author of Poems," the summit of the poetic mount itself is compared to a "giant king" that o'erglooms the hill, and a year later in "To a Young Friend," where the poetic mount is called a Hill of Knowledge, the surrounding plains are "subject" to it. As strange as it may seem to us, even this doctrinaire young democrat, when he gropes for poetic images to convey his sense of the nature of the poetic act, finds it necessary to employ the symbol of the king, and we should not let ourselves be misled by too great a knowledge of biographical fact. But this is not all. Though Kubla be even a tyrant, we must remember that Coleridge was capable of translating Στυγνὲ Τύραννε as "stern *genius*," and that even the rebellious angels, who in "The Destiny of Nations" "o'er dark realms arrogate power," still "train up to God" and are compared to the far-off *sun* in Lapland, darting his slant beam on unobeying *snows*, in a context where contradictories reconciled provide a glimpse of the absolute. Even a quite domestic mountain like "Blencartha" is "stern" and "perilous," its winds "tyrannous," and yet, in "A Thought Suggested by a View," it is associated with the supernal quiet of the sky in contrast to the noise and riot of earth. Skiddaw, another localized version of the poetic mount, is "stern and proud," capable of replying to questions "In sullen majesty" "from out his helm of cloud." Later in "A Stranger Minstrel," his voice is "like a monarch wooing." This rough equivalence between king and mountain will be good to remember as we read further in the poem. It is repeated again in the case of a greater mountain than Skiddaw—Mont Blanc, apostrophized as a potentate, a "most awful Form," regally silent amid turbulence, and possessing a "calm home, thy crystal shrine," his habitation from eternity. It becomes evident that for Coleridge, as for many others who may have opposed political absolutism, monarchy nevertheless furnishes a symbol of connection with some kind of absolute. Mont Blanc is the "Kingly spirit throned among the hills," a "Great Hierarch," a "Dread ambassador from Earth to Heaven." Here we would seem to be very near Knight's interpretation of Kubla as a symbol of God. In somewhat the same way Coleridge was capable of comparing a warship and a church, to the advantage of the former, in a connection not unrelated to a significance of Kubla's dome. One of "The elements of this picturesque effect of a Ship / a man of war, for instance" is "It's height upon a flat surface / if a Steeple be so uniformly pleasing on a diversified meadow, how much more the Masts of a man of war, referring as with a finger to the Sky, on this vast Level?" [17]

The poems can also help us with another problem concerning

[17] *Notebooks*, Vol. II, 2012 9.118, f38ᵛ (April, 1804).

Kubla. Coleridge is after all, among other things, a Romantic nature poet, a critic who insists upon the "organic" character of the poetic enterprise, and a philosopher who takes every possible occasion to inveigh against the mechanistic, against the products of the "mere understanding"; and Kubla, decreeing a pleasure-dome surrounded by a well-measured garden, is seen by some readers as a symbol of the artificial as opposed to the natural creator (represented by the poet in the latter part of the poem). But as early as 1792, in "An Effusion at Evening," we find the poet, under the influence of the song of a maiden recaptured by imagination, wishing his were "the wizard's rod" so that he could decree an arbor for his love. Creation by wizardry is certainly not artificial, not a product of the understanding, but neither is it organic, though what results, if the wizardry be really successful, would surely seem natural—that would be the miracle. And it is well to remember at this point that in "Religious Musings" Imagination, as contrasted to nature, is the source of the "arched dome" and costly feast, nursing the soul to forms of beauty. And the poem ends with an invocation to beings "of plastic power, that interfused / Roll through the grosser and material mass / In *organizing surge!*" The last phrase is, in many ways of thinking, an oxymoron, but it may be that we cannot understand "Kubla Khan" unless we can conceive the possibility that something that "surges" may at the same time "organize," or at least be organized. The point might serve as a reminder that knowledge of a poet's philosophical writings, indispensable though it be, can be as dangerous as knowledge of his biography or his "sources." Philosophical writings are, after all, a schematization, performed by someone whose first language is usually not that of philosophical elaboration,[18] and our reading of them is at best a further schematization. The result applied to the poetry is much too likely to be a reduction rather than an enrichment of the poetry. Even "Kubla Khan," incantatory as

[18] Among Romantic poets, one thinks first of Keats: it is possible at some moments to wish that his letters had never been published.

it is, has not always been able to withstand the critics' knowledge of Coleridge's distinction between Understanding and Reason.

More of Kubla's character, the Kubla of this poem, should become evident as we read further into the poem, though in the nature of things his character may become less rather than more distinct, depending upon how he is really being used in the poem. As for the site of his pleasure-dome, there would seem to be less difficulty. After all, the Kubla of Purchas, whom Coleridge declares himself to have been reading at the moment of composition, is said to have built a pleasure-house at Xamdu, Xaindu, or Xandu, so that the name was ready at hand, and was no doubt, as Lowes suggests, changed to Xanadu for purposes of euphony. But then Coleridge cannot be supposed to have been held to his sources, since, as Lowes demonstrates so thoroughly, he altered and combined them in the most complicated way; and since Xanadu is *in* the poem, it has a potential effect of which we may be more or less conscious as readers. Without going as far as Knight, who suggests that the letter "X," along with the "A" of Abyssinia–Abora and the "K" of Kubla Khan may represent first, middle, and last things [19] (there would seem to be nothing in the poem itself or in Coleridge's usual poetic practice to indicate the probability of such a strategem), we can note simply that, in addition to being highly euphonious, it is the name of a faraway and exotic place, like Abyssinia, like Tryermaine, like the southern polar regions and the south seas. In the words of Bernard Breyer, it is "a realm of delight set off from the regular course of life" (but not completely, as he goes on to explain).[20] Still other poems come to mind— "The Wanderings of Cain," perhaps "The Dark Ladié," "The Solitary Date-Tree," "The Garden of Boccaccio," all but the last of them fragments, and they seem all to be somehow of the same family, as distinguished from the far greater number of poems whose set-

---

[19] *The Starlit Dome,* p. 97.
[20] "Towards the Interpretation of *Kubla Khan,*" *English Studies in Honor of James Southall Wilson, University of Virginia Studies,* V (1951), 284.

tings are either domestic or at least very familiar. Perhaps the point to be gathered is that what Coleridge sought, and had glimpses of, was from as far away as anything can be—and at the same time in every wood and dale. And we ought to remind ourselves again of the curious equivalence between Worsdworth's task and Coleridge's in *Lyrical Ballads,* as reported in the *Biographia.*[21] In any case we may suppose that Coleridge would have been amazed to learn that there was a *road* to Xanadu.

Already at this point something of the density and organization of the poem becomes evident. We have considered only the first line, with its two images, and are about to come upon the pleasure-dome. Before finishing the first five-line section, we shall have encountered all but one of the elemental images of the poem as well as the predominating personal image, that of Kubla, and shall, in a sense, have read the whole poem.

> In Xanadu did Kubla Khan
> A stately pleasure-dome decree:

If we have been right so far in our estimate of the character of Kubla and the nature of the site he chose, I should suppose that, aided by the word "stately," what we see is at the very least an imposing piece of architecture; but since the character of this dome has been associated by readers of the poem with everything from the Elysian Fields [22] to Pandemonium,[23] we shall do well to pause. There is certainly no reason within the immediate context to suppose that Coleridge is using the word "stately" with any other than its usual meaning—majestic, grand, august. The difficulty comes, perhaps, from its juxtaposition with "pleasure"—if not from preconceptions concerning the rest of the poem. There is, for our ears at least, a kind of subdued paradox in the idea of "stately pleasure." And so either the word "stately" has been momentarily

---

[21] II, 5–6.   [22] Bodkin, p. 100.   [23] Beer, p. 226.

ignored and the pleasure-dome compared to the Empress Anna's ice palace, in which abhorrent orgies took place,[24] or the word "stately" has been read as connoting, along with "decree," a malign or misguided use of power.[25] The latter reading has been at least partially disposed of by our consideration of the character of Kubla himself, the decreer. The former is rendered a good deal less likely by the fact that, as Breyer points out,[26] in the whole description of Kubla's establishment there is no suggestion of appetite, sexual or alimentary, that, except for the incense, all the pleasures are visual (he seems to forget the "mingled measure" later on, but that is incidental).

Before going on to examine other Coleridgean domes, we can get some help in determining how the word "stately" fell upon his ears from a notebook entry of 1802. He is describing a lake and its environs, not a palace, though there is something comparable nearby:

> Coniston Lake a fine mixture of the aweful & the pleasing Simple— of one-colored dark Rocks, & pastoral Hills below.
> Coniston is doubtless a worthy Compeer of the Statliest / an equal Coheir of Nature with Keswick, Wyndermere, & Ulswater / Its distinguishing characteristic I think is its perfect & easy comprehensibility. . . . The Head of the Lake is an admirable junction of awful & of pleasing Simplicity. / it is beyond all other lakes perfectly intelligible— . . . The Houses, Gardens, fields, & woodland upon this crescent Hill are all in admirable *keeping,* various as heart can desire, yet all sweet Brothers & Sisters— . . . Add Coniston Hall as the first bold feature, with its four Round Chimneys, two cloathed so warmly cap a pie with ivy & down on the wall far below / [27]

---

[24] Woodring, "Coleridge and the Khan," pp. 365–66.

[25] Beer, pp. 222 and *passim;* George Watson, "The Meaning of 'Kubla Khan,'" *A Review of English Literature,* II, (1961), 28.

[26] "Towards the Interpretation of *Kubla Khan,*" p. 279.

[27] *Notebooks,* Vol. I, 1228 2.33 f31 (italics in text). See *Biographia Literaria* II, 11, for a discussion of this principle in another context—the making of a poem.

We have the familiar personification of a natural phenomenon—the lake is a Compeer, a Co-heir, and we remember all the mountains personified as kings, kings who *were* their palaces. A "stately" object is one that combines the awful and pleasing simplicity. The mystery is how an object doing that can at the same time excel in comprehensibility, intelligibility. But is it not possible that that is just the mystery presented, not solved, in "Kubla Khan"? In an actual vision, that mystery is solved, not by philosophic reasoning, but by sight.

In another context, the word "stately" is actually applied to a castle, a castle that, like Coniston, is both pleasing and awesome. The Knight in "The Dark Ladié" answers the Maid's plea for shelter by declaring,

> 'Nine castles hath my noble sire,
> None statelier in the land.

> 'The fairest one shall be my love's,
> The fairest castle of the nine!'   (35–38)

But in order to reach it they must pass through a romantic chasm, and the Maid is unwilling to go.

As for the word "pleasure," its use in the poems is quite inconclusive. It occurs many times, capitalized or not, denoting sensual vice, but just as often, and sometimes within the same poem, denoting the most elevated emotions, specifically the emotions associated with the poetic experience.[28] "Joy" was certainly the word Coleridge preferred in that connection, but it does not fit all metrical situations. Once, writing the word "PLEASURE," he compared its

---

[28] A cursory reading of the poems suggest this, but a check with the aid of the concordance confirms it. As Coleridge complains in the second essay "On the Principles of Genial Criticism" (*Biographia Literaria,* II, 224), "The term, pleasure, is unfortunately so comprehensive, as frequently to become equivocal: and yet it is hard to discover a substitute." On Coleridge's use of "pleasure" in "Kubla Khan" and elsewhere, see Breyer, "Towards the Interpretation," p. 278.

influence upon the mind to that of the Holy Spirit moving upon the waters, producing order out of chaos.[29] If stateliness is something like an eminently comprehensible combination of the awful and the pleasingly simple and pleasure a force producing order out of chaos, then the creation of a king like Kubla, devoted to the spread of knowledge, might very well be appropriately described as a stately pleasure-dome.

These considerations alone would lead to the conclusion that the stately pleasure-dome of Kubla Khan is at least something like what the ordinary reader takes it to be, a highly desirable locale, though he might be warned that it is both positively and negatively more than meets the eye. Actually, the problems of interpretation centering about the dome may be reduced to two, and we shall look to the poems for aid in approaching a resolution of them. One involves the question as to whether the dome of line two is identical with or opposed to the domes mentioned later in the poem, in lines 31, 36, and 46–47. This is a problem that I suspect occurs only to the most ingenious reader, but that is hardly a sufficient ground to dismiss it. Since it is a problem clearly intrinsic to the poem itself, it had better be postponed. The other involves the relation between this dome decreed by Kubla, a dome that the poet chooses to describe in considerable detail as we go through the poem, and the natural domes to be found throughout his poetry. The solution to the first problem depends in part upon the solution to the second, since one reason for supposing the domes in the poem to be essentially distinct is the opinion that one is "artificial," the other somehow "natural."[30]

The poems, as we have seen, abound in dome-like forms, from the "Ode" of 1792 to "The Garden of Boccaccio" of 1828, and a remarkable number of them have characteristics that clearly associate them with Kubla's stately pleasure-dome. The "Ode" is as

[29] "To the Rev. W. L. Bowles," ll, 11–14, *Poems*, p. 84.
[30] See Beer and Woodring.

good an example as any—its images correspond to images the length of "Kubla Khan." Its dome is a "giant Rock" impending over a fretful current amid waving foliage. It governs a precinct where "Reason's voice might swell / With whisper'd airs and holy spell," where passion "drinks the sacred balm," protected from the tumults of Conquest and ruthless war. Here the dome is simply a presiding presence. In "Songs of the Pixies," however, we get a more detailed picture, and one still closer to "Kubla Khan." Here the dome is formed, we remember, by the roots of ancient trees, their tops in the sunlight, the excavation cool, the trees' shadow floating on the waves of a river. Since it has been argued that even the "dome of pleasure" in line 31 of "Kubla Khan" is not the same as the dome decreed by Kubla,[31] it is important to note that in this version we find not only the sun-ice-shadow image of lines 31–36, but "old trees" and an "elfin-haunted grove." The dome here is the privileged retreat of poetic experience, of "Solemn Thought," of love.

Close examination of the many other natural domes of one kind or another to be found throughout the poems [32] reveals that virtually all of them have characteristics linking them in some specific way with Kubla's pleasure-dome, and further, that they are very nearly indistinguishable in character from the various man-made domes that appear, the temples, castles, mansions, etc.[33] Far from the natural dome's being preferable to the artificial or man-made one, the fact seems to be that Coleridge uses both to spur the imaginative creation of the artistic dome. Over and over, as we

[31] Beer, p. 246.

[32] See "Effusion at Evening," "To the Author," "Reflections on Having Left a Place of Retirement," "Religious Musings," "Destiny of Nations," "This Lime-Tree Bower," "Hymn Before Sunrise," among others.

[33] See especially "Reflections," where God makes a temple out of the landscape, imaging the whole world. Also, "Religious Musings," "Monody on the Death of Chatterton," "Osorio," "The Old Man of the Alps," "The Nightingale," "The Dark Ladié," "Catullian Hendecasyllables," "Love," "The Picture," "The Garden of Boccaccio."

have noted, he *sees* the natural dome in artificial terms. And so Miss Bodkin must be right in seeing the dome as on or merged with a mountain.[34] Whether decreed by Kubla as it were *ex nihilo,* or decreed by Coleridge out of the natural or artificial materials he sees before him, it is somehow above and beyond nature, though continuous with it.[35] We should remember in this connection that even Wordsworth sometimes shows a preference for a nature *remaniée,* a nature touched or seemingly touched by man—one thinks of "Tintern Abbey" and the Margaret story in "The Excursion." And Coleridge finds it satisfying that the landscape around Coniston is in such "admirable *keeping.*" In a notebook entry of April, 1804, he discusses with great subtlety the influence of literary associations in producing or inhibiting this impression of meaningful unity in nature. Under the right circumstances, the associations become one with Nature:

At certain times, uncalled and sudden, subject to no bidding of my own or others, these Thoughts would come upon me, like a Storm, & fill the Place with something more than Nature.—But these are not contingent or transitory / they are Nature, even as the Elements are Nature / yea, more to the human mind / for the mind has the power of abstracting all agency from the former, & considering as mere effects & instruments, but a Shakespeare, a Milton, a Bruno, exist in the mind as *pure Action,* defecated of all that is material & passive /. And the great moments, that formed them—it is hard & an impiety against a Voice within us, not to regard as predestined, & therefore things of Now & For Ever and which were Always.[36]

The whole passage might well be required reading for those engaged in assessing the importance of literary sources in the formation of poetry. In the essay "On Poesy and Art" Coleridge makes it

[34] *Archetypal Patterns,* p. 100. See also Knight, p. 96.
[35] On this point, see R. H. Fogle, "The Romantic Unity of 'Kubla Khan,'" *College English,* XIII (1951–52), 15.
[36] *Notebooks,* Vol. II, 2026   15.7, f7. We may be reminded of the Lady in "The Nightingale," who was "vowed and dedicate / To something more than Nature in the grove."

very clear that the difference between nature and art is, as it were, accidental, but, paradoxically, genius is required to render the identity evident:

> The wisdom in nature is distinguished from that in man by the co-instantaneity of the plan and the execution; the thought and the product are one, or are given at once; but there is no reflex act, and hence there is no moral responsibility. In man there is reflexion, freedom, and choice; he is, therefore, the head of the visible creation. In the objects of nature are presented, as in a mirror, all the possible elements, steps, and processes of intellect antecedent to consciousness, and therefore to the full development of the intelligential act; and man's mind is the very focus of all the rays of intellect which are scattered throughout the images of nature. Now so to place these images, totalized, and fitted to the limits of the human mind, as to elicit from, and to superinduce upon, the forms themselves the moral reflexions to which they approximate, to make the external internal, the internal external, to make nature thought, and thought nature—this is the mystery of genius in the Fine Arts.[37]

On the other hand, nature by itself can be even ludicrous, as we learn from another notebook entry:

> It is not only that the distant Mountains before me, all named "du" black, are of the wildest Shapes, one of them a bridge tumbling topsy Turvy, called mountain Croupean—all dark, of a hundred Shapes, & no shape of Grandeur, nothing combining—it is not only this, but the whole land thro' which the Road lies, is cloven & cut into a vast room left by Drunkards—short tables, & high Tables, & side Tables, & cushions in confusion—& the hundred Forms that can be brought into no Analogy. In short, I who adore Nature, was kept *grinning* at the Scene—& the Faces of the Highlanders like faces on wooden Sticks.[38]

As we all know, Ruskin did not invent the pathetic fallacy, he merely misnamed it.[39]

If, then, we can safely treat the domes, natural and man-made, as indistinguishable in import, what are their relevant characteris-

---

[37] *Biographia Literaria,* II, 257–58.

[38] Notebooks, Vol. I, 1946   7.45, f71–71ᵛ (September, 1803).

[39] On this general subject, see also *Biographia Literaria,* II, 257–58, 262.

tics possibly to be imported into the context of "Kubla Khan"? Those found in the "Ode" and the "Songs of the Pixies" give the first indication. A dome, as presented in those poems, is something set apart from the wide gamut of nature, not contrary to it, but affording a privileged refuge, to a finite being, for inspiration, for vision and delight. This is not after all an eccentric conception —poets and mystics from the beginning of time have felt a similar necessity, to be in contact with Nature, but protected from nature and the everyday world of men. Part of the universal appeal of "Kubla Khan," before any critical analysis, may derive from a general though more or less dormant nostalgia for such a retreat, which the poem reawakens and satisfies. Outside "Kubla Khan" itself, this aspect of the dome and its environs is perhaps most explicitly stated in "The Triumph of Loyalty," where we have a Mansion with "spacious pleasure grounds"—they must be spacious enough but, as we see a moment later, not too spacious—descending from a mountain. "Lawn and Grove, River and Hillock—it looked within these high walls, like a World of itself." Critics have noted the similarity of Earl Henry's illusory dome, the "Pillars of a Temple of sand . . . built by Omnipotence in its own honor"— to the dome in "Kubla Khan," but this Mansion with its spacious pleasure grounds has been neglected in this connection, and it is here that the ultimate fulfillment occurs. If the Temple of sand is like any dome in "Kubla Khan," it is most like the "dome in air" of the last section. Finally, among the many possibilities, an early poem, "Religious Musings," provides a quasi-metaphysical description of the process involved in the creation of the dome. The Philosopher and Bard are seen as leading unnumbered tribes to

> tame the outrageous mass, with plastic might
> Moulding Confusion to such perfect forms,
> As erst were wont,—bright visions of the day!—
> To float before them, when, the summer noon,
> Beneath some arched romantic rock reclined
> They felt the sea-breeze lift their youthful locks;   (246–51)

Surely Kubla's dome is for Coleridge one of those perfect forms, bright visions of the day.

The dome as the locale or the subject of vision reappears many times, most often in an environment that links it in some specific way to "Kubla Khan." We may think of the vision midway the slope of yonder hill in the "The Eolian Harp," a vision of divine omnipresence, or again of the mountain-dome in "Reflections," conceived as a temple, built by Omnipresence in its own honor and including the very being of the observer in its scope. In "The Destiny of Nations," Joan's vision includes the music-induced apparition of a reflected eminence described as an "ice-piled mount / And meteor-lighted dome," contrasted with the blood and suffering of a battlefield. There are many others, and all these visions, as is the way with visions, issue in knowledge and delight.

This association, at its ultimate state this equivalence, between knowledge and delight is so central to Coleridge's thinking, and therefore so central to the interpretation of a work like "Kubla Khan," that we ought to pause at this point and review the many contexts in which it is evident. As early as 1789, in the poem called "Life," we find a recognizably "Kubla Khan" landscape associated with "Knowledge" that issues in "rapture," thought suspended in a "blissful trance." In the "Ode" of 1792, it is Reason's voice, with whispered airs and holy spell, that quells the threat of war hanging over a privileged retreat. In "Songs of the Pixies," the Bard woos "the Queen of Solemn Thought" in a kind of pleasure-dome—and the dreams in the cave, "soothing witcheries," are tinctured with sunshine. In "The Eolian Harp" we find the record, both vivid and delicate, of orgasmic delight issuing in philosophical reflection, the vision itself more closely reminiscent of "Kubla Khan" than anything else in Coleridge's poetry, but in 1795 he had not quite learned that metaphysical Solution was a great Vice in Poetry.[40] The temple in "Reflections on Having Left a Place of

[40] *Notebooks,* Vol. I, 673   10.34 (February–March, 1800).

Retirement" *images* the whole world, and as a result, it is "a luxury,—to be!" In "Religious Musings," the vision of perfect form is like reclining under an arched romantic rock while the sea-breeze lifts one's youthful locks. Later in the same poem, in another close analogue to "Kubla Khan," a vision of paradise involves knowledge of the future. The relevance of the passage is so striking that we ought to have it again under our eyes:

> Such delights
> As float to earth, permitted visitants!
> When in some hour of solemn jubilee
> The massy gates of Paradise are thrown
> Wide open, and forth come in fragments wild
> Sweet echoes of unearthly melodies,
> And odours snatched from beds of Amaranth,
> And they, that from the crystal river of life
> Spring up on freshened wing, ambrosial gales!
> The favoured good man in his lonely walk
> Perceives them, and his silent spirit drinks
> Strange bliss which he shall recognize in heaven.
> And such delights, such strange beatitudes
> Seize on my young anticipating heart
> When that blest future rushes on my view!   (343–57)

What follows is again a kind of "metaphysical Solution," involving Milton, Newton, and Priestley, but the knowledge and delight of the vision are eloquently caught. In "The Destiny of Nations," the delight of "Strong music" on the harp induces a kind of Platonic apperception of reality (with political overtones), involving metaphysical knowledge, "For all that meets the bodily sense I deem / Symbolical, one mighty alphabet / For infant minds." (18–20) The poetic mount in "To a Young Friend" is a "Hill of Knowledge." The poet and his friend are to find "Our hopes, our knowledge, and our joys the same." In a fine paradox, as we noted in an earlier chapter, the mind *drinks* its fill of truth, but must be disciplined to "pure delight." In "This Lime-Tree Bower," delight is kindled as the poet in imagination stands "with swimming sense," seeing the Almighty Spirit through the veil of perfectly arranged natural forms.

The equivalence of knowledge and delight finds expression in an epithet in "Fears in Solitude," where the effects of a landscape bearing some resemblance to that of "Kubla Khan" induce a "meditative joy," in which the poet finds "Religious meanings in the forms of nature." Surely Coleridge intends a slightly oxymoronic shock in the term "meditative joy," and we should ponder a bit on what it can mean to find religious meanings in the forms of nature. If one has read a good deal of Romantic poetry, especially if one has read a good deal of commentary thereon, the expression may easily be assimilated without any question. But it *is* an ambiguous expression. It might mean, and sometimes does in Coleridge's poetry, a kind of allegorical taking off from some perceived or imagined relation among natural objects into metaphysical disquisition, discursive elaboration of philosophical ideas. But if it takes place in what can properly be called a "meditative *joy*," it must be a *seeing*, an *experience*, of a kind that can be rendered only in what Coleridge and many after him called "symbols," which, as he points out in the *Biographia*, "of necessity involve an apparent contradiction." [41] Once we realize that this kind of "seeing" *is* a kind of "making," we are, I think, very near to the real burden of "Kubla Khan."

At least two other poems deserve attention in this connection. One is "The Blossoming of the Solitary Date-Tree," in which Coleridge links "Science and song" in a list of his blessings, and the other is "The Garden of Boccaccio," in which he calls Philosophy a "fairy child," and says "She bore no other name than Poesy." He was fully aware of the necessary distinction between delight and knowledge, between poetry and science, as he made clear, for instance, in his essay "On the Principles of Genial Criticism con-

[41] I, 100.

cerning the Fine Arts," where he says that the common essence of all forms of poetry, whether of language, of the ear, or of the eye, "consists in the excitement of emotion for the immediate purpose of pleasure through the medium of beauty; herein contra-distinguishing poetry from science, the immediate object and primary purpose of which is truth and possible utility." [42] But as the poems we have been examining indicate, he was also aware of their identity on another level. Indeed, even in the essay cited he makes this clear, pointing out that the sciences may give a "high and pure pleasure," and that the fine arts may "lead to important truth," but the distinguishing characteristic of the arts, he points out, is indicated by the word "immediate" in his definition, to the "full force" of which the attention must be directed. [43] Part of that full force surely involves the sense "non-mediated." The "knowledge" derived from the poetic experience is non-mediated knowledge, knowledge by experience, by identification, what the scholastics and sometimes Coleridge called "connatural" knowledge, and this is the knowledge that for Coleridge is identical with delight.

All this is something of what the pleasure-dome would seem to have meant for Coleridge, and it is in the light of all this that we must understand what is involved, in the "Hymn before Sunrise," in referring to Mont Blanc, a king dwelling eternally in a "crystal shrine," as an "Ambassador from Earth to Heaven." That is surely what Coleridge conceived the poet might be. On occasion, in fact, the poet actually *becomes* the dome. In the early "Lines on an Autumnal Evening," under the influence of song, he changes into a flower-entangled arbor to shield his love from noon-tide's sultry beams. The same tendency is at work in "The Eolian Harp," where, in his pantheistic ecstasy he becomes identified with "the one Life within us and abroad," and where, lying on the midway slope, he becomes along with all of animated nature the lute

[42] *Biographia Literaria*, II, 221. [43] *Ibid.*, II, 224.

whereon the cosmic "intellectual breeze" plays its supernal melodies. The identification is made again at the end of "France: An Ode":

> —on that sea-cliff's verge,
> Whose pines, scarce travelled by the breeze above,
> Had made one murmur with the distant surge!
> Yes, while I stood and gazed, my temples bare,
> And shot my being through earth, sea, and air,
> Possessing all things with intensest love,
> O Liberty! my spirit felt thee there. (99–105)

Finally, in the "Hymn before Sunrise," the transfiguration is complete; addressing sovran Blanc, he says,

> Yet, like some sweet beguiling melody,
> So sweet, we know not we are listening to it,
> Thou, the meanwhile, wast blending with my Thought,
> Yea, with my Life and Life's own secret joy:
> Till the dilating Soul, enrapt, transfused,
> Into the mighty vision passing—there
> As in her natural form, swelled vast to Heaven! (17–23)

It is as if for a moment he *had* revived within him that symphony and song—the song of a mountain-king, the song of his own soul. There is a perfect blending of knowledge and delight, he passes *into* the vision, and assumes his natural form. If we remember that Cain also wanted to become "one with nature," we can begin to appreciate the ultimate crisis with which Coleridge is dealing in these poems.

On a less august level, the dome also seems to be a symbol of security and of fulfillments less than ultimate. In "To a Young Lady" (1794) there is reference to a "friendly dome," presumably the church at Ottery St. Mary. In "Monody on the Death of Chatterton," the sound of bells from distant spires and domes sounds "like a seeking Mother's anxious call, / Return poor Child! Home, weary Truant, home!" (14–15) And the various dome-like "bowers," as in *Osorio*, I, 30–45, and "The Old Man of the Alps," 27–36, much as they may resemble Kubla's exotic structure and its environs, are predominantly domestic in character. Indeed, it seems very probable, as a number of psychiatrically oriented critics have suggested,[44] that the dome was for Coleridge, if not precisely in the poem "Kubla Khan," a symbol of the breast, although on at least one occasion he explicitly distinguished between the two.[45] Douglas Angus, who departs from a diagnosis of Coleridge as the victim of an aggravated Oedipus complex with its attendant narcissism, succeeds in a very ingenious way in interpreting the whole poem on this basis, the dome as breast symbol, the river a river of milk, and of course the poem ends with the milk of Paradise.

Since "Kubla Khan," by virtue of the very richness of its imagery and its resistance to easy interpretation on other levels, especially attracts the psychiatric interpreter, some meditation on the subject seems in order. As long as the psychiatrist, in the pursuit of his peculiar ends, is using poetic images as an aid in the diagnosis of the personality of the *poet*—and even if the poet be dead psychiatrists no doubt have their legitimate purposes in diagnosing his case— only other psychiatrists have, strictly speaking, the right to object, and that on technical grounds of misdiagnosis. But there is a fairly widespread tendency among lay readers of poetry, some of them writers of criticism, to suppose that, once we have traced a given image to its source in a neurosis, we have arrived at its "meaning," and that other interpretations are superfluous if not downright misleading.[46] Practitioners of a more conventional kind of inter-

---

[44] See, for instance, Edmund Bergler, *The Writer and Psychoanalysis* (New York, 1950); and Douglas Angus, "The Theme of Love and Guilt in Coleridge's Three Major Poems," *Journal of English and Germanic Philology,* LIX (1960), pp. 655–68, who cites Bergler. From a somewhat different point of view, House makes a similar point (House, p. 118).

[45] Arriving at Lisbon on his way to Malta, he thus in part describes the scene: "still farther back some very large building, 2 towers visible to the naked Eye / Palace or Convent?—very high, just in a line with 5 or 6 breast-shaped Peaks / After this Cape Espeichal, with a grand *Dome*—shaped Mountain / &c." (*Notebooks,* Vol. II, 2021 9.127, italics in text).

[46] See, for instance, Robert Graves, *The Meaning of Dreams* (New York: Greenberg, 1925).

pretation are then likely to rise in its defense by attacking the *diagnosis,* a strategy facilitated by the fact that there is likely to be a number of conflicting diagnoses. Or they may impugn the psychiatrist's proper concern with poetry in general. And once the issue is really joined, the tones of voice tend to rise. But there must be a way to avoid this ill-joined dispute. The psychiatric interpretation of an image may be treated like any other "source," and like other sources it is of more or less interest to the reader of the poem depending upon how much of its content seems on intrinsic grounds to be operating *in* the poem.

But the situation here is perhaps especially complicated, and the handling of psychiatric "sources" of images in poems no doubt often involves some confused assumptions. For instance, the fact that my ideas and feelings about poetry, about love, about religion, have their "source," in some complex and as yet unexplained way, in the physical and emotional experiences of my infancy or in the infancy of the race, is not, in the first place, surprising. Actually, no one yet knows enough to say categorically that they have their "source" there in some simple, absolute way, but at the very least they are necessarily fleshed out, given their particular substance and color by the experiences that *I* have had. That I learn something of what I know about love in inextricable terms of the contact of my lips with my mother's breasts is an interesting fact from many points of view, but it in no way invalidates what I may know, nor can what I know be "reduced" to it.[47] Actually, only certain philosophers have supposed that "real" knowledge is only to be had in the manner of unembodied spirits. And further, it has never been a secret that, in what seems to be our "fallen" state, some of our most exalted knowledges have their roots at least entwined with experiences that from a hygienic or from a moral

[47] In 1797 or 1798, Coleridge jotted in a notebook: "all our notions husked in the phantasms of Place & Time, that still escape the finest sieve & most searching Winnow of our Reason & Abstraction.—" (*Notebooks,* Vol. I, 334   21.259).

point of view are highly undesirable. Coleridge knew a great deal about this, just as he knew that beauty often has its origin in evil— "the pearl, the beautiful ornament of the beautiful, is [the oyster's] disease." [48]

Thus, to say that the dome as breast symbol "fits the narcissistic pattern of Coleridge's personality" [49] is an interesting statement in itself, whether true or not clinically speaking, but it may or may not be of use to the reader of "Kubla Khan." As a matter of fact, it would seem (if the idea had not occurred to one for other reasons), the suggestion that the dome is a breast symbol might very well lead into highly relevant, poetically relevant, interpretations of its function in the poem. In any case, if, for other reasons, the domes in "Kubla Khan" and elsewhere seem to be operating as symbols of something like security, it is reassuring to have clinical corroboration. And in the most stubborn cases, the literary critic can always hope that the psychiatrist may be able to come to his aid by suggesting a clinically likely possibility. The problem remains, at what level the "security" is being conceived.

For the moment at least we can pass over the sacred river with very little comment. For once, virtually everything is in agreement —Coleridge's own use of rivers in other poems, the symbolic import of most of the rivers in his possible sources, the critics themselves, [50]

---

[48] *Biographia Literaria*, II, 245.

[49] Angus, "The Theme of Love and Guilt," p. 664.

[50] A recent exception is George Watson, who says categorically, "This is not the River of Life. It is the river of poetry," (p. 29) upbraiding Knight for reading the poem as an allegory of human existence instead of a poem about poetic creation. But surely it is "about" both, and the relation of one to the other. "The vast power of the river is allowed to rise," he says, "but only 'momently,' and then sinks back into silence, 'a lifeless ocean' [an unlikely reading of 'momently' if only because of all that happens in the poem between its rise and fall]." The river is "the poetic imagination which, under the old order, had been debased into a plaything and allowed its liberty only when 'girdled round.'" The passages quoted above concerning landscape should be enough to indicate that Coleridge's views of the relation between order and variety, art and nature, were not so simple as this interpretation would seem to presuppose.

and archetypal usage. The sacred river is the river of Life. No one, it seems to me, has written better and more succinctly on the subject than Humphry House:

> The bounding energy of its source makes the fertility of the plain possible: it is the sacred condition of human life. By using it rightly, by building on its bank, by diverting its water into his sinuous rills, Kubla achieves his perfect state of balanced living. It is an image of these non-human, holy, given conditions. It is not an allegorical river that would still flow across the plain if Kubla was not there. It is an imaginative statement of the abundant life of the universe, which begins and ends in a mystery touched with dread, but it is a statement of this life as the ground of the ideal human activity.[51]

There have been many interesting suggestions as to the source of the name Coleridge chose for his sacred river, from the Nile and the Alpheus [52] to the stream issuing from Wookey Hole in Somerset.[53] On all counts, the sacred river Alpheus seems the most likely origin of the name, and the poem is relevantly enriched if the associations clinging about that fabulous river in the many works where Coleridge was likely to have encountered it at least hover in the background of the reader's mind. It is more than likely that Coleridge had many of the suggested sources at least vaguely in mind, Virgil, Pausanias, Strabo, Ovid, Pindar, and others; but the most obvious one of all may have been uppermost in his mind: "Return Alpheus, the dread voice is past / That shrunk thy streams." The dread voice is at least distantly reminiscent of the ancestral voices heard from far in "Kubla Khan." Heard nearer by, they might well shrink the stream of the sacred river.

It may be, as Lowes suggests, that " 'Alpheus' has been docked of its syllabic excess, and dream-fashioned, as 'Alph,' into a quasi-equivalence with 'Nile.' " [54] Or, as Beer would have it, that the association is with the letter Alph in the Amharic dialect of Ethi-

---

[51] *Coleridge*, p. 121.   [52] Lowes, pp. 393 ff.

[53] Wylie Sypher, "Coleridge's Somerset: A Byway to Xanadu," *Philological Quarterly*, XVIII (1939), 353.

[54] *Road to Xanadu*, p. 396.

opic, regarded as a prototype of the Hebrew Aleph and the Greek Alpha,[55] all beginnings, origins. But the possibility must not be overlooked that, quite simply, Alpheus had too many syllables for the meter, just as Xamdu, Xaindu, and Xandu had too few. Like most poems, "Kubla Khan" is certainly indeterminably complex both in origin and import, but it must be remembered that the manner of construction of poems is not ordinarily similar to the manner of construction of Double-Crostics.

Consideration of the caverns measureless to man and of the sunless sea may be postponed until they recur later in the poem. In a way, the first five lines of the poem constitute a paradigm of the whole first section, lines 1–36.[56] What follows, in lines 6–36, fills in the picture in a most interesting and suitably surprising fashion. The garden proper is described in lines 6–11:

> So twice five miles of fertile ground
> With walls and towers were girdled round:
> And there were gardens bright with sinuous rills,
> Where blossomed many an incense-bearing tree;
> And here were forests ancient as the hills,
> Enfolding sunny spots of greenery.

The garden thus provides the means of extending the sheltered precinct—and the possibilities—of the dome, though still within strict limits. A dome, even a sunny pleasure-dome furnished miraculously with caves of ice, might seem to involve an almost stark simplicity. The problem, in the poem and outside poems, is to extend the possibilities of variety without losing the advantage of form. This is also, after all, the technical problem of writing a poem. And so the ground is fertile, because, as we find out later, it is watered by the sacred river, but it is precisely measured and surrounded by walls and towers (almost, one might hazard the guess, as the vital stuff of a poem is walled in by meter and rhyme). Fogle calls attention to the effective juxtaposition of the "measure-

[55] *Coleridge the Visionary*, pp. 207–8.
[56] See Breyer, "Towards the Interpretation," pp. 286–87, on this point.

less" caverns and the measured garden.[57] On his walking trips in
the mountains of England and Germany, Coleridge seems con-
stantly to have been "seeing" naturally walled gardens, paradises
to the practiced eye. Here is a typical passage, dating from 1802:

I now pass on, beyond the source of the hither Beck, to the top of the
Hill along which & up which my road had been ever winding, & see
behind me to my right a grand Seaview & the flat lands upon the Sea,
with 3 Hills, the largest of which looks like a Paradise in the wild, the
fields so sweetly shaped & so green, the smaller one is not unlike it, the
hither one is bleak / [58]

If there is still any doubt as to the character that such gardens
have in Coleridge's mind, we have only to refresh our memory of
the remarkable number of them to be found in the poems. As early
as 1789, in "Life," we find a verdant hill, with dreary steep, wood,
and meadow, and a stream symbolizing life, a "quick succession of
delight" producing ravishment and trance. And we should remember that real encinctured paradise in "Pantisocracy," with its
"fertile" land on the banks of the Susquehanna, where "dancing to
the moonlight roundelay, / The wizard Passions weave an holy
spell." In "Lines Composed while Climbing the Left Ascent of
Brockley Coomb, Somersetshire," a mountain landscape with
melody, green plots, precipices, fissures of native rock, dark green
boughs and flowering trees, as well as luxury, proud towers, and a
prospect-bounding sea, he finds an "Enchanting spot!" The opening vision in "Religious Musings" is of a landscape with vernal
mead, high grove, sea, sun, and stars, a natural garden, and it
reflects the divine order, "the supreme beauty uncreate." Of Chatterton he says in the "Monody," "On many a waste he bids trim
gardens rise." When he is for any reason disaffected, however, the

---

[57] "The Romantic Unity of 'Kubla Khan,'" p. 15. Coleridge once unaccountably said of himself, "I am no measurer" (*Notebooks*, Vol. I, 1218
2.12(b) f17ᵛ), but he must have meant that he was not an accurate measurer
or something of the sort, for his notebooks are full of measurements of all
kinds of things. He might almost be called a compulsive measurer.
[58] *Notebooks*, Vol. I, 1227   2.22 f30ᵛ.

finest scene fails to develop into a garden. In "Lines Written at Elbingrode" there is a "sovran height," "Woods crowding upon woods, hills over hills, / A surging scene and only limited / By the blue distance." There are even fir groves, bright green moss specked with sunshine, a waterfall and chattering brook. But the scene does not become a garden because there is no "finer influence from the life within." But almost always the miracle occurs, in the instances we have recorded, e.g., in "Fears in Solitude," "Hymn to the Earth," "The Picture," and "Hymn before Sunrise." And all these gardens are places of inspiration, of vision.

It should be noted that even the particular details of the garden, the sinuous rills, the incense-bearing trees, the ancient forests, and the sunny spots of greenery are not one-time inventions, are rather all but ubiquitous in the poems, and for the most part occur not in isolation but at least two or three together, always within a poetic garden. In "A Wish" (1792) the sinuous rills are in the form of a murmuring stream working its secret way through "vales irriguous," meandering until in a kind of tumult it "Embosoms in the Deep!" About midway the poetic mount in "To the Author of Poems" is a mead of mildest charm with an unceasing "rill," and other familiar accompaniments, and there are many others. The idea of the intricately diverted stream did not originate with "Kubla Khan."

Like a good many other images in "Kubla Khan," the incense-bearing trees are not at all unusual in the poetic tradition, or used in this poem in an unconventional way. We should certainly not be surprised to find flowering trees and od'rous boughs in any paradise. They occur in something like a score of Coleridge's paradises. The presence of this one nonvisual delight in the opening description of the garden may be thought of as providing the most rarified of sensual intensifications, and that there be some sensual intensification is important to the total effect. There may in addition be a slightly sacerdotal overtone in the use of "incense"-bearing trees in "Kubla Khan," not a frequent usage in Coleridge's poems. On the assumption that the poem is delicately balanced, this little weight ought to be noted. In "Hymn before Sunrise," which bears so many resemblances to "Kubla Khan," and where, since the subject is Mont Blanc, there is hardly a possibility of incense-bearing trees, Coleridge has the mount itself "rise like a cloud of incense from the Earth!"

The "sunny spots of greenery" enfolded by "forests ancient as the hills" call for some special attention. In the first place, the combination accounts for a good part of the total effect of the description. Each of the three pairs of lines (6–7, 8–9, 10–11) involves a kind of contrast: the fertile ground girdled by walls and towers, sinuous rills and incense-bearing trees, and finally, ancient forests and sunny spots of greenery. They are all in some way combinations of the free and the formed, but the last of the three is the most striking. In forests ancient as the hills, nothing could be more surprising, or more delightful, than to come upon sunny spots of greenery, and to heighten the sensation, Coleridge feels the ancient forests as "enfolding" the sunny spots of greenery. Douglas Angus points out that the words used to describe the garden are "consistently feminine: 'fertile,' 'girdled,' 'sinuous,' and 'enfolding,' " [59] and certainly these words do serve to reinforce the effect of shelter, of refuge; but if it is useful to identify the items of the description with the sexes, we must notice that both are present. Neither "walls and towers" nor "forests ancient as the hills" would seem in any ordinary symbolic lexicon to be "feminine" symbols. As the walls and towers "girdle" the fertile ground, so the ancient forests enfold the sunny spots of greenery (and the incense-bearing trees presumably stand erect beside the sinuous rills). Whether it was present to Coleridge's mind or not, such a sexual reading may lead *us* to a perception of the tensions involved in the passage. If the garden is a site and symbol of fulfillment, it is a vibrant, active kind of fulfillment.

[59] "The Theme of Love and Guilt," p. 664.

We should also be aware that Kubla was, after all, a somewhat Romantic gardener. This is not the garden of Versailles or Schönbrunn, but a combination of the natural and the contrived, and, especially in the last two lines, of the awesome and the temptingly secure. We should also notice that the ancient forests and the sunny spots are related to each other in a way analogous to the sunny pleasure-dome and caves of ice. Lowes finds the source of the particular "sunny spots" of "Kubla Khan" in Bartram,[60] and there is no reason to think that the passages he cites from the *Travels* were not in Coleridge's mind when he composed the poem. Coleridge himself, in a letter quoted by Lowes, characterizes the "divine repose" afforded by laudanum as "a spot of enchantment, a green spot of fountains, & flowers & trees in the very heart of a waste of Sands!"[61] But lest the knowledge of these two facts tend to circumscribe for us the possible reverberations of the image in "Kubla Khan," we must remind ourselves that this image, like so many others in the poem, is a perennial one with Coleridge. It begins to appear in the poems as early as 1795. In "Lines Composed while Climbing the Left Ascent of Brockley Coomb" we find "green plots o'er precipices" (along with the other familiar features noted a moment ago), and the whole scene is an "Enchanting spot!" In "Reflections on Having Left a Place of Retirement" there are really two places in question (as in "The Eolian Harp" and elsewhere). There is first the domestic garden, which is itself a "little landscape round / . . . green and woody." In fact, "It was a spot which you might aptly call / The Valley of Seclusion!" Then, on the poetic mount, "Grey clouds, . . . shadowing spot the sunny fields"—a kind of photographic negative of the image. The poetic mount of "To a Young Friend" is a "verdurous hill with many a resting place" and "nooks untrod," and the roaring dell in "This

[60] *The Road to Xanadu*, pp. 364–67.
[61] *Collected Letters*, I, 394. Letter 238, to George Coleridge [*circa* March 10, 1798].

Lime-Tree Bower" is "only speckled by the mid-day sun." And so in poem after poem there are "bright green vales," "sunny islands," sunshine spotting mossy rocks. And when Coleridge walked in the mountains, he saw these sunny spots of greenery everywhere, these "delicious green vales," sometimes even measured them, as once in Germany when he says that he "left the wood, descending—came to an exquisitely beautiful Rotund of Greenery, 170 strides in diameter." [62] Later during the same walk, on the way up to see the castle of the hill, he lay down "& looked back—there I saw again the beautiful spot of green, and woody Hills ranging over Hills—" In September of 1803 there is this note:

Wherever her eye turned, gladness came, like spots of Sunshine on green Moorland Hills, creating a new field in the Waste /—spots of sunshine seen thro' floating mists, or thinning Showers—[63]

It is easy to imagine with what delight Coleridge came upon the passage in Bartram, and how, when he sought a means of conveying the sweet free solace of laudanum he fixed upon a "green spot." Again, it would seem, we ought to look behind Bartram and laudanum.

The description of the garden proper ends on this note. It is as if the sunny spots of greenery were the very heart of what the garden meant. They provide a luminous seclusion within an already secluded spot.[64] And the many versions of the image in the poems and notebooks lead to the conclusion that it was a sacred seclusion, sacred to the poetic experience. What is to be said, then, to the readers who find in Xanadu a fallen world, and, like Beer, see the garden as an earthly paradise connected with the fall and the loss of the Skechinah,[65] basing their conclusions upon echoes of Milton,

---

[62] *Notebooks*, Vol. I, 411   3.21 f23ᵛ-f24.

[63] *Ibid.*, 1503   7.55 and n. See also, among many others, 410   3.20 ff 22–22ᵛ.

[64] What Coleridge in a very different context called a "Lacus in mare / Imperium in Imperio." (*Notebooks*, Vol. II, 2014   9.120 f 48).

[65] Beer, pp. 216–22.

Purchas, Jacob Bryant, and others? Perhaps Humphry House has
said all that need be said:

> Of course we have in "Kubla Khan" a fruit of Coleridge's Miltonising,
> . . . but because the Abassin kings and Mount Amara belong with one
> false paradise it does not follow that the Abyssinian maid and Mount
> Abora belong with another.

There is only one answer to those who want to make this a false
Paradise—that is, an appeal to the poem as a whole, its rhythmical development, its total effect as a poem of fulfillment, and to say "If you
still want to make that experience a spurious experience, do so: 'Thy
way thou canst not miss, me mine requires.' " Acceptance of the Paradise, in sympathy, is the normal response, from childhood and unsophis-
tication to criticism: to most people rejection would mean a ruinous and
purposeless wrench.[66]

After all the searching and the analysis that have gone on in
connection with these lines, it is perhaps ironical that we should
come at the end to appeal to something so "simple" as the tone of
the poem, but surely if these lines do describe an undesirable site, a
place that, properly disposed, we ought to avoid, we have to say
that Coleridge has been an extraordinarily bad rhetorician. Of
course it must be true, in a sense, that Xanadu exists in a "fallen"
world—since the ejection of Adam and Eve from Eden there has
been no other on this planet, and as the poem continues it becomes
evident that, as House maintains, this can not be either "the
earthly Paradise of Eden before the Fall or . . . the Heavenly
Paradise which is the ultimate abode of the blest." But in this sense
its location in a fallen world is something that "Kubla Khan" has
in common with all but a very few works in all of literature, and in
view of the many the echoes from Coleridge's own poetry suggesting the contrary, we should need something much more coercive
than echoes from Milton and Purchas to lead us to the conclusion
that the "fallen" character of the site constitutes its primary import.

[66] *Coleridge*, p. 120.

CHAPTER SIX

The Romantic Chasm

As we move into the second section of the poem, we see that the distinction between the "paradisal" element, the stately dome with its protected garden, and the "fallen," or simply other, aspects of the real world *within* which it lies, is made very explicitly in the poem, by means of a stanza division and a striking exclamation:

> And here were forests ancient as the hills,
> Enfolding sunny spots of greenery.
>
> But oh! that deep romantic chasm which slanted
> Down the green hill athwart a cedarn cover!

On one level, the description of the romantic chasm, with all it contains, is a further extension of the environs of the dome. First we see the garden, girdled with walls and towers, then we go further, but not much further afield. Although, as we noted earlier, it is not easy to determine the exact geographical relations involved, it is clear that the chasm is intimately related to the dome and garden—it is at least within earshot. But the exclamation serves notice that we are about to be shown a different aspect of things, and if the two aspects can be made to exist together the poem will be a success. There is perhaps not much use in trying to discuss the tone of a line, as such—agreement is too rare, even rarer than agreement on metrics, and poets do not, like composers, give us rough approximations—but I should read the opening exclamation of the second stanza in a tone of fascinated awe (if anyone knows precisely what *that* is), the "oh!" elongated, *ma non troppo*.

The word "romantic" might give us an initial hint of the

intended character of the place were it not so highly ambiguous a word, and there is no indication that Coleridge uses it in any especially precise sense. In the poems and notebooks it is associated with the "rude," the "old," the "melancholy," the "wild," [1] all seen in a favorable light. And "Romantic," as we see from what follows, does not suffice to characterize the place. It is a

> deep romantic chasm which slanted
> Down the green hill athwart a cedarn cover!
> A savage place! as holy and enchanted
> As e'er beneath a waning moon was haunted
> By a woman wailing for her demon-lover!

The words "slanted," "athwart," and "cover" already suggest a slightly sinister note, and the three following lines greatly intensify the impression. Much has been said about the contradictory character of the adjectives in this description. Lane Cooper, as we have seen, found it necessary to castigate Coleridge for the "unworthy, acquiescent admission of demoniac love within so-called 'holy' precincts." [2] Howard Parsons protests on logical grounds that "romantic," "enchanted," and "haunted," as he interprets those words, are all opposed to "holy." [3] Most modern readers will doubtless find Cooper's objection irrelevant (even if they agree with the moral precept underlying it). Parson's objection may likewise be considered irrelevant, and for a similar reason—both the immoral and the illogical may have their proper place in a poem that is itself neither (even on the assumption, not universally admitted, that poems may relevantly be said to be both).

More recent critics have been quite prepared to take the apparent

---

[1] See "To the Rev. W. J. Hort" (1795?), "To a Young Friend," (1796), "Religious Musings" (1794–96), "Lines Written at Elbingrode" (1799), and *Notebooks,* Vol. I, 411   3.21 f24, 412   3.23 f26, 1225   2.20 f25–26.

[2] "The Abyssinian Paradise in Coleridge and Milton," *Modern Philology,* III (1905–06), p. 328.

[3] "A New Interpretation of Coleridge's 'Kubla Khan,'" *Poetry Review,* XXXIV (1943), p. 113.

contradiction in stride, assuming that it is in some sense intentional, and to try to see in just what way it enriches the poem, but the accumulated results are confusing. Breyer [4] and Fogle [5] both find in the romantic chasm with its river a symbol of the supernatural—as opposed to the "natural" garden previously described. Miss Bodkin, not so recently, reads it as a description of Hades—as opposed to the paradise of the garden,[6] while Knight sees a blend of the romantic, the sacred, and the satanic, enhanced by the "mystic glamour of sex that conditions human creation." [7] Miss Mercer, reading out of Boehme, sees it as a symbol of the "great mystery of the abyss of God," the indeterminate stage between the paradise of Eden and potential rebirth.[8] And Beer, more nearly in Miss Bodkin's tone of voice than Lane Cooper's, maintains that all the images in the second stanza of the poem are "anti-types of the true paradise," though "it is also the wilderness through which man must pass if paradise is to be regained." [9] In spite of the variety of terminology and the very different reasons given for the conclusions (mostly in terms either of the common usage of the words involved or the supposed sources of the images), there seems at first to be a good deal of unanimity among these readings. So far they all observe in the passage an incursion of the supernatural, for better or for worse, and most of them agree that the chasm is in some way the origin or locus of potentiality, of creativity, either in spite of or somehow because of its sinister elements. Yet before trying to assess the state of the question, there is still another view to be considered, that of Carl Woodring, who opposes the chasm to the dome and garden as something natural opposed to something artificial, expressly minimizing the importance of the opposition

[4] "Towards the Interpretation," p. 280.
[5] "The Romantic Unity of 'Kubla Khan,' " p. 15.
[6] *Archetypal Patterns,* p. 96. [7] *The Starlit Dome,* pp. 91–92.
[8] "The Symbolism of 'Kubla Khan,' " p. 54.
[9] *Coleridge the Visionary,* pp. 242–45.

between supernatural and natural, finding both in the chasm, neither in the dome and garden.[10]

An exhaustive logical analysis of the relations among these interpretations might turn out to be at least as long as all the rest of this book, and I shall have to summarize it very briefly. That at least will be worth our while, since it would seem that the basic differences of interpretation of the poem as a whole are most clearly reflected in the positions taken concerning this second section, or, more precisely, concerning the relation of the chasm to the dome and garden. Thus in its most concise form, the problem has to do with the relation between parts one and two of the poem, whether they are diametrically opposed (and if so on what basis), or represent aspects of a continuous reality. In either case, whether they are opposites or aspects of the same whole, what are the elements either opposed or distinguished? To judge by the observations of these representative critics, the elements involved are the natural as distinguished from or opposed to the supernatural, the natural as distinguished from or opposed to the artificial, and in both cases, the good as opposed to the evil. As we have seen, these three pairs of variables have been combined in almost all of the possible ways by one critic or another. Some injustice is necessarily done to each of the critics in so drastic a summary of their positions, but each one *has* tried, as every reader must at least at one stage, to schematize, to see the issues drawn in a certain simplicity; and it may be that the range of disagreement among highly competent readers is due to the fact that the poem does not really lend itself to so distinct a partition between these two of its parts (in spite of the "But oh!").[11]

Rather than enter the dispute on a logical basis, let us again appeal to the notebooks and poems to see if they suggest limits

---

[10] "Coleridge and the Khan," pp. 363–64.

[11] Here it is well to remember *"And* that simplest Lute" is "The Eolian Harp."

within which the images in question may be operating in the poem. Our previous consideration of the dome and its garden, where the natural and the artificial, the natural and the supernatural or sacred, were seen to be combined in so interesting a way, would seem to indicate that we might expect the same amalgam here, perhaps merely with a different emphasis. Any reader of Coleridge's notebooks is aware that they are fairly teeming with chasms and ravines —Coleridge did a great deal of walking in mountainous country— and it should be useful to see how they struck him, in what tone he speaks of them. One of the most interesting may be taken as an echo of "Kubla Khan," since it was recorded during a walk in August of 1802:

when I first came, the Lake was like a mirror, & conceive what the re-flections must have been, of this huge facing rock, more than half a mile of direct perpendicular height, with deep perpendicular Ravins, from the Top two thirds down / other Ravins slanting athwart down / the whole wrinkled & torrent-worn and barely patched with Moss—and all this reflected, turned in Pillars, & a whole new-world of Images, in the water / [12]

The walk to this spot from his inn of the night before had been "exceedingly pleasing," and the expression "conceive what the reflections must have been" seems almost if not quite to correspond in tone to "But oh! that deep romantic chasm." When we learn that the ravines are "slanting athwart down," we know exactly where we are. This is all "natural" landscape, but Coleridge describes it as if it were a painting, framing it in the mirror of the lake. The next day, in a similar setting, he goes even further toward seeing into or making out of the natural landscape an artistically expressive object:

—O for wealth to *wood* these Tarns—Weeping Birches with Mountain Ash & Laburnum / with Hollies for underwood /

[12] *Notebooks,* Vol. I, 1213 2.9 f10ᵛ.

A gentle Madman that would wander still over the Mountains by the lonely Tairns (Lakes)—the like never seen since the crazy Shepherd, who having lost almost all his sheep in a long hard snow was repulsed or thought himself treated coldly by his Sweet-heart—and so went a wandering seeking his Sheep for ever / in storm & snow especially.[13]

If neither holy nor enchanted, this landscape is for Coleridge at least romantic, and haunted, and his wish for wealth to wood the tarns should make us wary of supposing he meant us to be repulsed by Kubla's "decree." This at any rate does not seem to be a landscape that would find itself in opposition of any kind to a stately pleasure-dome, if one were nearby.

Among the many earlier chasms, one described in 1799 deserves attention for its combination of beauty and terror:

Scale force— The first fall a thin broad white ribbon from a stupendous Height, uninterrupted tho' not unimpinged by, the perpendicular Rock down which it falls, or rather paralel with which there is no pool at the bottom, but a common shallow brook over small flattish pebbles— but the chasm thro' which it flows, is stupendous—so wildly wooded that the mosses & wet weeds & perilous Tree increase the ~~Hill~~ Horror of the rocks which *ledge* only enough to interrupt not stop your fall—& the Tree—O God! to think of a poor Wretch hanging with one arm from it / The lower Fall i.e. from the Brook is broader; but very low in comparison & only markworthy as combining admirably.

Before the great fall there are six falls, each higher than the other, the chasm still gradually deepening, till the great fall, of which the Heighth & Depth is sudden & out of all comparison / I never saw Trees on rock Zigzag in their Lines more beautifully—Trees white in bark & more than half patched with blackish Moss—Then the green moss upon the rocks mingled with flats & little precipices of grey Rock—& Trees again.[14]

Stupendous and wildly wooded, yet "combining admirably" with the less romantic features of the landscape, and the same chasm that inspires imaginary Horror is praised for the beauty of its Lines.

---

[13] *Ibid.*, Vol. I, 1214 2.10 f13 (italics in text).
[14] *Ibid.*, Vol. I, 540 5.118 f38 ff.

Coleridge's tendency is certainly to *fuse* the contradictories, to try
to realize "the perfect form of a harmonized chaos." [15] Two days
later he describes what seems to be a petrified version of the romantic chasm with its fountain:

Brooks in their anger—all the Gullies full & white & the Chasms now
black, now half hid by the mist, & ever and anon the waterfall in them
flashing thro' the mists. On one hill I counted 7 huge Gullies—a dark
misty thunder-murmured Scene—Remember all about the Sheep &
Larches.

7 Gullies but numberless Tapes, white tiny Streams to which the
mountains owe their colouring, in conjunction with the breaking &
frost chasms of Stone, with the Stone-cataract / the largest Stones still
at the bottom of this solid Stream—[16]

Again the familiar conjunctions, "& ever and anon the waterfall
in them flashing thro' the mists." On the same trip he makes the
point even more explicitly:

—the Woods on the right shadowy with Sunshine, and in front of me
the sloping up into Hills so playful, the playful Hills so going away in
snow-streaked savage black mountain—[17]

And in this landscape where the playful and the savage combine,
Coleridge describes one scene by making a list of its features, a list
that might almost be notes for "Kubla Khan":

1. The Cliff admirably wooded, one knob of grey Rock butting out in
the middle—
2. a Hill in a curve almost a straight line, green on the Top, but all
else black & precipitous snow-patched & snow-streaked all over.
3. The green Hill that rises off, & runs along the Lake opposite to the
Convex Semicircle.
4. A House or Outhouse, of most savage aspect—with a quite green
roof—three slender but stately Trees behind, the first at the gavel end
near me, the second at the other gavel, the third at an equal distance
close by the

[15] *Biographia Literaria*, II, 262.
[16] *Notebooks*, Vol. I, 54   5.119 f33, f32ᵛ.
[17] *Ibid.*, Vol. I, 549   5.121 f26ᵛ.

5. Stone fence, which runs in a trembling circle round a green Lawn.[18]

For good reasons Coleridge chose Xanadu as the locale of his poem, but what he saw there he had seen no further away from home than Ullswater; or "The Giants' Cave in the Banks of the Emont— 2 miles from Penrith, . . . Torquin lived here—A maiden (one of his Prisoners) escaped—leaped over a chasm, with a torrent underneath her, called the Maiden's Leap—"; [19] or Helvellyn, "its deep torrent chasmy crags bound the view, so high, so perpendicularly steep"; [20] or Scafell, where he found "the frightfullest Cove, with huge Precipice Walls," and sought a place where he might "look down into the wild *savage, savage* Head of Eskdale / Good heavens! what a climb! dropping from Precipices and at last should have been crag fast but for the chasm—" [21] There are many others in his accounts of the country he loved most. He finds them stupendous, awful, savage, he peoples them with creatures of legend or of his imagination, and he also finds them beautiful, feeling nothing strange in their being contiguous with the most delicate loveliness. Just so in the poems, as we have seen, from "Songs of the Pixies" with its "elfin-haunted grove" through the "time-haunted wells and groves" of "The Old Man of the Alps" (where there are also "sighs which chasms of icy vales outbreathe, / Sent from the dark, imprison'd floods beneath"), to the "fairy world" of Chamouni in "Hymn before Sunrise," which alternates the wildest appearances of nature with the softest and most beautiful, the Aveiron rushing from the glaciers like a giant mad with joy from a dungeon, the glacier sloping down into the valley, the river raging "ceaselessly," its streams perpetual wild torrents called forth from night and utter death.

In none of these places real or imaginary should we be surprised

---

[18] *Ibid.,* Vol. I, 549 f24.   [19] *Ibid.,* Vol. I, 560   5.55.
[20] *Ibid.,* Vol. I, 798   5½.42.
[21] *Ibid.,* Vol. I, 1218   2.12(b) ff 15ᵛ, 17 (italics in text).

to encounter a woman wailing for her demon-lover. It ought to be noted, of course, that the syntax of "Kubla Khan" does not make it quite certain that we actually encounter her as a character in the poem—she appears in a simile:

> A savage place! as holy and enchanted
> As e'er beneath a waning moon was haunted
> By woman wailing for her demon-lover!

The lines can plausibly be paraphrased in two ways, either "A place as holy and enchanted as any of the others that have, like this one, been haunted by woman wailing for her demon-lover," or "A place as holy and enchanted as any of the places that have been haunted by woman wailing for her demon-lover," with no implication that this one actually has been so haunted. Although the difference may not be important—the image exists in the poem, and the poem is neither narrative nor dramatic in form—the latter reading is the more likely one, if only because, with the possible exception of Kubla's "hearing" ancestral voices, or the speaker's "building" the dome in air with music loud and long, there is nothing in the poem that cannot on the literal narrative level be accepted as naturally possible. The "events," the phenomena, are all within the realm of the naturally possible (an instance, perhaps, of what Coleridge called "faithful adherence to the truth of nature," [22] in a surprising context); the preternatural effect derives from an "atmosphere" achieved in a quite unanalyzable way by the images and adjectives, and their juxtaposition. Coleridge attributed to Wordsworth "above all the original gift of spreading the tone, the *atmosphere,* and with it the depth and height of the ideal world around forms, incidents, and situations, of which, for the common views, custom had dimmed all lustre, had dried up the sparkle and the dewdrops." [23] He too possessed the gift, and if, in the light of all that has been said so far about Coleridge's *seeing* the more than natural in nature, we see "Kubla Khan" as, among

---

[22] *Biographia Literaria,* II, 5.   [23] *Ibid.,* I, 59.

other things, a version of quite "real" forms, incidents, and situations, as, for instance, a description of mountain scenery, then the poem constitutes a kind of ultimate extreme of what Coleridge was pleased to single out as Wordsworth's excellence, and his task in *Lyrical Ballads*. Again we see, from a different angle, that the two tasks are really the same.

But in spite of any syntactical quibbles, for most readers the woman is irrevocably *there,* wailing for her demon-lover, one of the sharpest and most telling images in the poem, in much the same way that for most readers the grove is "haunted," even haunted by a demon-lover,[24] though the word is obviously being used in the sense of "persistently visited," since it is the woman who is haunting it, not her lover—that presumably is why she wails (once you discover they are demons, they hardly ever come back). And she must be there in the lines to convey to us something about the character of the place. She is immediately associated with the romantic chasm, but if we have been right about the continuity of the first part of the poem, the whole (lines 1–36), including the dome, the garden, the chasm, and the river, constitutes one "place," and that place is the real world as seen in the "dream" of the speaker, the world as *he* lives in it, or would like to live in it. But it is very far from being the real world as it is seen and lived in by the ordinary mortal—it is both more beautiful and more terrible—and an ordinary mortal might hesitate or be unable to follow a lover into it, especially if the way in led through the savage chasm, and so might be left wailing on the slope of the green hill. And what more natural than that to her such a lover seem, nay be, a "demon"-lover. The reading has the *a priori* advantage of economy, of reducing the number of personages, and I think we shall see in the sequel that it reveals some significant symmetries within the poem. To readers who have remarked the series of women wailing for their lovers in the other poems, this reading should seem less

---

[24] See, for instance, Parsons, "A New Interpretation," p. 113.

gratuitous than it might to others. There are a great many of these
women, as we have seen, but a few among them are especially
instructive.

"The Dark Ladié," was written roughly in the same period as
"Kubla Khan," and linked by Coleridge, it is to be recalled, with
"Cain," "The Ancient Mariner," and "Christabel," [25] all poems
that involve the difficulties of "seers," a genus that for Coleridge
surely includes the poet, in their relations with ordinary mortals.
The Ladié here is shown in the process of discovering the demonic
character of her lover. He promises to lead her to the stateliest castle
in the land, but they must go through the *dark*. Whatever this
means to us, in her it induced a reaction of hysterical fear. The
fragment fails to inform us of the reasons for the lover's unexpected
requirement, but it is easy to see from the Ladié's closing description of what she *had* expected that the opposition is between the
conventional or normal and something that to her is outlandish
or mysterious, sinister.

The fragment "Cain," in addition to belonging with the group
of poems mentioned above, is clearly (or perhaps not quite
"clearly") connected with the poetic process by Cain's statement
in the alternative version that he is being punished by God "because
he neglected to make proper use of his senses," and we know that
this somehow involves his misrelations with Nature and God.
Each of these poems may be seen as treating the poet's status and
potentialities from a different point of view, with a different emphasis, and in Cain we seem to have him very nearly at his worst.
In the alternative version, if not a demon himself, Cain is literally
demon-beset. And we must remember that this is the version said
to have been planned as a narrative told by Cain to his wife. As the
story exists, the wife appears in a landscape a good deal more savage
than the chasm of "Kubla Khan," but similar to it in a number of
details. She is screaming, and surrounded by tigers, "determined to
follow her husband." Although Cain tells her his story, we are left

[25] *Biographia Literaria*, II, 6.

in doubt as to whether they are ultimately reunited. Here, even more than in "Kubla Khan," our sympathy goes out to the woman wailing—we know that her lover is the father of her legitimate children, and he is the most famous of criminals. In other contexts, the woman's role in the drama is subjected to closer scrutiny, and she turns out to be a not wholly innocent victim.

"Christabel," another poem of the same group, is perhaps the best example. In fact, it can be read as a poem whose heroine is the woman wailing for her demon-lover (although to read it only in that way would obviously be to miss a great deal in it). Although Christabel places herself in a situation suspiciously reminiscent of the romantic chasm (the very moon is "small and dull"), she is discovered innocently enough praying for her betrothéd knight, just as the Dark Ladié waits in a similar place for a lover she supposes to be unexceptionable. Like the Dark Ladié, but in an aggravated form, what Christabel finds is a demon, an exceedingly beautiful demon. And as the poem progresses, we see—it would be too much to say that we understand—how although she is innocent, she shares the responsibility borne by all good subjects of seduction. Although Christabel remains the focus of sympathy in the poem, there is more than a suggestion of compassion for Geraldine, and we remember the confusions of identity.

"The Triumph of Loyalty" affords still another perspective: we see a version of the demon-lover on his reluctant way to meet the woman wailing for him. He tells in considerable detail of their original encounter, and in doing so provides an insight into the ecstatic abysses that so attract and repel these women. His account deserves another reading at this point. He says he found in the original experience a "Joy above the name of Pleasure,"

> Deep self-possession, an intense Repose.[26]
> No other than as Eastern Sages feign,

---

[26] Cf., in "A Stranger Minstrel," "That repose divine
When the soul centred in the heart's recess
Hath quaffed its fill of loveliness. . . ."   (2–4)

> The God, who floats upon a Lotos Leaf,
> Dreams for a thousand ages, then awaking,
> Creates a world, and smiling at the bubble,
> Relapses into bliss.

Here the identification is with a greater than Kubla, and as in
"Kubla Khan," the dream is to result in creation, the creation of a
"world." Even this, at the extreme, might be tolerable to a lover, in
spite of the self-possession, but that he should smile at the "bubble"
surely makes a demon of him. And Oropeza reacts appropriately,
though the reaction is no guarantee that she will not subsequently
go wailing in that "gloomiest covert of the garden." She comes very
near it within the scene:

> Ah! was that bliss
> Fear'd as an alien, and too vast for man?
> For suddenly, intolerant of its silence,
> Did Oropeza, starting grasp my forehead.
> I caught her arms; the veins were swelling on them.
> Thro' the dark Bower she sent a hollow voice;—
> 'Oh! what if all betray me? what if thou?'

The correspondence between these two passages and the first two
sections of "Kubla Khan" is startling. Were it not for considerations of meter, one might expect the second passage to begin *"But
ah!"* If the overtones from these poems are to be heard in "Kubla
Khan," then the presence of the woman wailing for her demon-
lover is surely indispensable if the reader is to grasp the full effect
of the natural-supernatural-artificial world that is being described.
We may suppose that the slopes of Xanadu are thick with women
wailing. On the most literal level, the woman provides, along with
the ancestral voices and the weavers of circles in the last section, a
touchstone from the ordinary world, enabling us to gauge the distances involved.

In this perspective it is possible to agree with Beer [27] that this is woman after the fall, and that the duality of her feelings—wailing, yet wailing "for"—corresponds to the duality of the demon, seraph-saraph, a fallen angel, although the mythological machinery still seems inappropriate. When he goes on to specify that the angel in question is an angel of heat rather than light, but still the woman's only connection with the lost Shekinah, it is still possible to see how such a superstructure might be erected over the more immediate sense, if one began with certain presuppositions. It is not so easy, on the other hand, to see how we could make of the demon-lover a purveyor of lust rather than love (if the passages from other poems are relevant at all, this is the kind of place where they may serve as a check). Readers approaching the poem with biographical or psychological sources in mind seem at least in this connection to be closer to the text, more plausible, than those like Beer who approach it on the basis of examination of literary sources. When Robert Graves says that the image of the woman wailing for her demon-lover "refers to the former strong passion that Coleridge had for his wife who was now bitterly reproaching him for his supposed unfaithfulness," [28] it seems very likely that he is right, if we modify the statement with the kind of nuances that do not come naturally to Graves. "The Triumph of Loyalty," for instance, seems to contain quite transparent references to Coleridge's relationship with Sara, and we have just seen how close it is to "Kubla Khan" in imagery. And nothing is more likely than that Coleridge should have learned much of what he knew about the relation of love and poetry in the context of his experience with his wife. Whether she did reproach him with unfaithfulness, in the ordinary sense of the term, is hardly what is in question here. What Sara understood about the kind of "unfaithfulness" of which he was surely guilty, the kind that might make him seem a demon-lover, we can never know, but it is likely that any woman Coleridge

[27] *Coleridge the Visionary*, pp. 234–35.   [28] Graves, p. 157.

loved would finally utter the same reproach, feel deserted in the same way, however much or little she understood what was happening. It is interesting that both Beer and Graves seem to suppose that demon-lovers are to be associated with lust as opposed to love. It is a strange supposition, and in the context of "Kubla Khan" we should recall Breyer's observation of the nonsexual quality of its images.

But the woman wailing for her demon-lover is, after all, incidental to the romantic chasm, important as she is in suggesting its significance. Above all, the romantic chasm is the site of the mighty fountain, the source of the sacred river:

> And from this chasm, with ceaseless turmoil seething,
> As if this earth in fast thick pants were breathing,
> A mighty fountain momently was forced:
> Amid whose swift half-intermitted burst
> Huge fragments vaulted like rebounding hail,
> Or chaffy grain beneath the thresher's flail:
> And mid these dancing rocks at once and ever
> It flung up momently the sacred river.
> Five miles meandering with a mazy motion
> Through wood and dale the sacred river ran,
> Then reached the caverns measureless to man,
> And sank in tumult to a lifeless ocean:

If the chasm is savage, holy, and enchanted, likely to be haunted by women wailing for their demon-lovers, it must be because it contains the mighty fountain. It is sufficiently evident why the site of the fountain should be "holy"—the fountain is the source of the "sacred" river, the river of Life, and its sinister aspect is hardly less evident. The fountain, as Angus points out,[29] is a familiar symbol of birth, and Coleridge used it as such on a number of occasions, with imagery of parturition at least equally unmistakable. In "On a Cataract from a Cavern near the Summit of a Mountain Precipice,"

[29] "The Theme of Love and Guilt," p. 664.

the holiness of the process is emphasized. The cataract is apostrophized as

> Unperishing youth!
> Thou leapest from forth
> The cell of thy hidden nativity;
> Never mortal saw
> The cradle of the strong one;
> Never mortal heard
> The gathering of his voices;
> The deep-murmured charm of the son of the rock,
> That is lisp'd evermore at his slumberless fountain.
> There's a cloud at the portal, a spray-woven veil
> At the shrine of his ceaseless renewing;

The echoes are clear—the hidden supernatural source, the murmuring voices, the ceaseless renewing—and the site is a "shrine." Further on,

> The moonshine sinks down as in slumber,
> That the son of the rock, that the nurseling of heaven
> May be born in a holy twilight!

These lines may suggest as good a reason why the moon is waning over the romantic chasm as the proposal that it is symbolic of the loss of mother-love,[30] or indicates that "redemptive forces of nature are not in the ascendant." [31]

In "Hymn to the Earth," we have a detailed account of conception preceding parturition:

Say, mysterious Earth! O say, great mother and goddess,
Was it not well with thee then, when first thy lap was ungirdled,
Thy lap to the genial Heaven, the day that he wooed thee and won thee!
Fair was thy blush, the fairest and first of the blushes of morning!
Deep was the shudder, O Earth! the throe of thy self-retention:
Inly thou strovest to flee, and didst seek thyself at thy centre!

---

[30] *Ibid.*, p. 665.   [31] Beer, p. 233.

Mightier far was the joy of thy sudden resilience; and forthwith
Myriad myriads of lives teemed forth from the mighty embracement.

The wonder and the terror of this encounter between Heaven and
Earth, between the supernatural and the natural, are older than
Leda and Danae, and the "shudder" is as real as the "sudden
resilience." The torrents in the "Hymn before Sunrise," "rave
ceaselessly," and Mont Blanc is said to be "parent of perpetual
streams," but then comes the question:

> And you, ye five wild torrents fiercely glad!
> Who called you forth from night and utter death,
> From dark and icy caverns called you forth,
> Down those precipitous, black, jaggéd rocks,
> Forever shattered and the same for ever?
> Who gave you your invulnerable life,
> Your strength, your speed, your fury, and your joy,
> Unceasing thunder and the eternal foam?
> And who commanded (and silence came),
> Here let the billows stiffen, and have rest?

There is the whole course of the sacred river, from nothing to
nothing, through fury and joy.

Even fountains not explicitly associated with birth in Coleridge's
poems are likely to present this ambiguous character, the ambiguity essential to all *created* life. In "Religious Musings," contemplant spirits hover over "the immeasurable fount / Ebullient with
creative Deity" (the fountain as well as the caverns at the end is
immeasurable), but Property is a "twy-streaming fount, / Whence
Vice and Virtue flow, honey and gall." In "The Old Man of the
Alps" it is beside a torrent and beneath a wood that the maiden
seemed to see her fancies "realis'd in air," "within some sunny
dell," but after the catastrophe,

> If to her spirit any sound was dear,
> 'Twas the deep moan that spoke the tempest near;
> Or sighs which chasms of icy vales outbreathe,
> Sent from the dark, imprison'd floods beneath.

The "Two Founts" of the poem of that name are founts of Suffering and Cheer. And in the fragment "Mahomet," because Christians have veiled the Gospel of Jesus, Heaven, "Choosing good from iniquity rather than evil from goodness," looses hordes of destruction:

> the people with mad shouts
> Thundering now, and now with saddest ululation
> Flew, as over the channel of rock-stone the ruinous river
> Shatters its waters abreast, and in mazy uproar bewilder'd,
> Rushes dividuous all—all rushing impetuous onward.

The fury without the joy. Before reaching the caverns measureless to man, life can turn to nothingness. In short, the fountain is the very locus of the origin of life, that greatest and most utterly ambiguous of blessings, and so it is not strange to say that a "place" where one comes face to face with the mystery of creation, and the consequently mysterious ambiguity of created life, is savage, holy, and enchanted. In a natural reaction it is savage; in religious or superstitious reaction it is holy or enchanted.

It is in this neighborhood that Kubla places his dome and garden, not through choice, either wise or impercipient,[32] but because there is quite simply nowhere else to place it—were it only because there is no other source of water to irrigate his garden. The actual violence of the fountain is described, as Woodring points out,[33] in "natural" terms:

> Huge fragments vaulted like rebounding hail,
> Or chaffy grain beneath the thresher's flail:

But in keeping with the duality of the whole scene, one of these is a destructive image, the other productive, the former wholly

---

[32] Cf. Woodring, "Coleridge and the Khan," p. 364. He feels that Kubla's "choice of location, above the chasm, tumult, and prophecies of war, was as impercipient as the Mariner's shooting of the Albatross."

[33] *Ibid.,* p. 363.

"natural," the latter an instance of cooperation between nature and man; and the description has an interesting counterpart in the first published version of the poem later called "The Destiny of Nations." The Being of higher class than Man whose noble province was "by disposal of apt circumstance / To rear up kingdoms,"

> from the invisible World
> Burst on the MAIDEN's eye, impregning Air
> With Voices and strange Shapes, illusions apt
> Shadowy of Truth. And first a landscape rose
> More wild and waste and desolate, than where
> The white bear drifting on a field of ice
> Howls to her sunder'd cubs with piteous rage
> And savage agony. Mid the drear scene
> A craggy mass uprear'd its misty brow,
> Untouch'd by breath of Spring, unwont to know
> Red Summer's influence, or the cheerful face
> Of Autumn; yet its fragments many and huge
> Astounded ocean with the dreadful dance
> Of whirlpools numberless, absorbing oft
> The blameless fisher at his perilous toil.[34]

Joan is seeing a vision of the Romantic chasm, out of which, with her cooperation, a kingdom is to rise. And so we come upon the other aspect of the fountain. It is both the source and the type of human "creation." As we might expect, there is in the poems a series of fountains symbolic of the poetic act, including the poetic founts of legend, Castalie and Hippocrene. The reference to the latter strikes familiar notes:

> For not a hidden path, that to the shades
> Of the beloved Parnassian forest leads,
> Lurked undiscovered by him; not a *rill*
> There issues from the fount of Hippocrene,
> But he had traced it upward to its source,
> Through *open glade, dark glen, and secret dell,*

[34] *Poems*, I, p. 136 n. Cf. also *Notebooks*, Vol. I, 272 G.269, items [u] and [x], and 4.12   3.23 ff25-25ᵛ.

> Knew the gay wild flowers on its banks, and called
> Its med'cinable herbs. Yea, oft alone
> Piercing the long-neglected *holy cave,*
> The haunt obscure of old Philosophy,

(which, as we know from "The Garden of Boccaccio," "bore no other name than Poesy")

> He bade with lifted torch its *starry walls*
> *Sparkle,* as erst they sparkled to the flame
> Of *odorous* lamps tended by Saint and Sage.[35]

Late in life he remembered this fountain in a very different mood. "All Nature seems at work," he says,

> And I the while, the sole unbusy thing,
> Nor honey make, nor pair, nor build, nor sing.
>
> Yet well I ken the banks where amaranths blow,
> Have traced the fount whence streams of nectar flow.
> Bloom, O ye amaranths! bloom for whom ye may,
> For me ye bloom not! Glide, rich streams, away! [36]

For their full effect, these lines ought to be read along with one of the earliest descriptions of the poetic mount, with its "clear delicious fount":

> Thus rudely vers'd in allegoric lore,
> The Hill of Knowledge I essayed to trace;
> That verdurous hill with many a resting-place,
> And many a stream, whose warbling waters pour
> To glad, and fertilise the subject plains;
> That hill, with secret springs, and nooks untrod,
> And many a fancy-blest and holy holy sod.
> Where Inspiration, his diviner strains
> Low-murmuring lay; and starting from the rock's
> Stiff evergreens (whose spreading foliage mocks
> Want's barren soil, and the bleak frosts of age,

---

[35] "A Tombless Epitaph," *Poems,* I, 413.
[36] "Work without Hope," *Ibid.,* p. 447.

And Bigotry's mad fire-invoking rage!)
O meek retiring spirit! we will climb,
Cheering and cheered, this lovely hill sublime; [37]

But even at twenty-three he was able to warn Joseph Cottle that the stream circling the base of the poetic mount could also be a stream "which rolls in lazy flow / Its coal-black waters from Oblivion's fount." Higher up the mount, it becomes an "unceasing rill" that "Murmurs sweet undersong 'mid Jasmin bowers." [38] The fountain within, from which flow the passion and the life of poetic creation,[39] is, like the prototype, both sacred and dangerous.

And so the romantic chasm is both ominous and attractive, ominous because it seems incomprehensible and uncontrollable, attractive because its mysterious vitality is just what must be comprehended and controlled in some measure if the imaginative paradise is to be real, to be fertile, to be more than an empty shadow. The continuity between the garden and the chasm, as well as the contrast, is essential to the unity and the meaning of the poem. We have to do with an opposition within a single realm, the realm of this world as it now exists, characterized by an almost inextricable combination of the natural and the supernatural, of evil and good —it is on the path from the natural to the supernatural that good and evil lie in wait; and we have to do in this poem with man's adjustment to these antinomies through a poetic act that is a mysterious amalgam of the natural and the "artificial," of that which is "given," and that for which man is himself somehow immediately responsible—Coleridge never ended the debate with himself on the proportions involved, as indeed who has? Certainly Coleridge does, as Woodring suggests, "crusade for the divinity of Nature," [40] a nature with the supernatural as it were imbedded in it. It is up to

[37] "To a Young Friend," *Ibid.*, pp. 156–57.
[38] "To the Author of Poems," *Ibid.*, p. 103.
[39] "Dejection: An Ode," *Ibid.*, p. 365.
[40] "Coleridge and the Khan," p. 363.

the poet, through responses, through correspondences, to find the supernatural in nature, to experience it in an act of creation (and usually to make it manifest in poems). And this is artifice.

But at the same time that nature is the repository of the good and the beautiful, evil too is somehow *in* nature, or at least is seen to spring from our incomplete or misguided relations with nature, sometimes even when our intentions are at their best. As Coleridge tells us in the essay "On Poesy and Art," the beauty in nature, that in nature which the poet must imitate, is not "connected with the ideas of the good, or the fit, or the useful." It can inspire pleasure "without, and aloof from, and even contrarily to, interest." [41] So inextricable is the evil that it becomes involved in our very attempts to reach the absolute in nature. The closer we get, the more perilous the ground. Multiple texts could be cited from both Wordsworth and Coleridge in which the reach for the absolute in or behind nature is attended by fear and peril, even by a sense of sin. Though so many volumes have been written on the origin of evil, it is perhaps in the end not a proper subject for "metaphysical Solution." [42] In "Kubla Khan," at any rate, no "solution" is suggested—the images in all their richness are placed before us. The existence of the poem is, if one likes, a solution, a demonstration. Kubla's decree, like the decree of every "creator," is at the same time the most perilously presumptuous of all acts, and the act to which man is ineluctably called if he is to realize his highest possibility as a man.

In lines 25 to 36, we have a kind of recapitulation of the whole preceding scene, with at least two important details added, the ancestral voices and the caves of ice. Again there is room for doubt

---

[41] *Biographia Literaria*, II, 257.

[42] In *Aids to Reflections* (7th ed., London, Moxon, 1854, pp. 114-15), Coleridge explains that he refrains from treating the Trinity or "the still profounder mystery of the origin of moral Evil" because "these doctrines are not, in strictness, subjects of reflection, in the proper sense of this word . . ." and because he finds people in general little troubled about them.

as to the exact geographical relations involved, but this is, after all, an imaginary landscape, the landscape of a dream, in short, a symbolic landscape, and we may expect it to be more or less severely schematized:

> Five miles meandering with a mazy motion
> Through wood and dale the sacred river ran,
> Then reached the caverns measureless to man,
> And sank in tumult to a lifeless ocean:
> And 'mid this tumult Kubla heard from far
> Ancestral voices prophesying war!
>   The shadow of the dome of pleasure
>   Floated midway on the waves;
>   Where was heard the mingled measure
>   From the fountain and the caves.
> It was a miracle of rare device,
> A sunny pleasure-dome with caves of ice!

One simple solution was suggested earlier: the enclosure is five miles by five miles, the fountain on one side, the caverns on the other, and in its mazy motion the river covers the five-mile distance from one side to the other. Various objections arise (e.g., does the sacred river of life flow *only* through Kubla's garden? One possible implication is that *only* through art is the life-force really productive), but there is no atlas to which one can appeal. The implication that the sinuous rills of the garden are not tributaries of the sacred river, to be found, for instance, in Beer's statement that the river, "which should be a quiet steady welling up becomes an untamable force, a spirit of ruin, rising up in destruction, proceeding in tumult, and finally sinking to the lifeless ocean," [43] would seem to be virtually ruled out by the repetition of "five miles." It may very well be that the river is conceived to run *beside* the garden, with some of its water diverted into the sinuous rills, but it would at the very least be uneconomic for Kubla not to take advantage of it for irrigation. The sacred river is, to be sure, "unencompassable,"

[43] *Coleridge the Visionary*, p. 237.

not to be "confined" by walls and towers,[44] but that does not mean that it is impossible, however presumptuous it may be, to build on its banks and draw sustenance from it.[45]

Line 25 itself gives some difficulty, and seems to serve everyone's purpose. Burke associates the word "mazy" with "the malign principle in drug addiction," [46] and cites as precedent a passage in "Religious Musings," where a Fury bids "her serpent hair in mazy surge" lick a young despot's face. Knight finds in the image a symbol of "uncertain and blind progress," of the "spiritual complexities of human life," [47] while Breyer sees an indication of nature in the domesticated state.[48] As in the case of "pleasure," appeal to the concordance is in vain, since Coleridge uses the word with a wide variety of connotations, both as adjective and as noun. In 1790 it is interchangeable with "inebriate." [49] In 1828 it is used in what is obviously a favorable sense in describing Ovid's and Boccaccio's "mazy tales." [50] In between, there are among others the "maze of youth" and of manhood,[51] fancy's "maze and clue," [52] a garden maze on Parnassus, and a pathway in mazes leading to a temple of ecstasy.[53] And so we come back to the line:

> Five miles meandering with a mazy motion
> Through wood and dale the sacred river ran,

Whatever unfavorable connotations mazes may have, "meandering" is a pleasant word, connoting leisure and freedom from compulsion, and one effect of the line derives from its contrast with

---

[44] Woodring, "Coleridge and the Khan," pp. 368, 363.

[45] See House, as quoted above, p. 212.

[46] *The Philosophy of Literary Form* (Louisiana State University Press, 1941), p. 97.

[47] *The Starlit Dome*, p. 92.   [48] "Towards the Interpretation," p. 280.

[49] "The Progress of Vice," line 15 and n., *Poems*, p. 12.

[50] "Alice du Clos," line 37, *Poems*, p. 470; "The Garden of Boccaccio," line 102, p. 481.

[51] "Translation," line 2, *ibid.*, p. 66, and "Sonnet," 1.12, *ibid.*, p. 153.

[52] "On Donne's Poetry," line 3, *ibid.*, p. 433.

[53] "The Reproof and Reply," line 51, *ibid.*, p. 442, and "Catullian Hendecasyllables," line 9, *ibid.*, p. 307.

the turbulence (both in idea and sound) of the fountain and the caverns. This is the area, too, presumably, where one hears the mingled measure. The "m" alliteration is all but obtrusive, and though one may like to go no further in such a direction, "m" alliteration *is* soft, as compared with "t" alliteration for instance. If the alliteration in the line is the result of deliberate effort, it must be noted that no comparable effort was made anywhere else in the poem, in which alliteration accounts for a good deal of the effect. The effect here seems appropriate to an oasis between tumult and tumult, and we ought to remember in this connection the early translation called "A Wish":

> Lo! through the dusky silence of the groves,
> Thro' vales irriguous, and thro' green retreats,
> With languid murmur creeps the placid stream
> And works its secret way.
>
> Awhile meand'ring round its native fields
> It rolls the playful wave and winds its flight:
> Then downward flowing with awaken'd speed
> Embosoms in the Deep!
>
> Thus thro' its silent tenor may my Life
> Smooth its meek stream by sordid wealth unclogg'd,
> Alike unconscious of forensic storms,
> And Glory's blood-stain'd palm! (1–12)

There is a good possibility that the memory of Jesus Wood contributed something to the dream of Xanadu. At any rate it is clear that a river meandering with a mazy motion is not necessarily a sinister image in Coleridge's mind. In the context of "Kubla Khan" it seems to be the opposite.

Whether the caverns measureless to man had their origin in Cheddar Gorge,[54] in a scene near Bristol,[55] or in some undeter-

[54] See Wylie Sypher, "Coleridge's Somerset," p. 353.
[55] E. H. W. Meyerstein, "The Completeness of 'Kubla Khan,'" *Times Literary Supplement,* October 30, 1937, p. 803.

minable place in Coleridge's reading,[56] there has been little disagreement as to their import in the poem. They are in inverse
correspondence with the mighty fountain, their tumult matching
its turmoil. As the river of life is "called forth from night and utter
death," [57] so it sinks in tumult to a lifeless ocean. The dissolution of
life is as mysterious and as terrifying as its coming to be. At an inef-
fable command, the silence comes.[58] Like the fountain as a symbol
of birth, the sea as a symbol of death, of eternal nothingness, is not
an unusual one, but its near ubiquity in Coleridge's poetry must
be due in part to the geographical situation in which he found
himself, for he was, after all, an islander—beyond the shores of
England, the outer darkness. In all his walks, in the mountains,
among the lakes, even when it could not actually be seen, the sea
was a brooding presence beyond. As early as 1789, in "Life," he
has life ending in an "infinite expanse," and in "A Wish," quoted
just above, the stream of life "Embosoms in the Deep." In "Lines
Composed while Climbing the Left Ascent of Brockley Coomb,"
the description of a mountain landscape with many features reminiscent of "Kubla Khan" ends with the "prospect-bounding
sea!" "The distant sea" in "The Eolian Harp" "tells us of silence,"
although it seems to be a sea somehow *this* side of the measureless
caverns. The same thing is true of the sea's faint murmur in "Reflections on Having Left a Place of Retirement," but again the final
item in the landscape seen from the summit of the poetic mount
is the "shoreless Ocean." In the "Monody on the Death of Chatterton," at the end of a description of a scene of poetic inspiration
the poet "upon some rough rock's fearful brow / Would pause
abrupt—and gaze upon the waves below." There is no sea in the
landscape described in "To a Young Friend," but at the end of
the description of the poetic mount we find "the glad landscape
round / Wide and more wide, increasing without bound," and it
is precisely the "boundlessness" of the sea image that operates most

---

[56] See Lowes, pp. 387–93.   [57] "Hymn before Sunrise," line 40.
[58] *Ibid.*, line 47.

powerfully in "Kubla Khan," in contrast to the bounds of the privileged precinct of Kubla's garden. Sometimes the sea is explicitly associated with eternity, as in "France: An Ode": "Ye Ocean-Waves! that, wheresoe'er ye roll, / Yield homage only to eternal laws." In the last stanza of the poem the pines "made one murmur with the distant surge"—always the sea is the final item. In "Fears in Solitude," leaving a "surrounded nook," he finds himself on the brow of a hill and sees "this burst of prospect, here the shadowy main, / Dim-tinted. . . . " Again in "The Snowdrop," although there is no literal sea, "A sea-like sound the branches breathe" in a version of the poetic mount featuring symbols of both immortality (the phoenix) and oblivion (cypresses, Lethe). And so, although the symbolism is conventional, it is important to realize that for Coleridge this sunless sea, this lifeless ocean, was almost obsessive. In a poem devoted to life and art, it is the image of death.

Nothing could be more appropriate than that 'mid this tumult Kubla should hear from far "Ancestral voices prophesying war." Again, the symbolism is not bizarre, war as the type of threats to life, to life at its best as realized through the visions of the poet. And, as so often happens, House would seem to have stated the case most succinctly:

This is essential to the full unity of the conception: the Paradise contains knowledge of the threat of its own destruction. It is not held as a permanent gift; the ideal life is always open to forces of evil; it must not only be created by man for himself, but also defended by him. It is not of the essence of this paradise that it must be lost; but there is a risk that it may be lost.[59]

---

[59] *Coleridge*, pp. 120–21. Cf. Fogle ("The Romantic Unity of 'Kubla Khan,'" p. 16), who seems to feel that the destruction of the garden is inevitable; and Woodring ("Coleridge and the Khan," p. 363), who argues on the basis of past tenses used in referring to it that the dome has already been destroyed (but might we not use the same tenses in saying "In Agra did Shah Jehan the Taj Mahal decree . . ."?).

Other readings of the lines, e.g., those of Fogle, Beer,[60] and Wood-ring, seem based upon the assumption that these voices prophesy-ing war are peculiar to this particular landscape, that Kubla's estab-lishment is somehow uniquely vowed to destruction. But perusal of the poems reveals that almost all of the poetic mountains, the privileged retreats, are threatened in the same way, though the threat be not so beautifully expressed. As early as 1792, besides "A Wish," there is the "Ode," in which a nearly complete version of the "Kubla Khan" setting is threatened by the voice of war, which in turn is stilled by the fragrant whisper of this lilied vale and by Reason's "holy Spell." In "Religious Musings," a vision of divine order is interrupted by voices prophesying war, in the person of Lord Abingdon, a self-appointed ancestral voice in Parliament. "The world's vain turmoil" may be "left" on the poetic mount of "To a Young Friend," but it still hovers in the distance, and later, as noises of the world, supplies a "melancholy *theme*." Both "France: An Ode" and "Fears in Solitude" furnish detailed treat-ments of the threat of war, and, as in "Kubla Khan," the threat is definitely from without, though weaknesses in the internal struc-ture of the paradise that is England are freely admitted. In "De-jection," on the other hand, the voices are no longer heard from far—they have invaded the possible garden itself and are indistin-guishable from the wind of inspiration. Here, not in "Kubla Khan," the destruction is inevitable, but the threat is universal. Take the ancestral voices out of "Kubla Khan," and the dome becomes a bubble.

In the first published version of "Kubla Khan," that of 1816, lines 31–36 were printed as a separate section, and basing his argu-ment in part on this fact Beer maintains that "the dome of pleasure of line 31 is not the pleasure-dome which Kubla decreed, 'a temple built by Omnipotence in its own honor'—and thus liable to perish. It is the 'miracle' in which two seemingly irreconcilable principles

[60] *Coleridge the Visionary*, p. 241.

are held together: heat and ice." [61] But there is also the fact that the poem was printed as we now have it, with no division between lines 30 and 31, in three subsequent editions during Coleridge's lifetime, and it would seem that we ought to take his second, third, and fourth thoughts as conclusive. It is not hard to imagine why at one moment Coleridge may have thought it best to set this section off, for there *is* a kind of natural logical division: having just surveyed the whole landscape from the mighty fountain to the lifeless ocean, the account now returns to its center, and the division might help a reader to be more quickly aware of this strategy. But if this alteration in the paragraphing of the poem was indeed deliberate, what is far from certain, we must suppose that Coleridge decided the unity of the whole to be more important. It is also true, of course, that we learn here for the first time that the dome is "sunny" as well as "stately," and that there are caves of ice; but there is nothing to prevent the same dome's being both stately and sunny; and to have left the caves of ice to the end of the description, in proximity with the dome as "sunny," provides a fine stroke of surprise—whether Coleridge deliberately planned it that way or not.

Most readers have agreed, whatever their view of the poem as a whole, that this little section is somehow the "center" of the poem. It certainly does, as we have noted before, recapitulate what precedes it, and in a way it prepares for what follows. No one familiar with Coleridge's poems and notebooks can be surprised that

> The shadow of the dome of pleasure
> Floated midway on the waves;

for not only are the two major images of the poem, the dome and the river, thus united, but one of Coleridge's favorite phenomena is thus included. In describing landscapes he sometimes gives the impression that they are not really complete in beauty unless there

[61] *Coleridge the Visionary*, p. 246.

is a reflection in water. (In going over his description of a scene in Germany, a description ending "in nature all in harmony," he adds "O why no water?—") [62] A description already quoted gives some idea of what reflections meant to him, and his reaction is not, I think, an uncommon one:

> when I first came, the Lake was like a Mirror, & conceive what the reflections must have been, of this huge facing of rock, more than half a mile of direct <perpendicular> height, with deep perpendicular Ravins, from the Top two thirds down / other Ravins slanting athwart down them / the whole wrinkled & torrent-worn and barely patched with Moss—and all this reflected, turned in Pillars, & a whole new-world of Images, in the water / [63]

A whole new-world of Images in the water—the reflection makes a picture, makes art out of it, as if nature were imitating herself, doing the poet's work for him. Another time, Coleridge exclaims, when a pool "reflected all the scene in a Mirror—Gracious God /" [64] There is something breathtaking, as it were miraculous, about it. There are many such reflections in the poems. To recall only a few, in the "Songs of the Pixies" the shadow of the tall tree whose roots form the cave-dome sleeps upon the breast of the river.[65] In the "Monody" we find a star-beam glittering on Avon's slow sequestered tide, and it is said of the isle that appears in Joan's vision in "The Destiny of Nations" that "Its high, o'er-hanging, white, broad-breasted cliffs," were "Glassed on the subject ocean." Even in the poems, in at least two instances, Coleridge pauses to exclaim. Once in "This Lime-Tree Bower,"

> my friends
> Behold the dark green file of long lank weeds,
> That all at once (a most fantastic sight!)

---

[62] *Notebooks,* Vol. I, 533   5.125 f29ᵛ.
[63] *Ibid.,* Vol. I, 1213   2.9 f10ᵛ.   [64] *Ibid.,* Vol. I, 1495   7.44 f68.
[65] One cannot fail to regret that Douglas Angus did not analyze *this* passage for us. The possible reverberations are fascinating to think upon.

>   Still nod and drip beneath the dripping edge
>   Of the blue clay-stone.

In *Osorio* (II, 150 ff.), "There's a lake in the midst" of Albert's retreat,

>   And round its banks tall wood, that branches over
>   And makes a kind of faery forest grow
>   Down in the water. At the further end
>   A puny cataract falls on the lake;
>   And there (a curious sight) you see its shadow
>   For ever curling, like a wreath of smoke,
>   Up through the foliage of those faery trees.

If in "Kubla Khan" we take the dome to be a work of art and the river to be the river of Life, of nature, then the sight is more than curious or fantastic: the dome, first *seen* "out of" nature as it were, is now reflected back into it. If Coleridge never succeeded in writing a treatise that explained the relation of art and nature to his satisfaction, here he found an image to present it, and each reader can reflect upon it at his leisure.

As for the shadow floating "midway" on the waves, the simplest reading is that the dome was halfway between the fountain and the caverns, or caves, as Coleridge was forced to call them once for reasons of rhyme. So it is that we hear the "mingled measure" from the fountain and the caves, the mingled sound of the tumults of birth and death, creation and destruction.[66] It comes within few enough lines of the "caverns measureless" that the contrast is not lost upon us, just as on their first appearance the caverns measureless were contrasted with the five-mile limit of the garden. Measure is wrought out of the measureless, vitality brought within measure —still another image akin to that of the shadow of the dome floating upon the waves.

The final surprising paradox of this first part of the poem, the

---

[66] See Knight, p. 94, on this point.

"sunny pleasure-dome with caves of ice," has elicited a bewildering variety of interpretations. The most ingeniously extrapolated is perhaps that of Beer, who believes that "the dome and caves respectively represent a synthesizing of the ideals of monotheism and pantheism, which, separated, lead only to self-centered rationalism on the one hand or idolatry of nature on the other." [67] Even Miss Mercer, employing the seven forms of Boehme's *Aurora*, does not arrive at so abstractly explicit an interpretation: the dome corresponds to the seventh form, or God's complete manifestation, the Kingdom of Heaven, the corporeal Being of the seven forms, light, the Holy Ghost, while the caves of ice correspond to the first form, or contraction, sharpness, coldness, ice.[68] For Knight the opposition is between light and heat, the Eros fires of the mind, the lighted intelligence, and inorganic nature, ultimate being, death, the depths of the unconscious.[69] Miss Bodkin sees the dome as emblematic of supreme well-being, divine bliss, while the caves connote imaginative fear or loss and frustration, although it must be remarked that it is not entirely clear whether she is speaking of the caves or of the "caverns." [70]

The variety of these interpretations may derive from the apparent tendency of most interpreters, especially at this point, to take the image in isolation from its context and to depend too heavily upon the conventional import or upon some special literary import of its separate parts, the sun and the ice. As an antidote, it may be well to begin with as immediate and simple-minded an examination of the text as possible.

> It was a miracle of rare device,
> A sunny pleasure-dome with caves of Ice!

Almost everyone has dealt in one way or another with the paradox involved in the juxtaposition of sun and ice, but it is not so often

---

[67] *Coleridge the Visionary*, pp. 247–48.
[68] "The Symbolism of 'Kubla Khan,'" p. 52.
[69] *The Starlit Dome*, p. 95.   [70] *Archetypal Patterns*, pp. 114–15.

noticed that read in a certain way the couplet begins with what may be an even stranger paradox, a miracle of rare device, a miracle formed by design. But the longer one ponders line 35 the less certain one may be just how it ought to be read. The question is one of emphasis, not in the matter of metrical stress, for several readings might be accommodated by the fairly obvious meter of the line, but in the pitch as indicating import. This is the kind of problem that a public reader would have to decide upon with some deliberation. There are at least four possible readings, which can be rendered by metrical symbols if ˘ is taken to indicate level monotone and ´ to indicate a raising of the pitch. Thus,

$$\text{I}\breve{\text{t}} \ \text{wa}\breve{\text{s}} \ \overset{\wedge}{\text{a}} \ \acute{\text{mi}}\text{racle o}\breve{\text{f}} \ \text{ra}\breve{\text{re}} \ \text{de}\breve{\text{vice,}}$$

makes a simple intensive of "miracle" and puts all the logical emphasis upon "rare device," as if one should say, "It was a very *mir*acle how ingeniously devised it was—a sunny pleasure-dome with caves of ice!" Read thus, the line has the effect of a sheer superlative, with little or no specific import.

A second possible reading,

$$\text{I}\breve{\text{t}} \ \text{wa}\breve{\text{s}} \ \breve{\text{a}} \ \acute{\text{mi}}\text{racle o}\breve{\text{f}} \ \acute{\text{ra}}\text{re de}\acute{\text{vice,}}$$

might be paraphrased, "It was a miracle, and one of unusually or superbly ingenious design, to wit, a sunny pleasure-dome with caves of ice!" In this reading some point is made of its being in one sense or another a "miracle," and equal stress is laid upon the ingeniousness of its design, with no suggestion that there is any paradox involved in applying both epithets to it. It is as if being a miracle and being of sufficiently rare device were equivalent, or, if one supposes the whole section, lines 1–36, to be somehow symbolic of the poetic act, the line would be noting its indispensable elements, inspiration and artistry, and passing over their mysterious incompatibility.

Another reading puts the stress precisely on that incompatibility:

It was a miracle of rare device,

which may be rendered, "It was, as goes without saying, a miracle, but, what is most strange in a miracle, it was an ingeniously *devised* one—a sunny pleasure-dome with caves of ice!" If we think of the word "device" as implying a deliberate process of "devising," of something's being as it were planned or thought out, there is indeed a certain shock of incompatibility with the idea of a "miracle." The noun "device," however, at most leaves this to be vaguely understood (just as Kubla's "decree" in line 2 does not lead us to wonder much about the architects and contractors engaged). But once the reading occurs to us as a possible one, some trace of paradox is likely to linger in the line.

There is at least one more possibility:

It was a miracle of rare device,

This, like the third reading, assumes the miraculous quality of the phenomenon, and, like the second reading, implies no element of contradiction between "miracle" and "device": "Being a miracle, it was, like all miracles, devised, in the sense of being a departure from the usual course of things, but in this case departing in a most extraordinary and felicitous degree—it was a *sunny* pleasure-dome with caves of *ice!*" As in the first reading, all the emphasis here is upon the ingenuity of the structure, but the underlying assumptions make of this reading something more than a simple intensive.

Is the conscientious public reader obliged to choose among these readings? It would hardly seem practicable, since a clear choice of

any but the second—"It was a miracle of rare device"—would inevitably tend to distort the meter too obviously. This is, after all, one service that meter can perform. And from an analytical point of view it is probably best that the implications of all four readings be implicitly retained, without any one of them being emphasized to the exclusion of the others. We ought to feel the force of the sheer superlative of the first reading—each of the other readings echoes it in its own way. It ought further to be noted that to say of the structure that it is a "miracle" is to say something that has not quite been *said* in the preceding lines, and is only fully confirmed by the line that follows. Also, the paradoxical mystery involved in the implementation of miracles, which we may ordinarily think of as purely spontaneous, inconsistent with deliberation, ought surely to be felt in the line. If by chance the structure in question *is* a symbol of *poeisis,* it is thus, by virtue of its manner of origin as well as its qualities, a symbol in the properly Coleridgean sense that it "partakes of the reality which it renders intelligible" [71]—its miraculous reconciliation of opposites "gives *outness* to" [72] the basic paradox of all artistic creation. Finally, an exclusive stress upon "rare," as in the fourth reading, focuses our attention upon the peculiar qualities of the structure. Other kinds of buildings might conceivably have been erected beside the sacred river, and so we are invited to ponder the special significance of this one, a sunny pleasure-dome with caves of ice, which if nothing more specific, is a reconciliation of a set of ultimate opposites.

If line 35 can bear this weight of implication, then line 36—"A sunny pleasure-dome with caves of ice"—might easily stand as self-evident in import, needing no appeal to recondite symbolisms: a sunny pleasure-dome with caves of ice can stand by itself as an instance of the reconciliation of opposites. And within the poem itself are to be found kindred juxtapositions: the sunny spots of greenery as opposed to the ancient forests, the sunny dome itself as opposed, not to the caves of ice, but to the sunless sea. In short, the line would not be a loss, would justify its place, if it conveyed no more than a concrete instance of the coexistence of opposite quali-

---

[71] *Statesman's Manual,* p. 437.   [72] *Notebooks,* Vol. I, 1387 8.106.

ties.[73] But it would be surprising, in what seems to be so tight a poem, if the choice of specific opposites had no further significance, and something of that significance can be gathered from an examination of Coleridge's use of similar elements elsewhere.

We have to go as far back as 1789 to find the first instance of a similar combination. In the undergraduate burlesque "The Nose" we saw that the combination of fire and ice was associated with destructive inspiration and madness, and there are at least two other, and more serious, instances of what seems to be adverse usage. In "To a Young Friend" the foliage of the ancient forests on the poetic mount "mocks / . . . the bleak *frosts* of age, / And Bigotry's mad *fire*-invoking rage." The two extremes at their harmful worst are things to seek protection from. So in *Osorio* Ferdinand likens the effect of the evil chasm where he is to meet his death to "needle-points of *frost* / Upon a *fever*ish head" (IV, 35–36). All of these may be taken as instances of *un*reconciled opposites. Thus in a notebook entry of 1802 we find "Devil at the icy end of Hell warming himself at the reflection of the fires in the Ice."

But there are also early favorable uses of the contrast between cold and heat. In "Songs of the Pixies" the Pixies' cool cave is contrasted to the sultry heat of the noonday sun, which bathes the tops of the trees whose roots form the grot. And it is there that the Bard has dreams that are "tinctur'd" with the sun under the influence of "soothing witcheries." Cool dreams tinctured with the sun are just the sort one might imagine in that sunny pleasure-dome with caves of ice, and this way of describing them may be a poetic version of what Wordsworth was trying to convey in speaking of emotion recollected in tranquility. It seems obvious, at any rate, that Coleridge is here deliberately manipulating the two elements in the effort, not entirely successful, to communicate some-

---

[73] House points out (*Coleridge,* p. 121) that one of Coleridge's examples of the reconciliation of opposites in the *Biographia* (II, 255–56) is "the heat in ice."

thing about the character of the poetic experience. In "Effusion at Evening," Imagination flings flowers of *Spring* "o'er *Winter's* icy plains" (Coleridge's italics), and in the later version, "Lines on an Autumnal Evening," the poet imagines becoming an arbour in order to shelter his love "from Noontide's sultry beam." As in "Songs of the Pixies" (if we ignore the sun-tinctured dreams), the favorable emphasis is upon the cool rather than the sunny, although the coolness is valued just because it somewhat miraculously co-exists with the sun.

But as we proceed, the equivalences are not so neat, and the warm side of the contrasting pair comes in for approbation. In "Religious Musings" omnipresent Love is compared to a day-spring rising in the poet's heart "As the great Sun, when he his influence / Sheds on the frost-bound waters—the glad stream / Flows to the ray and warbles as it flows." Here the sun prevails and the effect is positive and pleasing, but not really miraculous. In the "Monody" there is no ice at all, but "floating high in air, / Glitter the sunny visions fair," and we are again reminded of the dreams tinctured with the sun, of the "bright visions of the day" in "Religious Musings" (line 248), as well as of "that dome in air / That sunny dome" in the second part of "Kubla Khan." It is tempting to see in all this a kind of groping toward the realization of lines 35-36 of "Kubla Khan," where, with all these implications understood, the full-fledged miracle can be decreed outright; and perhaps we would not be entirely wrong if we read no conscious deliberation into the process.

Although the kindred images in "The Destiny of Nations" seem literally closer to "Kubla Khan" than those just examined, the contrast is still not quite unequivocal. The action of rebellious angels training up to God is compared to the "far-off Sun" darting his slant beam on "unobeying snows." The implication is that a closer sun, the real sun of which these fallen angels are tarnished approximations, would melt the snows—and there would be no miracle. But under the actual circumstances the pseudo suns and the snows do coexist, and afford a hint of the Absolute. In "Kubla Khan" we presumably have the real sun, and still the ice does not melt! In one version of "The Destiny of Nations" Joan is said to have seen in one of her visions an "ice-pil'd mount / And meteor-lighted dome."

The language of "This Lime-Tree Bower" in no way suggests the miraculous dome of "Kubla Khan," but it is worth noticing that the juxtaposition of a damp and "unsunn'd" dell (at least only "speckled by the mid-day sun") and a burning landscape issues in a perception of the Almighty Spirit. The experience produces "delight," and through that delight the poet is enabled to see in his little bower the abode of Love and Beauty. The sequence is close to that of "Kubla Khan"—vision involving sun and shade, heat and cool; delight; creation.

There is not really a direct confrontation of sun and ice in "The Ancient Mariner." They appear rather in succession, first the "ice, mast high, came floating by, / As green as emerald," the snowy clifts sending a dismal sheen, and only later, "like God's own head, / The glorious Sun uprist." The ice mast-high reminds one of the caves of ice, but the scene is one of tumult, more like the fountain and the caverns of "Kubla Khan." Coleridge seems to be working with some of the same images in the two poems, but rather clearly in different ways, toward potentially distinguishable symbolic ends. The most important thing to notice for our present purpose is that the realm of ice in "The Ancient Mariner" serves to *separate* from the ordinary world, the world of beasts and men, but that it produces the Albatross, that vehicle of blessing and curse. One is suddenly reminded that there are no beasts or men in Kubla's dome and garden, although in Coleridge's declared source the garden contained "all sorts of beasts of chase and game," [74] and

---

[74] *Purchas his Pilgrimage* (London: fol. 1626), Bk. IV, chap. xiii, p. 418, cited by E. H. Coleridge, *Poems,* p. 296 n.

that the vision responsible for its re-creation will leave the visionary in a state of delight and at the same time the object of holy dread. Whether Knight's formulation for the three great poems—Hell, Purgatory, Paradise—is literally acceptable or not, it seems clear that on the symbolic level they are somehow connected, and probable that they deal at least in part with different "moments" or different views of one great process—poetic contact with the Absolute, with all its attendant joys and perils. In the state, or alternatively, from the point of view, depicted in "The Ancient Mariner," there is nothing comparable to the sunny pleasure-dome with caves of ice as an accomplished fact.

Perhaps because it was written after "Kubla Khan," the "Hymn before Sunrise" contains the most specific reminiscences of the images we are just now concerned with. Mont Blanc *is* a king, dwelling in a "crystal shrine," a symbol of "the Invisible alone." Whatever his political reservations concerning tyrants and the Russian dynasty in particular, Coleridge leaves no doubt in this poem of the positive symbolic import of a "potentate" inhabiting a structure built partially or wholly of ice. The contemplation of it has so powerful an effect that he *becomes* the dome rather than building it, and its features are quite familiar: there are "Green vales and icy cliffs," "sunless pillars deep in Earth," and a countenance filled with "rosy light." The king, the mountain, and the dome are completely fused in this post-"Kubla Khan" vision, and the whole, into which the poet is himself fused, is an "ambassador from Earth to Heaven." There is perhaps no more authoritative, or explicit, commentary on the import of "Kubla Khan."

CHAPTER SEVEN

The Vision

The first part of the poem, as we have seen, begins and ends with the dome, revealing in the concluding couplet the miraculous characteristics that warrant such attention, a very plausible poetic strategy, we may note in passing, which in no way implies that the dome of lines 31–36 is not identical with that of lines 1–2. Our survey of Coleridge's other uses of heat and cold, of sun and ice, leads to the conclusion that for him it is not primarily in the separate qualities of each element that the significance lies, but in the very fact of the juxtaposition. Without any recourse to specific literary or mythological sources, it is sufficiently evident that for Coleridge the site of such an imagined juxtaposition was perennially associated with dreams, with visions involving approximation to the Absolute, perception of the Almighty Spirit, a perception amounting at most to a union with the Invisible. If the two elements are to be considered separately, it would seem that the sun is most often associated with love and light (in connection with the latter we may recall the element of Knowledge associated with the poetic mount), and ice with isolation and tranquility. It is as if it were necessary to be coolly isolated from the *ordinary* passions to receive and bear the effulgence of the Absolute.[1]

The whole of lines 1–36 seems thus to form a unit, and in the light of so many ramifications in Coleridge's poetry over so extended a period before and after "Kubla Khan," it is very hard to believe that the general import of the section is negative, as, in one way or another, Beer, Woodring, and Watson would have us

---

[1] House seems to present the most plausible interpretation of these lines. See *Coleridge*, pp. 121–22.

suppose. The relation between the two main parts of the poem is so important to the interpretation of the whole that as we move from the first to the second part it may be well to consider one recent opinion on the matter, that of Watson. Whereas Beer, as we have seen, interprets the first part (for him, lines 1–30) as the description of a fallen world in the theological sense, and Woodring sees Kubla's whole enterprise as typical of overweening tyrannical pride, Watson contrasts the first part and the second as instances of false and true poetry, the former actually produced, the latter merely promised (without, it is true, suggesting an explanation of Coleridge's devoting thirty-six lines to the false exhibit and only eighteen to the true):

"Kubla Khan," then, is not just about poetry: it is about two kinds of poem. We have one of them in the first thirty-six lines of the poem; and though we do not have the other, we are told what it would do to the reader and what it would do to the poet. The reader would be able to visualize a palace and park he had never seen; and the poet would behave after the classic manner of poets, like a madman. The second poem—the poem that does not exist—is so evidently the real thing that it is clear that the poem we have, in ll. 1–36, is not the real thing—not quite a poem at all, in Coleridge's terms.[2]

Watson's argument is that the first part is "factual, detailed, matter-of-fact," and so falls under Coleridge's condemnation in the *Biographia* (Chap. XXII) of Wordsworth's occasional matter-of-factness. In spite of the measurements given (themselves imprecise enough to have given rise to much dispute), and what House calls the "plain clear statement"[3] of the first part, it may never before have occurred to a reader to take these lines as an instance of unpoetic matter-of-factness. Perhaps the only answer is to be found in reading one of the passages from *The Excursion* to which Coleridge alludes, and seeing if, on the face of it, this seems to be poetry of a kind with the first part of "Kubla Khan":

---

[2] "The Meaning of 'Kubla Khan,' " pp. 25–26. [3] *Coleridge*, p. 117.

    Upon a semicirque of turf-clad ground,
The hidden nook discovered to our view
A Mass of rock, resembling, as it lay
Right at the foot of that moist precipice,
A stranded Ship, with keel upturned,—that rests
Fearless of winds and waves. Three several Stones
Stood near, of smaller size, and not unlike
To monumental pillars: and, from these
Some little space disjoined, a pair were seen,
That, with united shoulders bore aloft
A Fragment, like an Altar, flat and smooth: (III, 50–60)

Watson is evidently asking us to suppose that Coleridge deliberately composed lines 1–36 of "Kubla Khan" as an illustration of this
poetic defect, a defect as Coleridge saw it, "of laborious minuteness
and fidelity in the representation of objects, and their positions, as
they appeared to the poet himself." [4] If this was indeed his intention, perhaps all we can say of the lines is, what a meaningless
failure!

The fact seems to be that none of the efforts to read an adverse
meaning into the first part of the poem stands up in the face of an
examination of Coleridge's other uses of the images found there,
or even simply in the face of most readers' spontaneous reaction to
the lines. Such efforts may have their origin in a sense of the abrupt-
ness of the transition between the two parts of the poem. The last
line of the first part, "A sunny pleasure-dome with caves of ice!"
singling out the dome and its caves as the prime object of the whole
image, leaving behind the gardens and all the other details, does
prepare us for the reference in the second part, where only the
dome and its caves are mentioned. But the opening of the second
part still seems abrupt:

                A damsel with a dulcimer
                In a vision once I saw:
                It was an Abyssinian maid,

[4] *Biographia Literaria,* II, 101.

> And on her dulcimer she played,
> Singing of Mount Abora.
> Could I revive within me
> Her symphony and song,
>   To such deep delight 'twould win me,
> That with music loud and long,
> I would build that dome in air,
> That sunny dome! those caves of ice!

There may have been various reasons for Coleridge's disposing the lines as he did, and it may or may not be possible to decide what those reasons were, but, given the lines as we have them, there is in fact nothing logically abrupt about the transition. Having just presented us, at the climactic end of the first part, a sunny pleasure-dome with caves of ice, in the second part of the poem he tells us, with perfect logical consequence, "I would build that dome in air, that sunny dome, those caves of ice, with music loud and long, if I could be won to such delight as I would be by reviving within me the symphony and song sung by an Abyssinian maid whom I once saw in a vision playing on her dulcimer and singing of Mount Abora." If this rearrangement tends to make a lover of the poem wince, it may be not only because, like any such rearrangement, it seems very clumsy in comparison with the original, but because any rearrangement is superfluous, because the poem is quite all right as it is.

But not *quite* all right—too many good readers have felt the jolt, and too many of those who have have accounted for it either by reading the first part of the poem in ways belied by its obvious tone and its affiliations within the corpus of Coleridge's poetry, or, like Miss Schneider, by supposing that we have to do with two poems, one a postscript to the other. If there really *is* no logical inconsequence, then these reactions must be the result of some rhetorical infelicity, since they are too many and too impressive to be dismissed. Perhaps the poem is too *short* to allow of the rhetorical strategy actually employed, too short for the logical inversion to take its proper effect, too short to enable the reader, with so little help, to connect the apparently new images of the second part (the Abyssinian maid and Mount Abora) with those of the first part. In this sense, no matter how hard put we might be to suggest additions, it may be that the poem is a "fragment." It is probably also true, for reasons difficult to specify, that two-part structure is especially difficult to bring off, more difficult than, for instance, three-part structure. The most notable exception is the Italian sonnet, though many relative successes in that form doubtless owe much to our sense of the conventional form itself. It might even be suggested to readers of "Kubla Khan" that they try to read it as a somewhat expanded Italian sonnet.[5] In any case, it would seem the more prudent course to convict Coleridge of a partial rhetorical failure, if we must, than either to rewrite his poem or to make of it two poems.

Still in connection with the relation between the two main parts of the poem, it may be well at this point to go back for a moment to the alternate title: "A Vision in a Dream." The reference of "Vision" and "Dream" is not immediately clear. Because the word "vision" is used in connection with the Abyssinian maid, it might at first appear that that is the vision alluded to in the title, "Dream" referring to the whole poem, in which this vision occurs. But in fact, the vision of the damsel with a dulcimer does not occur within the time of the poem at all, any more than the woman wailing for her demon-lover—it is a vision, the speaker tells us, that "once I saw." And here is what Coleridge has to say at the end of his prefatory note, after telling of the interruption by the person from Porlock:

Yet from the still surviving recollections in his mind, the Author has frequently purposed to finish for himself what had been originally, as

[5] *Pace* Alan Purves, whose metrical analysis convincingly reveals a highly symmetrical division of the poem into seven parts. See "Formal Structure in 'Kubla Khan,'" *Studies in Romanticism*, I (1962), 187–91.

it were, given to him. Σαμερον αδιον ασω: but the to-morrow is yet to come.

As a contrast to this vision, I have annexed a fragment of a very different character, describing with equal fidelity the dream of pain and disease.[6]

When he speaks of "what had been originally, as it were, given to him," as when he speaks of "this vision," it would seem that Coleridge is referring to the whole poem, in any case that the reference is not specifically and exclusively to the vision mentioned in line 38. Earlier in the note he says that "all the images rose up before him as *things*" (Coleridge's italics), and surely the images that rose up before him as things are preeminently the images of lines 1–36, all of which are together presented directly, not as things seen once or perhaps to be re-created for others in the future.[7] In a sense, the whole prefatory note may be taken as a substitute for such an infelicitous opening as "I dreamed that . . ." and the alternate title, "A Vision in a Dream," as equivalent to "what I saw in a dream,"[8] and what he saw, what the poem presents as *things*, are above all the images of part one. The vision was so real, so vivid, that it is described as one would describe an actual occurrence— "In Xanadu did Kubla Khan / A stately pleasure-dome decree." The prefatory note gives us the not entirely indispensable information that these events occurred in a dream, a dream furnished, as we have seen, by many years of seeing into, of feeling, and of making landscapes to "give outness to" the vision.

But although we shall see that the two parts of the poem are inextricably bound together, that they form one poem as surely as, say, the two "parts" of Wordsworth's Intimations Ode, still there *is* a distinct change in point of view. The shift from the third person in part one to the first person in part two is sufficient to render the

---

[6] *Poems*, pp. 296–97.

[7] As Miss Bodkin points out (*Archetypal Patterns*, p. 95), the damsel with a dulcimer is never "spontaneously visualized."

[8] Cf. Bard Bracy's vision in a dream in "Christabel" (lines 523–40).

change dramatically evident, especially in so short a poem as this one. But this change in itself neither furnishes evidence that the first part is a negative image, as Beer, Woodring, and Watson would have it, nor indicates that, as Miss Schneider suggests, the second part is a mere postscript explaining why the poem cannot be completed. Rather, both the external evidence and, I believe, close analysis of the whole poem suggest that, simply enough, the first part presents a vision, a beautiful and complex vision subtly compounded—just how deliberately we can never know—of a whole train of symbols gradually enriched and integrated in the poet's mind over many years, and that the second part offers a kind of commentary on the significance of that vision, not a philosophical elaboration but a commentary realized in terms as symbolic, as poetic, as the vision itself. To convince oneself of the necessity of this commentary, one need only try to imagine the poem ending at line 36. What is left is a beautiful series of images, delicately articulated, and thoroughly unified in its A-B-A structure (lines 1–11, 12–24, 25–36). But as always with dreams and visions, one asks, what do you think it means? With a certain sophistication, what one asks is, what does it mean to *you?* And if the dreamer is wise, he answers by telling another dream. At any rate, that is what Coleridge does in the second part of "Kubla Khan."

A reexamination of the first thirty-six lines of the poem will reveal that, within the confines of the poem itself, taking all of the images in their more or less conventional signification, there is little or no warrant for any of the interpretations concerning "life" and "poetry" that have either been made or quoted above—except in the light of the last section, lines 37–54. It is as if the first thirty-six lines were "pure image" (if such a thing were possible), and the last eighteen devoted, though in a very different way, to what Miss Schneider calls making the meaning explicit.[9] We have the vision,

---

[9] I must confess to being greatly reassured by the discovery of a way to find Miss Schneider in the right, since it seems in the nature of things unlikely that she is quite wrong.

in fascinating detail, and in saying that he could re-create the miraculous dome, giving the circumstances in which that would be possible (if he could recover the song of the Abyssinian maid), specifying the means to be employed (music loud and long), and predicting the results, Coleridge makes it as obvious as possible in symbolic language that the poem as a whole has to do with poetry-making, with the poet, the poetic experience, the poem, and the world in which they so strangely, and alarmingly, exist. This much would seem obvious on the surface. But the last eighteen lines of the poem are not a philosophical elaboration, do not make the meaning "explicit" in that way, and careful attention to the images involved may enrich the understanding of these lines as well as the first thirty-six.

A great many literary sources have been suggested for the Abyssinian maid, the damsel with a dulcimer, and they all turn out to have something at least vaguely in common. Beer cites Porphyry's version of the Cave of Nymphs in Homer, found in Taylor's translation of Proclus, pointing out that the nymphs were the guardians of knowledge; and the troglodytes of Abyssinia, also guardians of knowledge, treated in Bruce and Herodotus, by the latter just after a description of the Fountain of the Sun. There is the additional interesting fact that the troglodytes are said to have invented the *sambuca*, an instrument whose name was translated as "dulcimer" in the eighteenth century and whose music was thought to be of a feminine character. Beer also mentions Isis as a possibility.[10] Both Miss Bodkin[11] and Fogle[12] suggest a connection with the Miltonic Urania, and Miss Mercer sees the damsel as an avatar of Boehme's Heavenly Virgin, embodying Wisdom, Sophia, the Logos, pure imagination, and the divine spirit as well as grace.[13] It seems very likely that one or more

---

[10] *Coleridge the Visionary*, pp. 251–55.   [11] *Archetypal Patterns*, p. 99.
[12] "The Romantic Unity of 'Kubla Khan,'" p. 17.
[13] "The Symbolism of 'Kubla Khan,'" p. 52.

of these figures was at least in the background of Coleridge's mind, since all of them seem in some way to be symbols of knowledge, and there is much indication that no song lacking that note would be likely to win the speaker of "Kubla Khan" to the requisite delight. And further, the Abyssinian maid is clearly some kind of muse, a source of inspiration.

Maidens throughout Coleridge's poems perform this function of purveyors or embodiments of inspiration (a highly conventional function for maidens), most often when seen in visions (also usual and understandable). Since the project is in some sense to re-create the dome, and since, as we have seen, that dome, like the many other domes and mountains, is a work of art *seen in* nature, the record and embodiment of a preternatural contact with the Intelligible in nature, a contact most simply between the soul of the poet and what is outside it, nothing is more likely than that the vision of a *maid,* a being available in the most special way to love, to connatural contact, should initiate the process. The lines are in a way simply a means of talking about the relation between love, love between the sexes that is, and poetry. And so in addition to the various literary maids there are doubtless in the background various real ones as well. Angus suggests Dorothy Wordsworth, because, if the poem was written in 1798, no other likely maid was available.[14] But there is a sense in which it is more appropriate to take the various real maids in Coleridge's life as reflections of the Abyssinian maid than to fix her identity in relation to them. Long before the date of the poem there was Mary Evans, and at the time, if Miss Schneider is right about the date, there was Sara Hutchinson. Most probably after, there were Perdita Robinson and Matilda Betham. Surely all of these, before, during, and after the time of "Kubla Khan," had a crucial part of their value for Coleridge as approximations of one kind or another to what in "Kubla Khan" appears as the Abyssinian maid.

[14] "The Theme of Love and Guilt," p. 667.

In this connection it is well to remember the cases in which there is a certain confusion between the maid and the poet. The most notable is perhaps to be found in "The Eolian Harp," where the lute and the maiden player are one and the poet is substituted for both. In *Osorio* the confusion is most baffling: Maria compares herself to a Moorish maid [15] playing her lover's lute over a spring in the mountain cleft. Under the inspiration of this once-heard music produced by herself, she imagines building a bower in paradise. In "Love" the *maiden* is inspired by the doleful song of the *lover,* a simple reversal. In "The Garden of Boccaccio" the maid sings while the poet plays the lute. Who is to say, including the poet himself, how much inspiration, in the proper sense of that word, derives from without, and how much is produced of the self? And no one, it may be assumed, has conclusively weighed the component of aspiring narcissism in love of any kind. In short, as was suggested much earlier, there is a sense in which the Abyssinian maid corresponds not just to various people real or imaginary that the poet loved or wanted to love, but to the poet himself, to that in him that could be in contact with what he most wanted to be in contact with. Here we should look back at "The Mad Monk" (1800), a story of the rape by means of murder of the Abyssinian maid. The monk ends his story with the line, reminiscent of Cain: "Oh, let me lie in peace, and be forever dead." And the speaker ends the poem with the reflection:

> Here ceas'd the voice. In deep dismay,
> Down thro' the forest I pursued my way.

How deep the dismay really was we can perhaps know better through a reading of "Kubla Khan" than even through a reading of "Dejection." Certain parts of "Dejection" might be read as

---

[15] We must remember that Coleridge himself was once a "lone Arab" ("Love's Apparition and Evanishment"), once a "blind Arab" ("The Blossoming of the Solitary Date-Tree"), both times listening for a familiar voice.

amounting to the confession—I have murdered the Abyssinian maid.

By this stage of the poem it becomes very difficult to talk about the images one by one, for one begins to sense the amalgamation of them all. Since one must both be and not be something else in order either to love it or to experience it poetically, and since this contradiction is not to be reconciled logically, amalgamation *in a poem* is the only solution, and the multiple identities gradually make themselves felt. The poet *is* the maid; the maid *is* her instrument (in "The Eolian Harp"), just as all of animated nature may be thought of as organic harps played upon by an intellectual breeze; her music is *like* the mount she sings of ("The Stranger Minstrel" and "Hymn before Sunrise"); the poet both creates the mount and *becomes* it ("Effusion at Evening" and "Hymn before Sunrise"). And so one might go on until one had identified all of the major objects of the poem with one another.

That music should be inspirational is no more unusual than that maidens should, and even the combination is not uncommon: perhaps Coleridge's "faith that there's a bond / Between the female mind and measured sound" ("To Matilda Betham") has some foundation. In his essay "On Poesy or Art," he says that

> Music is the most entirely human of the fine arts, and has the fewest *analoga* in nature. Its first delightfulness is simple accordance with the ear; but it is an associated thing, and recalls the deep emotions of the past with an intellectual sense of proportion.[16]

This is precisely what he is expecting of the song of the Abyssinian maid, that it shall recall the deep emotions of the past with an intellectual sense of proportion. Elsewhere he speaks of music's "aloofening" the mind,[17] and in contemplating an "Ode to Music" he even thought of its "bringing me back to primary Feelings" in

---

[16] *Biographia Literaria*, II, 261.   [17] *Notebooks*, Vol. I, 1296   8.45.

such a way as to "make moral regeneration." [18] Since music "has the fewest *analoga* in nature," it is all the more remarkable when, as in "A Stranger Minstrel," it "resembles" a mountain (in being "soft, various, and sublime"), or when, as in "Hymn before Sunrise," a mountain is "like some sweet beguiling melody" that blends with our thought:

> Yea, with my Life and Life's own secret joy:
> Till the dilating Soul, enrapt, transfused,
> Into the mighty vision passing—there
> As in her natural form, swelled vast to Heaven!   (20–23)

And as a result he builds the dome in air, complete with sunless pillars, a countenance filled with rosy light, perpetual streams, and dark and icy caverns.

The poems, of course, are full of references to music from the very beginning. As early as 1790, in "Pain," the muse's lyre is associated with "delight," and in the "ode" of 1792 a fall of harmony provides a "sacred balm." Music is "strange," "wild," "impetuous," "unearthly," "witching," "magic." It is also "solemn," "sweet," "divine." The "strange" notes sung by the boy in *Osorio* were taught him in a dream. The "unearthly minstrelsy" of "Reflections" is "then only heard / When the soul seeks to hear; when all is hush'd / And the Heart listens." The "unearthly melodies" of "Religious Musings" are wild fragments of a vision of paradise, resulting from molding confusion to perfect forms. For paradise *is* formed nature, exhaustively intelligible nature, a nature we can only glimpse in this world, and we must celebrate and try to fix those glimpses:

> Awake, my soul! not only passive praise
> Thou owest! not alone these swelling tears,

---

[18] *Ibid.*, Vol. I, 1505   7.57. It should be remembered that the evidence of salvation in "The Ancient Mariner" comes as music, natural, instrumental, and angelic, and that Enos recognizes Abel by his "sweet voice."

> Mute thanks and secret ecstasy! Awake,
> Voice of sweet song! Awake, my heart, awake!
> Green vales and icy cliffs, all join my Hymn!
> ("Hymn before Sunrise," 24–28)

By 1802 one seems to detect a note of desperation, but the impulse is perennial.

Perhaps the least expected, and most frequent, characteristic of the music in Coleridge's poems is loudness. The Otter, in "The Songs of the Pixies," sings, somewhat redundantly, a "loud unquiet song." In "The Eolian Harp" it is when the strings are "boldlier swept" that we hear the music of Paradise, evoking the One Life within us and abroad. "The Destiny of Nations" opens with "song" and "symphony," characterized as "strong music," and it constitutes a "soliciting spell." In "Christabel," Bard Bracy, having had a vision in a dream of a green snake strangling a dove, wants to exorcise the wood with "music loud," with "music strong and saintly song." In "The Nightingale," the music of the birds is like "a hundred airy harps," and in "Dejection" Joy is "this strong music in the soul." It is possible to think that the line in "Kubla Khan" may have started out ". . . with music loud and strong" and been changed for musical reasons. If music, with the fewest *analoga* in nature, is to inspire the architecture of that sunny dome, those caves of ice, it must needs be loud and long.

The maid who sings this music is singing of Mount Abora. Perhaps we may take a certain satisfaction in no one's knowing where the mountain is. The suggestions have been legion, but we must face the possibility (1) that "Abora" is a complete fabrication, and that, even if we could know them, the reasons for Coleridge's having come out with *these* particular syllables rather than others that might fit the meter and sound pattern just as well, are quite irrelevant to the task of interpreting the poem; or (2) that even if in fact he adapted the name more or less consciously from something like Amara, Abola, Astaboras, Abor, Pelorus, Beth Abara,

Amhara, or Abur,[19] it would not automatically follow that characteristics or ideas associated with those names in their sources were for him or are for us relevant to the significance to be attributed to Mount Abora in the poem. As with all other allusions in poems, it is the reader's problem to determine how much (anywhere from none to all) of the original freight belonging to the borrowed image is to be imported into the present context. It is worthy of remark that in the case of Mount Abora the readers who have suggested possible sources of the name have not thought it worthwhile to record any curiosity about Coleridge's reasons for altering the name, from whatever they think might be its original form or forms, to "Abora," if we except Lowes's hook-and-eye theory, which would reduce to a minimum the probable significance of the sources for interpretive purposes. The case may be the same as with Xanadu and Alph, and although Coleridge may have had some or all of the suggested sources in mind, the ultimate significance of the name may be that it is slightly out of *this* world, though not quite.

We have seen the ubiquity of the mount in the poems, its interchangeability with the dome, its identification with the king, the peril of ascending it, its special significance as the locale of inspiration, as the poetic mount, the ambassador from earth to

---

[19] While we are at it, another possible source may as well be recorded. Beer notes (*Coleridge the Visionary,* p. 256) that " 'Abor' appears on the second page of Holwell's mythological dictionary with the comment that 'the sun was called Abor, the parent of light.' " Since "Abor" is one of the closer approximations to "Abora," it is interesting to know that this form occurs in the work of an author Coleridge is known to have been acquainted with and may well have read (see *Notebooks,* Vol. I, 497 5.23). Jacob Bryant, in his *New System* . . . , 3d ed. (London: J. Walker, 1807), II, 40, notes that "out of Kir-Abor, from *ķir,* place, and ab-or, the father of fire, which had been the name of a temple situated near the mouth of a subterranean cave, they [the ancient Greeks] fashioned Cerberus, the three-headed dog guarding the gates of hell." I am indebted for this information to Nancy Ruth Warshaw, "Jacob Bryant and William Blake," unpublished master's thesis, Columbia University, 1962.

heaven. And at the ultimate stage, the poet becomes the mount. A notebook entry of September, 1802, is eloquent in this context:

Poems.—Ghost of a mountain / the forms seizing my body, as I passed, became realities—I, a Ghost, till I had reconquered my Substance /.[20]

Coleridge, of course, was not the only one who felt toward mountains in something like this way. Bernard Blackstone, appealing to "Agrippa and Burton and their speculations on the medium in which mind and elements act and react upon one another," points out how for Keats "mountains and lakes are also manifestations of the great Power, like mighty poets; and how the task of the poet is to quintessentialize the mountain-intellect into poetic forms for the benefit of mankind," and he directs us to Keats's often-quoted letter to his brother Tom, written during his tour of Scotland in 1818—one cannot help thinking of Mont Blanc in "Hymn before Sunrise," and of Mount Abora:

What astonishes me more than anything is the tone, the colouring . . . or, if I may say so, the intellect, the countenance of such places. The space, the magnitude of mountains and waterfalls are well imagined before one sees them; but this countenance or intellectual tone must surpass every imagination and defy any remembrance. I shall learn poetry here and shall henceforth write more than ever, for the abstract endeavour of being able to add a mite to that mass of beauty which is harvested from these grand materials, by the finest spirits, and put into etherial existence for the relish of man's fellows. I cannot think with Hazlitt that these scenes make a man appear little. I never forgot my stature so completely. I live in the eye; and my imagination, surpassed, is at rest.[21]

It is out of an inspiration surely not entirely unkin to this that a poem like "Kubla Khan" may grow. To speak of the "countenance" of a landscape is not very different from saying that it is "in

---

[20] *Notebooks,* Vol. I, 1241 21.254.
[21] Blackstone, *The Consecrated Urn* (London: Longmans, Green, 1959), pp. 113, 210–11. Blackstone's occasional tendency to disparage Coleridge's sensibility to the benefit of Keats seems unfortunate and unnecessary.

admirable *keeping,"* and its "intellect" must be something very like its "comprehensibility." It occurs to Keats also that the experience is such as to "defy any remembrance," but he has nevertheless great confidence that it can be revived within him, and though Blackstone would have us interpret "etherial" in a technical, hermetic sense, to put a mite of the beauty into ethereal existence for the relish of one's fellows is perhaps not so different a thing from building that dome in air, that sunny dome, those caves of ice, that all who hear may see them there. For Coleridge as for Keats the experience of mountains is an ennobling rather than a belittling one, speaking as he does of

> the dilating Soul, enrapt, transfused,
> Into the mighty vision passing—there
> As in her natural form, swelled vast to Heaven!

And the final result for him, as for Keats, is rest:

> No *wish* profan'd my overwhelméd heart.
> Blest hour! It was a luxury,—to be!
> ("Reflections on Having Left a Place of Retirement," lines 41–42)

And yet there is one wish for both of them, the wish to re-create the mount.

For Coleridge, having brought together the maid, the music, and the mount, with all the associations they had for him coalesced, the aspiration expressed in the lines that follow seems inevitable:

> Could I revive within me
> Her symphony and song,
> To such deep delight 'twould win me,
> That with music loud and long,
> I would build that dome in air.
> That sunny dome, those caves of ice!

It would seem fruitless to argue further as to the precise import or the tone of the conditional clause, although to superadd a negative

on biographical grounds—to suppose that the meaning is, I would
if I could but I can't—seems quite unjustified. Whatever the tone,
the syntax clearly says, could I do one thing the result would be
such that I would do something else: if I could revive within me
her symphony and song, it would win me to such delight that
I would build that dome in air. "But I cannot" is nowhere implied
in the poem. There is still, of course, the question of tone, and there
is no reason why that may not be open to a variety of simultaneous
interpretations. Since we *do not know* when the poem was written,
and since the moods reflected by the various possible tones are of a
kind that may change from day to day, it were best, perhaps, to
leave biographical considerations out of account. But there is
within the structure of the poem itself a kind of correspondence
that may be relevant—the speaker: Abyssinian maid = the woman
wailing : her demon-lover. The correspondence enriches the poem
in many ways, and here it lends a note of longing, with a certain
pathos, that is surely not inconsistent with the context. And there
is the somehow nice fact that, except for Kubla, the correspondence
embraces all of the figures mentioned in the poem, with Kubla
as it were presiding over them.

Another, and easily complementary, tone is suggested by a
notebook entry of 1804 (?), certainly some time after the composition of the poem but not for that reason necessarily irrelevant, since
it is unlikely that Coleridge forgot this poem. He is transcribing
some passages from William Cartwright's *The Lady Errant,* and
fixes upon this one:

> Would you had
> Been there yourself! Would you had drank in all
> The Looks, Words, Graces, and Divinities
> That I have done! I am like the Priest, that's full
> Of his inspiring God! am fill'd possessed,
> With such high Raptures, that *methinks I could*
> Bear myself up without a wing or chariot

And hover o'er the Earth, still dropping something
That should take root in Kingdoms & come up
The Good of the People! [22]

I have not been able to consult the edition of Cartwright that
Coleridge used, but Miss Coburn indicates his departures from the
text, and it would seem that the italics appear in the original. It is
not hard to imagine the whole passage being transcribed in recollection of "Kubla Khan" ("The Good of the People" at the end
takes us back to the notebook entries concerning Kubla Khan
himself), and "methinks I could" is certainly one plausible way of
taking "Could I. . . ." Something between "methinks I could"
and "if only I could" probably strikes the right tone.

We have already noticed the repeated association of "delight"
with the state of ultimate communion with Nature or with the
Absolute, and we ought now to be in a position quite simply to
believe that a revival within him of a *song* by a *maiden* about a
mount would induce that experience, and have the expected results.
As we have seen, so remarkable a number of his poems and notebook entries seem to record, celebrate, or result from just such an
encounter. But the next lines occasion some difficulties nevertheless.

That with music loud and long,
I would build that dome in air,
That sunny dome! those caves of ice!

After all of the domes that we encounter in the poems, domes he
saw or imagined building or became, it would seem most immedi-

---

[22] *Notebooks*, Vol. II, 1931   21.424 and n. The next entry, also a transcrip-
tion from Cartwright, may also be related:

            those that come fresh from Visions:
What saw you there?
            That which I still see, that
Which will not away. I saw a face that did
Seem to participate of Flames & Flowers
Eyes in which Light combined with Jet to make
Whiteness be thought the Blot, & Black hereafter
Purchase the name of Innocence & Glory.   (1932   21.425)

ately plausible to paraphrase "in air" as "in words, in poetry," with Knight,[23] or less literally, "in spirit" [24] or "imaginatively." [25] The latter readings gain some support from lines in "The Old Man of the Alps," which dates from the same general period as "Kubla Khan":

> And oft she prattled with an eager tongue
> Of promised joys that would not linger long,
> Till with her tearless eyes so bright and fair,
> She seem'd to see them realis'd in air!
> In fancy oft, within some sunny dell,
> Where never wolf should howl or tempest yell,
> She built a little home of joy and rest,
> And fill'd it with the friends whom she lov'd best: (29–36)

This may be all the weight the lines will bear, but other possibilities occur to one. In the first place, since it is always best to read as literally as possible in a given context, it ought to be noted that "in air" does not in itself require any paraphrase at all: with the rarest exceptions, all domes are built "in air." And so we have to face the alternative that the statement "I would build that dome in air" is a quite literal statement. If by any chance it is so to be taken, then the final section of the poem is saying something more daring than has ordinarily been supposed, but something that other Romantic poets would understand very well. Like Amphion, he would build with music an actual structure that all could see. It would, built in this way, be a miraculous structure in its origin as well as its characteristics, and a symbol of what the seer-poet, the seer-maker, posits in the actual world for "the Good of the People." Here is Coleridge's version of Keats's "vast idea," his "idea of doing some good in the world" through knowledge wrought into poetry, of Shelley's poets as "legislators or prophets," of Byron's "feeling of a Former world and Future."

[23] *The Starlit Dome*, p. 95.
[24] Mercer, "The Symbolism of 'Kubla Khan,'" p. 52.
[25] Woodring, "Coleridge and the Khan," p. 364.

There is the further question of the relation between this final dome and the dome decreed by Kubla in the first lines of the poem. It would almost seem that attention to one word in line 46 ought to settle the matter: "I would build *that* dome in air." What dome? In the same meter (if not with quite the same sound effect), he might have written, "I would build a dome in air, / A sunny dome, and caves of ice." The simplest answer would seem to be, he would build the dome he has been talking about throughout the poem, the pleasure-dome of Kubla Khan. But this is not quite satisfactory. He can't build *that* dome, since Kubla has already built it by decree, and so the expression "that dome" must be equivalent to "a dome like that." Kubla's dome, like all the others, is just one approximation to *that* dome, the ultimate ambassador from earth to heaven that one *becomes*. Such an interpretation renders a little less likely the reading of "in air" as "in poetry," and indeed, if Watson is wrong in his view that "the poem we have, in ll. 1–36, is not the real thing—not quite a poem at all . . ." [26] then the dome has already been built in poetry of surpassing beauty.

Readers of the poem who see the first part as an unfavorable image and the last part as a favorable one naturally have some difficulty with the concluding lines (49–54):

> And all should cry, Beware! Beware!
> His flashing eyes, his floating hair!
> Weave a circle round him thrice,
> And close your eyes with holy dread,
> For he on honey-dew hath fed,
> And drunk the milk of Paradise.

Beer has nothing at all to say about the cry "Beware! Beware!" For Woodring, the beholders "turn from the Khan and cry: 'Have awe of poets!' " [27] But the Khan has been dead for a long time, and "to have awe of" is a good deal less than to perform a ritual

---

[26] "The Meaning of 'Kubla Khan,' " p. 25.
[27] "Coleridge and the Khan," p. 368.

exorcism. Other readers as well seem to find the lines puzzling in one way or another. Burke finds a "suggestion of Medusa in the 'floating hair,' " but then he has the *poet* cry "Beware! Beware!" [28] Miss Mercer sees in the three-fold circling an acknowledgment of the poet's three-fold sanctity (love, the expression of love, and the experience of paradise),[29] but this gives no account of the cry to beware: conventionally, at least, sheer sanctity does not give rise to such a cry.

But those who have read the other poems with "Kubla Khan" in mind will not be surprised that a performance inspired by "such delight" should be both impressive and ambiguous in character. We should look back first, perhaps, to the passage in "Religious Musings," which is one of the closest in mood to "Kubla Khan":

> *Such delights*
> As float to earth, permitted visitants!
> When in some hour of solemn jubilee
> The massy gates of *Paradise* are thrown
> Wide open, and forth come in *fragments wild*
> Sweet echoes of *unearthly melodies,*
> And *odours* snatched from beds of Amaranth,
> And they, that from the *crystal river of life*
> Spring up on freshened wing, ambrosial gales!
> The favoured good man in his lonely walk
> Perceives them, and his silent spirit *drinks*
> *Strange bliss,* which he shall recognise in heaven.
> And *such delights, such strange beatitudes*
> Seize on my young anticipating heart
> When that blest future rushes on my view!   (343-57)

"Strange" bliss, "strange" beatitudes, and we remember the "de-

---

[28] *The Philosophy of Literary Form,* p. 97. Perhaps correctly, but surely quite irrelevantly, N. B. Allen, in "Note on Coleridge's 'Kubla Khan,' " *Modern Language Notes,* LVII (1942), 110-11, suggests the flashing eyes and floating hair constitute an accurate physical description of the poet himself at the time.

[29] "The Symbolism of 'Kubla Khan,' " p. 53.

licious" surges of the lute in "The Eolian Harp," music that results
in the creation of a paradise, and also, as the poem finally stands, in
a rebuke for heresy. Likewise in "The Wanderings of Cain," the
evil spirit imitating Abel in the alternative version, tempting Cain
to sacrifice his eyes, says that God requires an example, and that this
will be furnished "by his terrible appearance, at the same time he
will be gratified with the most delicious sights and feelings." Each
situation is different, but a menace always seems to hover.

The awe- and fear-inspiring figures of the poet, of whom Cain
is the ultimate example, are both conventional and frequent in
Coleridge's poetry. In the same poem in which the good man
drinks "strange bliss," the poet sees the phalanx of unnumbered
tribes molding confusion to such perfect forms as they as youths
have seen in visions when "They felt the sea-breeze lift their youthful locks" ("Religious Musings," line 251)—here the poet and all
who hear are identified, the context is a rather strainedly optimistic
one, and there is no occasion for alarm at the floating hair. Nor is
there when Chatterton's "eyes have glorious meanings" in the
"Monody," and "More than the light of outward day shines there"
(lines 53–54), or according to a variant version, "as floating high in
air, / Glitter the sunny visions fair, / His eyes dance rapture and
his bosom glows!" But we know in the sequel how the "hard
world" reacts to him, and the more dire result. Lamb, of all people,
turns up, we remember, as a "wild-eyed boy" when he is seen as a
dedicated poet. In "Ode to the Departing Year," a music-induced
vision produces "no unholy madness" in the poet, as a result of
which he raises "the impetuous song." The double negative introduces the note of doubt. Later in the same poem there are actually
"eyeballs flashing"—they belong to nature in painful childbirth,
bringing forth Equality and Peace, and if the building of the dome
has the full import I have been suggesting these political implications are not foreign to it. There are other more or less close
analogues to the figure of the poet as presented in these closing

lines—in *Osorio,* "The Old Man of the Alps," "The Triumph of Loyalty," and elsewhere—but perhaps the most significant of all (along with Cain) is the Ancient Mariner himself, the sight of whom, immediately after his voyage, sends the Pilot's son mad, thinking he has seen the devil, and who ever after holds his chosen interlocutors with his "glittering eye." He too has seen the supernal, under different circumstances and a very different guise, and has come back to make others see it. The effect he has upon them is something very like "holy dread."

There would seem to be several distinguishable elements in this complex image. On the most obvious level, any incursion of the supernatural is likely to inspire a combination of wonder and dread. But it ought to be noted that it is not the sight of the musically built dome and caves themselves that calls forth the reaction:

> And all who heard should see them there,

quite simply; then,

> And all should cry, Beware! Beware!
> His flashing eyes, his floating hair!

It is the seer, not the vision, that inspires dread. So it is with the Mariner; so it is no doubt universally—one thinks of Oedipus at Colonus. The purveyors of vision (outside the Christian and certain other orthodox traditions) are both blessed and accursed. What they bring is a blessing, but to their means of attaining it is always attached a kind of impiety, from Prometheus and Philoctetes to Faust. One would presumably have to submit the unconscious of the race to analysis in order to "know" why the fact of having fed on honey-dew and drunk the milk of Paradise necessitates a ritual of purification and protection. In the poem there is a sense in which the speaker has *become* the demon-lover, or alternatively, in which the Abyssinian maid, judging by the final result of encounter with her, stands to the speaker as the demon-lover to the woman wailing, an equation we have noted previously. On another but still related level, there is surely here an allusion to the misunderstanding, even persecution, to which the poet, the seer, is perennially subjected by the "poor loveless ever-anxious crowd." Here is a theme especially congenial to Coleridge's Romantic peers.

The last two lines, of course,

> For he on honey-dew hath fed,
> And drunk the milk of Paradise

are among the most "magical" in this or any poem. Is it either too personally or too culturally subjective to see part of their attraction in the contrast one may feel between the delicate beauty of the images and a certain sense of the forbidden, the sinful? One may agree with Miss Schneider in minimizing the influence of opium upon the composition of the poem and still feel that Meyer Abrams has done it no disservice in calling his book on the subject *The Milk of Paradise.*[30] For us, at any rate, the sense of *stolen* pleasure associated with opium may render something of this connotation of the lines, and it seems very likely that the same thing would be true for Coleridge.

The *New English Dictionary* gives as one of the early uses of "honey-dew" a passage from Samuel Purchas, not, tantalizingly enough, the Samuel Purchas whom Coleridge declares himself to have been reading when "Kubla Khan" came to be written, but a sixteenth-century pastor at Sutton in Essex who died about 1658 and was the author of *A Theatre of Political Flying-Insects.*[31] Chapter XXI of this work is entitled "Of the Hony-dew," and there is to be found (p. 125) the passage cited in *NED:*

Pliny affirmed the Hony-dew to bee either the sweat of heaven, or the slaver or spittle of the stars, or the moisture of the aire purging itself.

[30] (Cambridge: Harvard University Press, 1934).
[31] (London: Thomas Parkhurst, 1657). The work concerns bees, and includes moral and theological meditation on every aspect of their life.

A curious combination of the supernal and the excretory. Elsewhere Purchas cites authorities saying that the word "honey-dew" signifies the Kings-evil and is the same thing as the manna of the Israelites, noting concerning the latter that

In *Persia,* they call Manna Xirquest, Xir in *Persian* is Milk, and Quest is the name of the tree which produceth it, or rather where of it is gathered; the best comes from *Ormuz,* and from thence throughout all the East; it is white, soft, sweet, and in grains like Incense or Mastick.[32]

A post-"Kubla Khan" notation of Coleridge's own is interesting in another way. As Miss Coburn informs us, following H. Oldroyd, he is roughly transcribing descriptions of the metamorphosis of butterflies and moths from caterpillars, found in the Preface to Moses Harris's "The Aurelian: or Natural History of British Insects . . ." (1766). The passage is a long one and ends with the statement: "The Hens of some moths do not feed at all, nor have any discoverable organ for food—the rest feed on honey & honey-dew.—"[33] It's a fine thing, and must have appealed to Coleridge, not to feed at all or to feed on honey-dew, having metamorphosed from the state of a worm to that of a moth, ready for flight within the hour, as the immediately preceding sentence points out. The equivalence or interchangeability of honey and honey-dew here suggests the relevance of another notebook entry in which only

[32] Purchas cites his source here as Pedro Teixeira [*Relaciones*] . . . *de los Reyes de Persia* [Antwerp: Hieronymo Verdussen, 1610], Book I, Chap. VII. This work was translated into English by John Stevens as *The History of Persia* . . . (London: Jonas Brown, 1715). I know of no evidence that Coleridge read either Purchas or Teixeira, though nothing could seem more likely, but if such evidence could be found, still another source of Mount Abora would be open: in Book I, Chap. I of Teixeira's work he discusses the religious practices of the Zoroastrians surviving in Persia and notes that "they serve the sun, and fire, which they preserve with great care, so that in more than three thousand five hundred years it has not been extinct for an instant. This is on a mountain one day's march from Yazd, called Albors Kuyh, or Mount Albors, and also Atèx quedah, or the 'House of Fire.' And there are always many people attending on it." (*The Travels of Pedro Teixeira,* trans. William F. Sinclair [London: Hakluyt Society, 1902], p. 196.) The verbal echo is as close as most of those suggested and the context is amenable.

[33] *Notebooks,* Vol. I, 1378   21.237 f46, and n.

the former is mentioned, but which, as Miss Coburn points out, has other interesting affinities with "Kubla Khan." Coming as it does in 1806, when Coleridge was revising his poems for a new edition, she thinks it may even indicate an attempt to continue "Kubla Khan." The entry in question is one of several references to Pindar, this one labeled "Picturesque Passages in Pindar," and bringing together passages from two *Olympian* odes, in which each of the three details singled out may be seen as corresponding to an image in "Kubla Khan": (1) the story of Heracles having brought trees from Istria to adorn the precinct of Zeus—one remembers Bonaparte, that layer out of a World-garden, and Kubla, in whose decreed precinct trees are the most prominent features; (2) "—the steep banks of the Alpheus, & distant mountains"—one is looking down into the romantic chasm; (3) "Evadne with the new-born babe, the wild wood, on a bed of yellow & purple violets —Lucina—the Parcae—the two Serpents feeding it with honey— one holding the honey comb in his folds & gyves, as in a vase / a slant ray thro' a small opening in the Trees, falling full on the face &c of the Infant / the Mother feeble, retiring, with reverted face, full of mother's yearning.—Introduce the scenery of Antist: γ . lines 6.7.8&9 to 'σωμα.' " [34] The last notation, about introducing the scenery of Antistrophe γ, certainly does make this sound like notes for a projected poem, and Miss Coburn may very well be right that the poem in question was to be a continuation of "Kubla Khan," but if that was the case I think we can be grateful that the project did not come to fruition—we really do not seem to need Heracles *et al.* in Xanadu. But the feeding on honey from the folds and gyves of serpents—grey-eyed serpents in the original—strikes a familiar note. Miss Coburn gives the Sandys translation of the passage: "two grey-eyed serpents tended the babe with the bane, the harmless bane, of the honey-bees." The bane, the harmless bane, honey from a serpent . . . the slaver or spittle of the stars . . . the only

[34] *Ibid.,* Vol. II, 2882 11.14, and n.

food of the worm transformed into a moth: one can begin to see how the image is consistent with the rest of the poem, almost every image in which may be seen as delicately balanced between beatitude and perdition.

Finally, there are expressions in the poems that throw some light upon the associations that feeding on honey-dew and drinking the milk of Paradise must have had for Coleridge. In the early "Ode" (1792), "Passion with a languid Eye / Hangs o'er the fall of Harmony / And drinks the sacred Balm" in a setting reminiscent in a number of respects of "Kubla Khan," but there is not yet the ambiguity of honey-dew. In "The Eolian Harp" we are much closer:

> Where Melodies round *honey*-dropping flowers,
> Footless and wild, like birds of *Paradise,*
> Nor pause, nor perch, hovering on untam'd wing! [35] (23-25)

The poem continues, "O! the one Life within us and abroad," as it now stands, but later, we know, there is the rebuke of "These shapings of the unregenerate mind." In passing we should recall that in "Christabel" it is said of *Geraldine,*

> For she belike hath drunken deep
> Of all the blessedness of sleep!

But the most telling case is the only one in which the word "honey-dew" is actually used, when the two spirits in "The Ancient Mariner" are discussing the Mariner's fate. The one accuses:

> The other was a softer voice,
> As soft as honey-dew:
> Quoth he, 'The man hath penance done,
> And penance more will do.   (406-9)

During his fit, the Mariner says,

[35] Milley calls attention to this parallel ("Some Notes," p. 53).

> I heard and in my soul discerned
> Two voices in the air.   (396–97)

His whole experience, as I have said before, is of a very different character from that of the speaker in "Kubla Khan," but surely not unrelated. The last two lines quoted try to get something very complex said—he *heard* and *in his soul discerned* two voices *in the air*. The situation seems to be very much like that of the speaker in "Kubla Khan" reviving *within* him the song he has heard in a vision, a song that, as we have seen, is in a sense the song of his own soul united with the Absolute. The Mariner's penance is presumably for his gross violation of the vision vouchsafed him, but the penance is announced by a voice in air "As soft as honey-dew." And part of his penance is just his glittering eye, which causes the Wedding-Guest to fear him. The reverberations between the two poems are delicate, and finally mysterious. Cain and the Prometheus-like disciple of Kubla are brothers after all, for both in their very different ways have fed on honey-dew and drunk the milk of Paradise. Both are aspects of the poet, as Samuel Taylor Coleridge knew him.

This, then, is one reading of "Kubla Khan," using its author's words as the gloss. Its very complexity, doubtless only suggested in these pages, is an effective bar to the temptation to paraphrase. Like all great poems, it can be more and more "understood" by enriching one's apprehension of the density of its parts and then reviewing them in the context of the whole, but it resists paraphrase. Avoiding that attempt, some general, summary observations may be in order. The indications are that there are some half a dozen ways in which the poem may be read, half a dozen "levels" of significance—it is that far from being glorious nonsense. None of these ways quite accounts by itself for all that is in the poem, none, that is, finds in its own terms a place for every image and for the relations among them as they exist in the poem.

Perhaps the least satisfactory in this respect is the autobiographical reading, with Sara Fricker as the woman wailing for her demon-lover, the poet alienated by wanderings in a realm she cannot understand and fears to enter, and someone like Mary Evans or Sara Hutchinson as the Abyssinian maid. One could go further, no doubt—some other suggestions of this sort have turned up as we went along—but the strain begins to tell. There is, however, no reason to suppose that this literally autobiographical element does not exist behind the poem, or that keeping it at the edge of our consciousness will not help us penetrate it.

There are also the elements of a love poem here, in a not quite autobiographical way. In a fairly conventional tradition, though hardly "conventional" in manner, it gives an account of what can be accomplished under the inspiration of love, suggests its dangers, and constitutes an appeal for response—if an Abyssinian maid would sing that song again, then perhaps. . . . In this reading, the details of the landscape fall remarkably well into focus.

The poem can also be read in political terms, but in a subtle and, for Coleridge as politician, a paradoxical way, since it seems clear that Kubla is most unlikely to be the villain of the piece, in spite of Coleridge's hatred of tyrants. What he might detest in Russia is quite another thing in Xanadu. If there is politics in the poem, it would seem to come near the end and to be of a singularly rarefied order. But if we are willing to classify all concern for human welfare, for human enlightenment, as a species of politics, then, indeed, the whole poem, in all its details, may be read as political.

More integral than any of these readings, though not excluding them, is that which sees the poem as an introspective account of the elements of personality involved in the poetic experience, an anatomy, as it were, of the poetic experience, its antecedents, and its results. Then we have the *poem* as symbol, partaking of the reality it would render intelligible, *being* what it is *about*. On this reading the poet, the speaker, is *all* of the personages in the poem, or better, each of the personages in the poem "gives outness to" an aspect of his personality, to one of its ways of being related to the universe of things, the universe of people, itself, and the Absolute. Yet at the same time it need not be read "psychologically," for by the same tokens it is a treatise on the identity of Knowledge and Delight—it is a vision.

There is still at least one other way of reading the poem, and perhaps it is the best, if it were unhappily necessary to choose. In this connection we should recall once more Coleridge's account of the division of labors between himself and Wordsworth in the poems of *Lyrical Ballads*. "Kubla Khan" may be read as a description of mountain scenery, Coleridge doing superlatively well what is described as Wordsworth's job:

Mr. Wordsworth, on the other hand, was to propose to himself as his object, to give the charm of novelty to things of every day, and to excite a feeling analogous to the supernatural, by awakening the mind's attention from the lethargy of custom, and directing it to the loveliness and the wonders of the world before us; an inexhaustible treasure, but for which, in consequence of the film of familiarity and selfish solicitude we have eyes, yet see not, ears that hear not, and hearts that neither feel nor understand.

Seen in this way, "Kubla Khan" is a remarkable concentration of perceptions, and may be paraphrased very briefly: *This* is the way all mountains would look, if. . . . Then we have to repeat the poem, with all we know of its depths.

Bibliography

Selected works contributing more or less directly to the interpretation of "Kubla Khan."

Abrams, Meyer H. The Milk of Paradise. Cambridge: Harvard University Press, 1934.

Allen, N. B. "Note on Coleridge's 'Kubla Khan,' " *Modern Language Notes,* LVII (1942).

Angus, Douglas. "The Theme of Love and Guilt in Coleridge's Three Major Poems," *Journal of English and Germanic Philology,* LIX (1960).

Beer, J. B. Coleridge the Visionary. London: Chatto & Windus, 1959.

Beyer, Werner W. The Enchanted Forest. New York: Barnes & Noble, 1963.

Bodkin, Maud. Archetypal Patterns in Poetry. London: Oxford University Press, 1934.

Bostetter, Edward E. The Romantic Ventriloquists. Seattle: University of Washington Press, 1963.

Breyer, Bernard. "Towards the Interpretation of 'Kubla Khan,' " *English Studies in Honor of James Southall Wilson, University of Virginia Studies,* V (1951).

Burke, Kenneth. The Philosophy of Literary Form. Revised ed. New York: Vintage Books, 1957.

Cooper, Lane. "The Abyssinian Paradise in Coleridge and Milton," *Modern Philology,* III (1905–06).

Fogle, R. H. "The Romantic Unity of 'Kubla Khan,' " *College English,* XIII (1951–52).

Graves, Robert. "Dreams and Poetry," The Meaning of Dreams. New York: Greenberg, 1925.

House, Humphry. Coleridge. London: Rupert Hart-Davis, 1953.

Knight, G. Wilson. The Starlit Dome. London: Oxford University Press, 1941.

Lowes, John Livingston. The Road to Xanadu. Boston, New York: Houghton, Mifflin, 1927.

Mercer, Dorothy F. "The Symbolism of 'Kubla Khan,' " *The Journal of Aesthetics and Art Criticism*, XII (1953).

Meyerstein, E. H. W. "The Completeness of 'Kubla Khan,' " *Times Literary Supplement*, October 30, 1937; December 1, 1951.

Milley, H. J. W. "Some Notes on Coleridge's 'Eolian Harp,' " *Modern Philology*, XXXVI (1938–39).

Muirhead, J. H. Coleridge as Philosopher. London: Macmillan, 1930.

Parsons, Howard. "A New Interpretation of Coleridge's 'Kubla Khan,' " *Poetry Review*, XXXIV (1943).

Purves, Alan. "Formal Structure in 'Kubla Khan,' " *Studies in Romanticism*, I (1962).

Schneider, Elisabeth. Coleridge, Opium, and Kubla Khan. Chicago: University of Chicago Press, 1953.

Schulz, Max F. The Poetic Voices of Coleridge; A Study of His Desire for Spontaneity and Passion for Order. Detroit: Wayne State University Press, 1963.

Sypher, Wylie. "Coleridge's Somerset: a Byway to Xanadu," *Philological Quarterly*, XVIII (1939).

Warren, Robert Penn. "A Poem of Pure Imagination," in edition of The Rime of the Ancient Mariner. New York: Reynal & Hitchcock, 1946.

Watson, George. "The Meaning of 'Kubla Khan,' " *A Review of English Literature*, II (1961).

Whalley, George. Coleridge and Sara Hutchinson and the Asra Poems. London: Routledge & Kegan Paul, 1955.

Woodring, Carl. "Coleridge and the Khan," *Essays in Criticism*, IX (1959).

—— Politics in the Poetry of Coleridge. Madison: University of Wisconsin Press, 1961.

Index